Essential Steps to College Success

Review this list, and work to complete each task during your first few weeks of college. These are important first steps to ensure that you will get off to a good start.

☐ Meet with your academic adviser. Make sure you feel comfortable with him or her.

☐ Figure out how to access your campus e-mail, your school's learning management system, and any other technological tools that you'll be expected to use in your courses or across campus.

☐ Be sure you know important deadlines, such as those for dropping or adding courses and due dates for upcoming quizzes, papers, and exams. Write them down in your planner, or add them to your electronic calendar.

☐ Create a weekly schedule that includes time for study, recreation, and sleep.

☐ Purchase all your textbooks, and keep up with reading assignments.

☐ Find an upper-level student whom you can talk to and ask for advice.

☐ Make an appointment to talk to one or more of your instructors outside class.

☐ Find a quiet place to study. You might need to negotiate with a roommate for dedicated study space and time.

☐ Find a club or some other organization you would be interested in joining.

☐ Learn about academic support available on your campus, and make an appointment to visit the academic support center.

☐ Create a budget, and monitor it regularly to make sure you're sticking to it.

☐ Join or form a study group, especially for your most challenging courses.

☐ Get some exercise every day.

☐ Check back over this list weekly, adding any items you deem necessary for your personal success.

Step by Step
to College and Career Success

Eighth Edition

Step by Step
to College and Career Success

Eighth Edition

John N. Gardner

Chief Executive Officer and Chair, John N. Gardner Institute for Excellence in Undergraduate
  Education
Brevard, North Carolina

Distinguished Professor Emeritus, Library and Information Science

Senior Fellow and Founding Director, University 101 Programs, National Resource Center for
  The First-Year Experience and Students in Transition
University of South Carolina, Columbia

Betsy O. Barefoot

Senior Scholar

John N. Gardner Institute for Excellence in Undergraduate Education
Brevard, North Carolina

Fellow, National Resource Center for The First-Year Experience and Students in Transition
University of South Carolina, Columbia

bedford/st.martin's
Macmillan Learning
Boston | New York

For Bedford/St. Martin's

Vice President, Editorial, Macmillan Learning Humanities: Edwin Hill
Senior Program Director for College Success: Erika Gutierrez
Program Manager for College Success: Allen Cooper
Marketing Manager: Amy Haines
Director of Content Development: Jane Knetzger
Development Editor: Bethany Gordon
Associate Editor: Melanie McFadyen
Editorial Assistant: Kathy McInerney
Senior Content Project Manager: Peter Jacoby
Workflow Project Manager: Lisa McDowell
Production Supervisor: Robert Cherry
Media Project Manager: Sarah O'Connor Kepes
Senior Media Editor: Tom Kane
Project Management: Lumina Datamatics, Inc.
Composition: Lumina Datamatics, Inc.
Text Permissions Manager: Kalina Ingham
Text Permission Researcher: Arthur Johnson, Lumina Datamatics, Inc.
Photo Permissions Editor: Angela Boehler
Photo Researcher: Kerri Wilson, Lumina Datamatics, Inc.
Director of Design, Content Management: Diana Blume
Text Design: Jerilyn Bockorick, Cenveo Publisher Services
Cover Design: William Boardman
Cover Image: Mads Perch/Getty Images
Printing and Binding: LSC Communications

Manufactured in the United States of America.

1 2 3 4 5 6   23 22 21 20 19 18

For information, write: Bedford/St. Martin's, 75 Arlington Street, Boston, MA 02116 (617-399-4000)

ISBN 978-1-319-10727-7

Brief Contents

Contents

Alexandr III/Shutterstock

03 Managing Your Time 33

IDesign/Shutterstock

04 Learning and Thinking in College 51

09
Considering Majors and Careers 137

Introwizi/Shutterstock

10
Connecting with Others in a Diverse World 157

WonderfulPixel/Shutterstock

11 $ Managing Money 173

Fenton one/Shutterstock

12 Staying Healthy 191

Preface

Anyone who teaches beginning college students or works with them closely knows how much they have changed in recent years. We can observe some of the perennial ways that college students remain unchanged. Today's students are overwhelmingly career-focused, skilled in using technology, concerned about the future, and anxious about their present. More than ever, they worry about how they will pay for college. According to the *Wall Street Journal* and *USA Today*, young people have expressed doubts about the value of college, citing concerns about how student debt delays them from starting families and businesses and even living independently.[1] Such reports raise serious questions about whether money spent on a college degree is worth the return on investment or would be better invested in a start-up business or travel.[2] While it is tempting to focus on the few individuals who can find an alternative path to a successful future other than through college completion, we know that for the overwhelming majority of individuals, a post–high school credential, especially a college degree, is more essential than ever before.

Today we are seeing diverse students of all ages and backgrounds enrolling in both two- and four-year institutions, bringing with them the hopes and dreams that a college education can help fulfill. And we are more optimistic than ever that success in college is a strong predictor of success in life. This textbook is written for students of any age at any type of college, pursuing a variety of educational and professional objectives. We present comprehensive and helpful information on every aspect of the college experience for a range of student audiences, from those straight out of high school to returning adult learners, from commuters to on-campus residents, from students who were born in the United States to immigrants and Dreamers. We provide examples that are relevant to students and do not make assumptions about the realities of their lives.

Step by Step to College and Career Success is specifically designed to give *all* students the practical help they need to set goals, succeed, and stay in college. As our briefest text, it is written to be to the point yet comprehensive. We've pared away the extras covered in our more extensive books to focus on the most crucial skills as well as the important choices students need to make in order to succeed in college and beyond. The eighth edition covers pressing topics that affect students' lives and how they learn, such as active learning, test taking, career preparation, relationships, and technology, and we have expanded on the book's themes of motivation, persistence, resilience, and decision making.

We also want to ensure that students think about long- and short-term goals so that they're able to take the steps necessary to do well in this course, their other courses, and their careers. In addition, the text covers a broad range of academic and life skills, including time management, learning styles, critical thinking, listening and taking notes, reading, communication, testing, money management, diversity, health, and majors and careers.

We show our respect and admiration for our students in our writing while recognizing their continued need for challenge and support. Our text is grounded in the growing body of research on student success and retention. Simply put, we do not like to see students fail. We are confident that if students both read and heed the information herein, they will become engaged in the college experience, learn, and persist to graduation.

Whether you are considering this textbook for use in your college success course or have already made a decision to adopt it, we thank you for your interest, and trust that you will find it to be a valuable teaching aid. We also hope that this book will guide you and your campus in understanding the broad range of issues that can affect student success.

---

[1] Douglas Belkin, "Recent Grads Doubt College's Worth," *Wall Street Journal*, September 29, 2015, www.wsj.com/articles/recent-grads-doubt-colleges-worth-1443499440.

[2] Oliver St. John, "Kids Skip College—Not Worth the Money," *USA Today*, April 22, 2013, www.usatoday.com/story/money/personalfinance/2013/04/21/avoiding-college-avoiding-debt/1987309.

Key Chapter Changes

- **A revised introductory chapter** has been reorganized to serve as a road map to get students off on the right foot, as the title, **"Taking the First Step,"** suggests. It offers a new section, "Thriving in College and Life," which gives students a better understanding of the value of college and making choices. Coverage of goal setting has been expanded to place more emphasis on exploring purpose and planning ahead. The "Connecting with Others" section provides a broadened view on maximizing relationships with instructors and other types of students, including those who teach and learn online.

- **Chapter 4, "Learning and Thinking in College,"** combines what had been two separate chapters in the seventh edition. The chapter now covers how people learn (formerly Chapter 4 "Understanding How Your Learn") and college-level thinking skills (formerly Chapter 8 "Thinking in College"). Content is streamlined and logically organized. This updated chapter provides new coverage on adapting to different learning environments, as well as a new subsection, "College-Level Thinking Is Critical Thinking," which provides greater focus on critical thinking.

- **Chapter 8, "Developing Information Literacy and Communication Skills,"** now features the section "Communicating with Others in a Digital Age" (formerly Chapter 10) to tie together ways of communicating, researching, and consuming information online.

- **Chapter 9, "Considering Majors and Careers"** (formerly Chapter 13), now appears earlier in the book to provide students with timely coverage on academic planning. Coverage of academic planning (formerly in Chapter 1) has been expanded and moved to Chapter 9 under "Working with an Academic Adviser."

- **Chapter 10, "Connecting with Others in a Diverse World,"** now includes a subsection on gender and sexual identity that explains, in detail, new understandings of the gender spectrum. The chapter also includes up-to-date information about sexual harassment, acknowledging the impact of the #MeToo movement and the way it is changing our knowledge and attitudes about this pervasive societal problem.

Features of This Edition

- **A powerful LaunchPad course space.** Available with the eighth edition, LaunchPad Solo for *Step by Step* is home to dozens of prebuilt assignable and assessable digital resources designed to help students engage with key course concepts and prepare for class, including ACES self-assessment reports, LearningCurve adaptive quizzing, video activities, case study quizzes, and links to further online resources, such as apps and podcasts. Easy-to-use and easy-to-assign modules based on essential college success topics prompt students to apply the strategies discussed in class and are easily adaptable to your own course material, such as readings, videos, quizzes, and discussion groups.

- **A stronger focus on technology** that reflects how students and instructors use technology to achieve educational and career goals. More coverage of online learning is woven throughout the narrative and appears in topic-specific pop-out articles, new Tech Tips, and ACES review features.

  - Pop-out articles focus on specific aspects of online learning.

  - New Tech Tips in every chapter help students leverage technology for their success. These Tech Tips feature timely subject matter, such as identifying fake news, networking online, and using digital tools to manage your time.

  - The Academic and Career Excellence System (ACES) measures student strengths in twelve critical areas and prompts students to reflect on their habits, behaviors, attitudes, and skills. Norm-referenced reports indicate whether students are at a high, moderate, or low skill level in particular areas. For more information, go to **launchpadworks.com**.

- **A carefully executed and updated design and art program** that keeps students focused and engaged with the content by including images that reflect the experiences of all students in the course so that they will feel comfortable and connected. Captions invite students to think critically about the content.

- **A fun and compelling approach.** The text is streamlined, focused, and readable.

New student stories reflect a diverse range of students' life experiences. Inviting pop-out articles address important real-world topics of pressing concern to students. New articles in the eighth edition cover such topics as making choices (Chapter 1), online learners (Chapter 1), emotional intelligence (Chapter 2), learning with a learning disability (Chapter 4), being an engaged learner (Chapter 5), reading online (Chapter 6), information literacy (Chapter 8), using research in writing and presentations (Chapter 8), finding and using campus resources (Chapter 9), and sexual harassment (Chapter 10).

Features and teaching techniques that engage students:

- **ACES self-assessment guidance** is now integrated into this edition through the "Review Your ACES Score" feature at the beginning of each chapter. A new appendix on "Using the ACES Progress Report" shows students using LaunchPad Solo how they can check their progress at the end of the semester to see the areas where they've grown.

- **Chapter content** incorporates coverage of technological tools and skills, digital examples and models, and more in-text examples that feature social media and apps in an effort to reflect the roles of these tools in students' lives.

- **Tech Tips** help students leverage technology for their success, featuring timely topics such as identifying fake news, networking online, and using digital tools to control your time.

- **Try It! boxes encourage students to interact with what they are learning.** Focusing on four themes—managing time, feeling connected, setting goals, and making good choices—each Try It! box explains a specific action for students to try, the benefit of doing so, and first steps to get started. The Try It! boxes that reinforce setting goals also carry an emphasis on motivation. These boxes can be used for student self-direction or as assignments in or outside the classroom. Examples include Feeling Connected: Share Your Story

(Chapter 2); Managing Time: Don't Waste Time Fussing and Fuming (Chapter 2); Setting Goals: "I've Got to Get My Priorities in Order!" (Chapter 3); Making Good Choices: Make Up Your Own Mind (Chapter 4); Feeling Connected: Two (or More) Are Better Than One (Chapter 6); Managing Time: Time Flies—Especially during an Essay Test (Chapter 7); Making Good Choices: Ponder Your Choice of Academic Major (Chapter 9); Setting Goals: Exhaust All Avenues (Chapter 11); and Managing Time: Making Time to Stay Fit (Chapter 12).

- **Streamlined chapter-ending sections.** These include a "Reflect on Choices" writing prompt; an Applying What You've Learned section with application opportunities; and a Use Your Resources section that encourages students to seek out peers (online or in person), use social media, take advantage of instructors' office hours, join study groups, access campus resources, and consult references like books and websites. These features encourage students to take the initiative in answering a variety of common questions and solving different kinds of problems.

Resources for Instructors

For more information on these resources, please visit the online catalog at macmillanlearning.com/stepbystep.

- **LaunchPad Solo for *Step by Step*, Eighth Edition.** LaunchPad Solo for *Step by Step* is home to dozens of prebuilt assignable and assessable digital resources designed to help students engage with key course concepts and prepare for class, including LearningCurve adaptive quizzing and video activities. Prebuilt units are easy to assign or adapt with your own material, such as readings, videos, and quizzes. LaunchPad Solo also provides access to a grade book that provides a clear window on performance for your whole class, for individual students and individual assignments. For more information, go to **launchpadworks.com**.

- **LearningCurve for *Step by Step*, Eighth Edition.** LearningCurve is an online, adaptive, self-quizzing program that quickly learns what students already know and helps them practice what they haven't yet mastered. LearningCurve motivates students to engage with key concepts before they come to class so that they are ready to participate; it also offers reporting tools to help you discern your students' needs. An updated version of LearningCurve, available with Launchpad Solo for *Step by Step*, features a larger question pool with new multiple-choice questions.

- **The Academic and Career Excellence System (ACES).** This instrument measures student strengths in twelve critical areas and prompts students to reflect on their habits, behaviors, attitudes, and skills. Norm-referenced reports indicate whether students are at a high, moderate, or low skill level in particular areas. An instructor's guide to ACES provides strategies for personalizing your instruction to your class and individual students based on their unique ACES scores.

- **Ordering information.** LaunchPad Solo is available to package at a significant discount. Please contact your Macmillan Learning representative for more information. To order LaunchPad Solo for *Step by Step* packaged with the book, use ISBN 978-1-319-24341-8.

- **Instructor's Manual.** The Instructor's Manual includes chapter objectives, teaching suggestions, an introduction to the first-year seminar course, a sample lesson plan for each chapter, sample syllabi, final projects for the end of the course, and various case studies that are relevant to the topics covered in the text. The Instructor's Manual is available online.

- **Computerized Test Bank.** The Computerized Test Bank contains more than seven hundred multiple-choice, true/false, short-answer, and essay questions designed to assess students' understanding of key concepts. An answer key is included. A digital text file is also available.

- **Lecture Slides.** Available online for download, lecture slides accompany each chapter of the book and include key concepts and art from the text. Use the slides as provided to structure your lectures, or customize them as desired to fit your course's needs.

- **Curriculum Solutions.** Our Curriculum Solutions group brings together the quality and reputation of Bedford/St. Martin's content with Hayden-McNeil's expertise in publishing original custom print and digital products. With our new capabilities, we are excited to deliver customized course solutions at an affordable price. Make *Step by Step to College and Career Success*, Eighth Edition, fit your course and goals by integrating your own institutional materials, including only the parts of the text you intend to use in your course, or both. Please contact your local Macmillan Learning sales representative for more information and to see samples.

- **Bedford Select for College Success.** The Bedford Select database allows you to create a textbook for your college success course that reflects your course objectives and uses just the content you need. Start with one of our core texts, and then rearrange chapters, delete chapters, and add additional content—including your own original content—to create just the book you're looking for. Get started by visiting **macmillanlearning. com/csSelect**.

- **Student Store.** You want to give your students affordable rental, packaging, and e-book options. So do we. Learn more at store.macmillanlearning.com.

- **TradeUp.** Bring more value and choice to your students' overall first-year experience by packaging *Step by Step to College and Career Success*, Eighth Edition, with one of a thousand titles from Macmillan publishers at a 50 percent discount. Contact your local Bedford/St. Martin's sales representative for more information.

- **The Macmillan Learning College Success Community** is our online space for instructor development and engagement. Find resources to support your teaching, including class activities, video assignments, and invitations to conferences and webinars. Connect with our team, our authors, and other instructors through online discussions and blog posts at https://community.macmillan.com/community/the-college-success-community.

Resources for Students and Packaging Options

For more information on these formats, please visit the online catalog at **macmillanhighered.com/stepbystep**

- **LaunchPad Solo for** *Step by Step*, **Eighth Edition.** LaunchPad is an online course solution that offers acclaimed content, including the e-book, ACES, LearningCurve adaptive quizzes, and videos. For more information, see the Resources for Instructors section.

  - **LearningCurve for** *Step by Step*. LearningCurve for *Step by Step* is an online, adaptive, self-quizzing program that quickly learns what students already know and helps them practice what they haven't yet mastered.

  - **Ordering information.** LaunchPad Solo is available to package at a significant discount. To order LaunchPad Solo for *Step by Step* with the book, use ISBN 978-1-319-24341-8.

- **E-book Options.** *Step by Step 8e* is available as an e-book for use on computers, tablets, and e-readers. See **macmillanlearning.com/ebooks** to learn more.

- **Bedford/St. Martin's Insider's Guides.** These concise and student-friendly booklets on topics critical to college success are a perfect complement to your textbook and course. One Insider's Guide can be packaged with *any* Bedford/St. Martin's textbook. Additional Insider's Guides can be packaged for an added cost. Recently published topics include the following:

  - *Insider's Guide for Adult Learners*

  - *Insider's Guide to College Etiquette*

  - *Insider's Guide for Returning Veterans*

  - *Insider's Guide for Transfer Students*

  - *Insider's Guide to Credit Cards*, Second Edition

  - *Insider's Guide to Getting Involved on Campus*

  - *Insider's Guide to Time Management*, Second Edition

For additional topics, or for more information on ordering one of these guides with the text, go to **macmillanlearning.com/collegesuccess**.

About the Authors

Scott Treadway/John N. Gardner Institute

John N. Gardner brings unparalleled experience to this authoritative text for first-year seminar courses. His first college teaching experience was at a two-year public college in a small rural town in South Carolina. That experience was so inspiring that he made a lifetime commitment to continue serving such students. John is the recipient of the University of South Carolina's highest award for teaching excellence. He has twenty-five years of experience directing and teaching in the most respected and most widely emulated first-year seminar in the country, the University 101 course at the University of South Carolina. John is universally recognized as one of the country's leading educators for his role in initiating and orchestrating an international reform movement to improve the beginning college experience. He is also the founding leader of two influential higher education centers that support campuses in their efforts to improve the learning and retention of beginning college students: the National Resource Center for The First-Year Experience and Students in Transition at the University of South Carolina (www.sc.edu/fye), and the John N. Gardner Institute for Excellence in Undergraduate Education (www.jngi.org), based in Brevard, North Carolina. The experiential basis for all of John Gardner's work is his own miserable first year of college on academic probation, an experience he hopes to prevent for this book's readers. Today, as a much happier adult, John is married to fellow author of this book, Betsy Barefoot.

Scott Treadway/John N. Gardner Institute

Betsy O. Barefoot is a writer, researcher, and teacher, whose special area of scholarship is the first year of college. During her tenure at the University of South Carolina from 1988 to 1999, she served as codirector for research and publications at the National Resource Center for The First-Year Experience and Students in Transition. She taught University 101, in addition to special-topics graduate courses on the first-year experience and the principles of college teaching. She conducts first-year seminar faculty training workshops around the United States and in other countries, and she is frequently called on to evaluate first-year seminar outcomes. Betsy currently serves as senior scholar at the John N. Gardner Institute for Excellence in Undergraduate Education. In her role at the institute, she led a major national research project to identify institutions of excellence in the first college year. She currently works with both two- and four-year campuses in evaluating all components of the first year.

Acknowledgments

Although this text speaks with the voices of its two authors, it represents contributions from many others. We gratefully acknowledge these contributions and thank these individuals, whose special expertise has made it possible to introduce new college students to their college experience through the holistic approach we deeply believe in. We are indebted to the following reviewers who offered us thoughtful and constructive feedback on this edition:

Cecelia Brewer, University of Central Missouri; Kathy Clark, Florida SouthWestern State College; Michele Everett, Coastal Carolina University; Alisha Francis, Northwest Missouri State University; Barb Garrett, Pikes Peak Community College; Tracey Glaessgen, Missouri State University; Kelly Herbolich, Saint Louis University; Paige Huskey, Clark State Community College; Noemi Iraci, Palomar College; Christopher Lau, Hutchinson Community College; Stacy Macchi, Western Illinois University; Maureen O'Connor, CUNY–Hunter College; Paul Romo, Glendale Community College; Kerry Tew, Arkansas State University; Joel Thomas, Ancilla Domini College; and Richard Underwood, Kirkwood Community College.

We would also like to acknowledge and thank the numerous colleagues who have contributed to this book in its previous editions: Catherine Andersen, Gallaudet University; Kathryn Arrington, Baton Rouge Community College; Erin Barnett, Eastern Kentucky University; Elaine Barry, Central Maine Technical College; Michelle Murphy Burcin, University of South Carolina at Columbia; Tom Carskadon,

Mississippi State University; Audra Cooke, Rock Valley College; Christine Deacons, Eastern Michigan University; Michael Dunn, Radford University; Peggy Dunn, New River Community College; Jerry Eddy, Sinclair Community College; Kathleen Fitzpatrick, Daniel Webster College; Juan Flores, Folsom Lake College; Gina Floyd, Shorter University; Philip Gardner, Michigan State University; Eric Gene-Shrewsbury, Patrick Henry Community College; Britta Gibson, University of Pikeville; Chris Gurrie, University of Tampa; Jeanne L. Higbee, University of Minnesota, Twin Cities; Nancy Hunter, Maysville Community College; Darby Johnsen, Oklahoma City Community College; Tony Jones, Milligan College; Natala Kleather (Tally) Hart, Ohio State University; Christopher Lau, Hutchinson Community College; Kristina Leonard, Daytona State College; Jonathan Long, Central Missouri State University; Tawana Mattox, Athens Area Technical Institute; Eileen McDonough, Barry University; Von McGriff, Polk State College; Stacey Murray, Sonoma State University; Brandi Neal, Coastal Carolina University; Mary Ellen O'Leary, University of South Carolina at Columbia; Adenike Oloyede, Lake Michigan College; Richard Robers, Virginia Western Community College; Rajon Shore, Blue Ridge Community College; Chris Strouthopoulous, San Juan College; Jacques Surrency, Fort Valley State University; Kate Trombitas, Ohio State University; Michelle Van de Sande, Arapahoe Community College; Keron Ward-Myles, Mountain View College; Peggy Whaley, Murray State University; Lenora White, Baton Rouge Community College; Michael Wood, Missouri State University; Andrea Zick, University of Wisconsin; and Edward Zlotkowski, Bentley College.

As we look to the future, we are excited about the numerous improvements to this text that our creative Bedford/St. Martin's team has made and will continue to make. Special thanks to Edwin Hill, Vice President of Editorial Humanities; Erika Gutierrez, Senior Program Director; Allen Cooper, Program Manager; Tom Kane, Senior Media Editor; Bethany Gordon, Development Editor; Melanie McFadyen, Associate Editor; Kathy McInerney, Editorial Assistant; Amy Haines, Marketing Manager; William Boardman, Senior Design Manager; and Peter Jacoby, Senior Content Project Manager.

Most of all, we thank you, the users of our book, for you are the true inspiration for this work.

01

Taking the First Step

Congratulations—you are going to college! You've joined about two million other students who are starting college this year. No matter your age, background, academic skills, or economic circumstances, whether you succeed will depend on your motivation, commitment, and willingness to take advantage of all that your college or university has to offer.

College is the most important investment of time, money, and energy you will make in your life, and for some students, the college experience can be transformative. What do we mean by "transformative"? For most college students, completing a degree will have a significant positive effect on their employment opportunities and income over a lifetime. But far beyond that, college can have an impact on

how you think about and understand the world around you. You're on an exciting journey that will take you to new places and introduce you to new ideas and new people. You will also learn more about your purpose for attending college and how to harness your particular strengths and interests to achieve goals you have always had and those you may discover.

This book is a step-by-step guide to college success. Reading, remembering, and practicing the information and strategies in each chapter will help you accomplish your goals and avoid the kinds of problems that sometimes trip up even the best students in their first year. What you learn from this book will also be valuable to you throughout your college experience and in life.

LaunchPad Solo
macmillan learning

To access ACES, the LearningCurve study tool, videos, and more, go to LaunchPad Solo for *Step by Step*.
launchpadworks.com

1

Review Your ACES Score

With this book, you'll have access to **ACES (Academic and Career Excellence System)**, an online self-assessment that will help you learn more about your attitudes, skills, habits, and needs for improvement across twelve key skill areas. You'll have an opportunity to review your ACES score at the beginning of each chapter and respond to a reflection prompt so that you can approach each chapter with an understanding of your current strengths and areas where you need improvement.

Score:

○ High
○ Moderate
○ Low

To take the assessment, log on to LaunchPad Solo for *Step by Step* at **launchpadworks.com**.

Identifying Your Strengths and Setting Goals in College

SpeedKingz/Shutterstock.com

"Here's the thing: I'm not planning to stay in college," I tell my academic adviser, Dr. Beene, at our first meeting. "I'm just here for a year to get my parents off my back. College is a big deal for them; they were the first ones in their families to go, and my dad has always regretted dropping out before he got his degree. So, right now I'm just here to have fun."

"There's nothing wrong with fun, Cameron," Dr. Beene says. "But don't forget that college is a huge investment of time, money, and energy. Have you thought about how college can help you meet your long-term goals?" He must have known by the blank look on my face that I really didn't have any long-term goals, but he didn't give up. "Some students have goals focused around a career or how they want to live their life in the future," Dr. Beene adds. "But most students are like you—they're still trying to settle on their goals. Your college success course will help you figure out what you value most, and a visit to the career center here on campus will help you match your values, strengths, and special abilities with a possible career path."

Cut to the end of the first term: I'm back in Dr. Beene's office. "Remember how during our last appointment I told you my only reason for being in college was to have fun?" I say. "Well, the very next week in our college success course we did this values exercise, and I learned that I value being a leader and taking charge of whatever situation I'm in. I'm pretty competitive, and I want to make my own decisions. I've decided that I want to be an entrepreneur and run my own business, and I want my college courses to help me learn the skills I need to make good business decisions."

How do Cameron's reasons for being in college compare with yours? What experiences did Cameron have that pointed him toward a goal? What steps should he take to ensure that his goal of owning his own business makes sense for him?

Thriving in College and Life

As authors of this textbook, our overarching goal is not only that you be successful in college and life, but that you *thrive* in both. Thriving means going beyond the minimum requirements to meet and even exceed your goals. Thriving is your discovery of talents and abilities you didn't know you had. Thriving is about achieving your highest possible level of performance and deriving the maximum amount of excitement, self-satisfaction, and pleasure.

Depending on who you are, your life situation, and your reasons for enrolling, college can mean different things. Whatever led you here, college will be a time when you take some appropriate risks, learn new things, connect with important people, and set goals for yourself—all in a supportive environment with people who will help you thrive so that you become the person you want to be.

So hang on for the exciting ride that is beginning right now.

The Value of College

American society values higher education because receiving a college degree provides the opportunity to achieve your goals and dreams regardless of your race or ethnic background, national origin, immigration status, family income level, family history, or personal connections. Today, new technologies and the information explosion are changing the workplace so drastically that to support themselves and their families adequately, most people need some education beyond high school. Higher education allows people to improve their lives by obtaining new skills, learning to perform different jobs, and establishing successful careers. Making more money isn't the only reason to go to college, but as Figure 1.1 shows, the

Figure 1.1 ▽ Education Pays

Earning a college degree will improve your earning potential. This figure breaks down unemployment rate and weekly earnings according to education level. Use this information as motivation to make the most of college.

Source: U.S. Department of Labor, Bureau of Labor Statistics, *The Economics Daily*, accessed June 22, 2017, https://www.bls.gov/careeroutlook/2014/data-on-display/education-still-pays.htm. *Bureau of Labor Statistics*

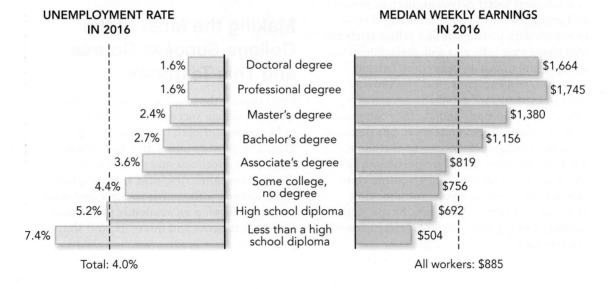

UNEMPLOYMENT RATE IN 2016 | MEDIAN WEEKLY EARNINGS IN 2016

	Unemployment Rate	Median Weekly Earnings
Doctoral degree	1.6%	$1,664
Professional degree	1.6%	$1,745
Master's degree	2.4%	$1,380
Bachelor's degree	2.7%	$1,156
Associate's degree	3.6%	$819
Some college, no degree	4.4%	$756
High school diploma	5.2%	$692
Less than a high school diploma	7.4%	$504

Total: 4.0%   All workers: $885

> **In addition to increasing your earning power, college is about helping you become a better thinker and a leader in your community, workplace, and profession.**

TRY IT!

MAKING GOOD CHOICES ▷
Your Decision to Become a College Student

List five reasons you chose to go to college at this time in your life. Share what you wrote with a classmate, and see how many of your reasons are the same or different.

more education you have, the more likely you are to be employed and the more you will earn.

In addition to increasing your earning power, college is about helping you become a better thinker and a leader in your community, workplace, and profession. Your college experience will be filled with a set of experiences and opportunities that will help you further define your goals and achieve your own purpose. In short, college can change your life for the better.

Opportunities in College

Being in college will provide numerous opportunities for you to develop a variety of formal and informal social networks, both in person and online. You will enjoy meaningful relationships with instructors and fellow students who share your interests and goals. Social networking sites, such as Instagram, Twitter, Snapchat, and Facebook, will also provide ways to expand your interactions with students on your campus and at other campuses as well; most colleges and on-campus organizations have online presences where students share information. If you are participating in an online program or taking an online class, take advantage of free videoconferencing tools, such as Google Hangouts, Skype, and Zoom, to connect with your peers and instructors "face to face."

In addition to developing lifelong friendships and professional networks, college is about gaining and practicing academic skills that will benefit you in your personal life and future career. College will help you understand how to become a careful and critical thinker, someone who doesn't believe everything that he or she hears or reads but instead looks for evidence before forming an opinion.

While college is an experience you will remember fondly throughout your life, it is also a lot of work. Being in college means studying for hours each week, staying up late or getting up early to complete assignments and prepare for class, taking high-stakes exams, and probably working harder than you ever have. For many students, college is like a job, with defined opportunities, duties, expectations, and obligations.

Making the Most of the College Success Course and This Textbook

Even though the exact name of the course can vary, all college success courses show you how to be successful both in college and in life. They also provide you with a safe place to share your successes and your challenges, get to know other first-year students, build relationships with your instructor and other students, develop an academic plan based on your strengths and interests, and shape your plans after graduation.

Both this course and this text are based on extensive research in the field of student success, which investigates what students need to know in order to thrive in college. Student success research has also helped identify the strategies and attitudes of the most successful students. What have we learned from the research? Research shows that students who take *and complete* a college success course such as this one are more likely to earn better grades, remain in college, and graduate than students who don't. Not only do these students know where to get help, but they actually seek it out and use it when they need it. And perhaps most important, these students make better choices overall while they're in college.

As individuals with years of experience working with first-year students, and as former first-year students ourselves, we know that starting college can be challenging. However, if you apply the ideas in this book to your everyday life, you are more likely to enjoy your time in college, graduate, and achieve your goals. While you attend class and read this textbook, you will get valuable advice that applies not only to your college success course but to all your college courses this year and in the future. Think of this course as a kind of laboratory for what to do in all your college courses to be successful. ■

The Choices You Will Make

You will make choices every day of your college career, both big and small, and being successful in college has a great deal to do with the choices you are making, will make, and should not make, often on a daily basis. Think about it. You are your own boss in college. Therefore, you can choose to be a person with an internal *locus of control*. This refers to individuals who exercise control over their lives. They don't see themselves being made to do things by others or outside forces. Instead, they take responsibility for their own actions.

Students are like other human beings—they make some good choices, and they make some poor ones. And the poor ones can cost them a lot of time, money, and heartache. Some college and university educators are now recommending—or even requiring—that students take a "pathway" or a "guided pathway": a prescribed set of courses leading to certain majors and degrees. These pathways are based on the use of analytics—information about whether students like you will be more or less likely to complete certain courses successfully. With limited choices, you will be able to avoid courses in which you would likely be unsuccessful, and you will ultimately save time, money, and energy by taking courses that are right for you.

Beyond the big choices you will make in college, there will also be little choices you will make every day that will affect your success in college for the better or worse. Consider the following questions: How much time will you devote to homework today? Are you going to get up in time for your first class, or sleep in and skip it? Are you going to eat breakfast and exercise today? Will you visit your instructor during office hours to get some questions answered? These may seem like minor decisions, but depending on how you answer these questions, your actions will interact with one another and either support or sabotage the achievement of your larger goals. This book will outline what strategies and habits will help you be more successful, so you can be aware of the choices you make and choose ones that support your future.

Exploring Purpose and Setting Goals

You may be very clear on why you are in college and what you hope to achieve, or—like Cameron in the opening example—you may still be trying to figure this out; either way, you are in charge of making the most out of your college experience. Wherever you are, achieving your purpose requires that you set goals along the way.

Considering Purpose

Your sense of purpose will drive many outcomes. It will give you motivation for today, this week, this term, college overall, and life.

It will shape many of the decisions you make. Purpose provides clarity, direction, commitment, and meaning. People who have a clear sense of purpose know how their past experiences have made them who they are. Purpose also connects to motivation, and this motivation plays out each day for college students in terms of the choices they make.

While some students come to college with a clear sense of purpose, others do not. For many students, a sense of purpose builds over time, and that's OK. College will provide you with a set of experiences that will help you clarify your purpose and achieve your

△ **Begin with the End in Mind**
Imagine that you've arrived at your graduation day and you're looking back over the years. How long has it taken you to get to this point? Describe what you feel most proud of. What plans do you have? We want to help you convert your ideas to reality through a plan to achieve the particular end you have in mind. In this section, we'll explore the most important driver of motivation and success in college: purpose. pixelheadphoto digitalskillet/Shutterstock.com

goals. It is possible that as you discover more about yourself and your abilities, your reasons for coming to college will change. In fact, a majority of college students change their academic plans at least once during their college years.

To gain insight about your purpose for being in college, reflect on the following questions: Why am I going to college? Is this college a good fit for me at this time in my life and for my goals? Do I have a strong sense of purpose for going to college and for my life at this time?

Your answers to these questions will drive most of the decisions you make in college, decisions that will likely affect the rest of your life. Because knowledge expands all the time, college won't teach you everything you will ever need to know, but it will teach you how to think and how to keep learning throughout your life.

Getting Started with Goal Setting

For most students, a central purpose for college is gaining the knowledge and experience that will lead to success. So what does success mean to you? Is it about money, friendship, or power? Is it about achieving excellence in college and beyond, or is it about finding a sense of purpose in your life? For most people, success is a combination of all these factors and more. First and foremost, your success will be the result of intentional steps you take and your accomplishments. So where do you get started?

Identify your personal strengths.
Everyone is good at doing something, and your strengths can help you choose the right path. Are you a good reader, and do you enjoy constructing an argument? If so, you might want to consider a career in the legal field. Are you a good science student, and do you enjoy working with your hands? If your answer is yes, dentistry is a profession that might be a good fit for you. You campus career center can help you discover your unique strengths—and

weaknesses—which can influence your direction as you explore course and career choices.

Ask yourself questions. Am I here to find out who I am and to study a subject that I am truly passionate about, regardless of whether it leads to a career? To engage in an academic program that provides an array of possibilities when I graduate? To prepare myself for transfer, a graduate program, or immediate employment? To obtain specific training in a field that I am committed to? To gain specific skills for a job I already have?

Begin establishing your goals. As you identify your strengths, it makes good sense to establish goals—personal and career goals for today, this week, this month, this term, this year, and beyond. Students who prefer to go with the flow and let life happen to them are more likely to waste their time and less likely to achieve success in college or in a career. So instead of simply reacting to what college and life present to you, you should take more control over the decisions and choices you make now, literally every day, to achieve your goals. While making general plans is easy, you need to determine which short-term goals are necessary if those plans are to become a reality.

> " As you identify your strengths, it makes good sense to establish goals—personal and career goals for today, this week, this month, this term, this year, and beyond. "

TRY IT!

MANAGING TIME ▷ How Will You Get Where You Want to Go?

The decisions you make today about how you will reach your goals will determine whether you can describe yourself as successful in ten years. List the skills and habits that will make you a successful and competent person. Did you include time management? Consider ways that you can improve your competencies as you prepare for life ten, twenty, or thirty years from now.

A short-term goal might be to read twenty pages from your history text twice a week to prepare for an exam that will cover the first hundred pages of the book. A long-term goal might be to begin selecting which elective college courses you should take to help you attain your career goals.

Follow the SMART Goal-Setting Guidelines

Here are guidelines that break down the aspects of goal setting. We call these the SMART goal-setting guidelines, designed to set goals that are *Specific*, *Measurable*, *Attainable*, *Relevant*, and *Timely* (**SMART**):

1. Be **specific** about what you want to achieve, why, and when.

2. State your goal in **measurable** terms. This means how many steps you will need to take to obtain your goal, and how you will know when each step is complete.

3. Be sure that the goal is **attainable**. If you don't have the necessary skills, strengths, and resources to achieve your goal, change it. Be sure that the goal is something you really want to reach. Don't set out to work toward something only because you want to please others.

4. Be able to state the **relevance** of the goal to your life—that is, why the goal matters. Make certain your goal will help move you forward.

5. Consider whether the goal is **timely**—achievable within a reasonable period of time considering the difficulties you might face. Plan ways you might deal with problems.

For instance, let's assume that after you graduate you want to get a good job. This goal isn't very specific and doesn't state a particular deadline. A more specific goal would be to decide which major will prepare you for the job or position you are interested in. What short-term goals will help you reach this longer-term goal? Once you choose your major, the next goal might be to look through the course catalog to identify courses that you need to take. An even more specific goal would be to prepare your academic plan and identify which courses you should take each term. You can meet with an academic adviser who can help you create a program plan for your major, specifying which courses you need to take and in what order. Remember that dreaming up long-term goals is the easy part. To reach your goals, you need to be specific and systematic about the steps you will take. Use Figure 1.2 to set SMART goals for this term. ∎

Figure 1.2 ▽ Practice Setting SMART Goals

What are your goals for this term? Using the SMART goal-setting guide, try to set one goal in each of the four areas listed: academic, career, personal, and financial. An example is provided for you.

Type of Goal	S	M	A	R	T
	What is my SPECIFIC goal?	What MEASURABLE steps are needed?	Why I can ATTAIN the goal?	How is this RELEVANT to me?	Is the goal TIMELY? What potential difficulties will arise, and how will I deal with them to stay on track?
Academic	Complete my academic plan this term based on my chosen major.	• In the next two weeks, review the college catalog to select a major that interests me and prepares me for my future job/career. • Select my required courses and map every term. • Choose my elective courses. • Meet with an academic adviser to make sure my academic map makes sense.	• I am organized. • I have a manageable range of interests.	• I can't use my time in college well if I don't know where I am headed. • An adviser can give me ideas for how I can apply my interests to a major.	• Meet with an academic and a career adviser by the middle of the term. • Obtain all the necessary signatures to finalize my academic plan. • Have the plan all ready to go by Thanksgiving break. **Potential Difficulties:** • I do not know an academic or career adviser. • I have not made a decision about the major I want to study. **How to Deal with Difficulties:** • Visit the academic and career advising centers to work with advisers. • Discuss my academic and career goals with the advisers and ask for their advice regarding the major I should select.
Career					
Personal					
Financial					

Connecting with Others

When you talk to college graduates and ask them what part of college was most memorable and influential, they will often tell you that it was the people. In college, fellow students, instructors, administrators, advisers, and other staff members will be important resources who can give you support in navigating college as well as enrich your overall experience. Let's consider the opportunities and challenges you will encounter when interacting with each group of people and how they can influence your college experience.

Students

Of all the different types of people on campus, the ones who will likely have the most influence on you and the choices you make are your fellow students. Other students are tremendously important to your success, so it is important that you get to know one another; your fellow students can be of traditional college age, older, veterans, those who come from another country, or part time. They can also be taking all or a few of their courses online.

Traditional students. If you are a traditional student, meaning that you are around eighteen years old and have just graduated from high school, the transition you are making will involve adjusting to some significant differences between high school and college. For instance, in college you will most likely be part of a more diverse student body, not just in terms of race and ethnicity but also in terms of age, religion, political opinion, sexual or

△ **You Aren't Alone**
You can develop social and learning relationships with other students through participating in study groups, joining an organization related to your major, or engaging in student activities. It's not wise to go it alone as you approach your first year of college; you will learn more deeply by interacting with other students. You will also develop friendships that will last through your college experience. *The Washington Post/Getty Images*

gender orientation, identity, and life experience. College is a perfect time and place to step outside your comfort zone and peer group. You will find your college experience significantly enhanced by time spent with those who are nontraditional or different from you in some other way.

Nontraditional students. If you are a nontraditional or adult student, you might have experience in the job market, and you might have a spouse or partner and children. You might be returning to college or beginning college for the first time. You will face a special set of challenges, such as trying to relate to younger students and finding enough time to juggle the important, competing responsibilities of work, caring for a family, and being in college. Remember, though, that nontraditional students have determination that comes with maturity and life experiences, and they appreciate the value of an education. You will have the advantage of approaching college work with a very clear purpose for why you are there, which your instructors will notice and appreciate. You may be intimidated by the advantages many younger students seem to enjoy because they were in school more recently, and you may also be intimidated by technology. But you and other nontraditional students also have many advantages as well, and you need to build your college success on those advantages.

Veterans. You might be one of hundreds of thousands of veterans who have come to campus after serving during the Iraq and Afghanistan conflicts or in other areas of the nation and world. If you are a veteran, you may have traveled the world, met all kinds of people, and faced life-threatening experiences. You may have already started college while you were on active duty. You likely made sacrifices, such as leaving your family behind, and you may have suffered either visible or invisible injuries. We believe that others on campus will find you and the stories you share about your time in the military very inspiring. Your knowledge and global experiences will enrich classroom discussions, and your perspective will be appreciated. Speak up and join in as much of campus life as your time will permit. Finally, we urge you to take advantage of special support services for veterans on your campus. Your school's veterans' affairs office is there to help

you maintain good grades and keep up with changes in your veterans' benefits, as Congress regularly revises benefits legislation.

International students. If you are a student who has come to the United States from another country, learning the unique language, culture, and expectations that exist at a U.S. college or university can be a challenge. Seek out English as a second language (ESL) courses or programs if you need help with your English skills. Also, visit the international student center on your campus to find out how you can continue to increase your understanding of life in the United States, both on and off campus.

As an important member of the college community, you will help U.S. students better understand and communicate with people from other countries. You will add a diverse perspective to class discussions and introduce students to what it might be like to work in a multinational organization. International students like you also play an important role in furthering peace and understanding among all peoples of the world.

Part-time students. If you are a part-time student, you are part of a large cohort in U.S. higher education. Students decide to enroll part time for many reasons. Maybe you have other obligations in your life, such as a family and a job, and need the flexibility of a part-time schedule. Or perhaps you are learning new skills to move forward in your current job. No matter what your age or particular characteristics, you will bring certain strengths to your college experiences that will help both you and others. Part-time students are motivated individuals who are experts at time management, often juggling work, education, and home responsibilities. However, if you, like many part-time students, commute to campus or take courses online, it can be challenging to feel part of the college community. It is also important to note that your financial aid options will be more limited than those of a full-time student. Be sure to talk to a financial aid adviser and analyze what it would cost you to move from part-time to full-time status in terms of the debt you would take on versus the income you would ultimately gain. If you decide that remaining a part-time student is the best option for you personally, professionally, and financially, know that college is just as real for you as it is for full-time students.

Online Learners

Some students will come to college with experience taking online courses in high school. For them, the idea of learning in an online setting will be easy to comprehend. But if you are a nontraditional student, this may be a totally new and confusing experience for you. Today, almost six million U.S. college students take courses online—about 28 percent of all enrolled students.[1] A few years from now, as more students want the flexibility and lower cost that online learning provides, the overall number of online students will be even larger.

Being an online learner will give you some advantages—for instance, you can take a class from home without having to travel to a college or university campus. If you are shy or reluctant to speak in class, online courses will make participating in class discussions or chats easier than in a face-to-face environment. Some students even report that they find it easier to concentrate in online courses because they are not distracted by other students.[2] Many online courses offer synchronous sessions in which you and your instructor meet online at a regular predetermined time. But the majority of online courses are asynchronous, meaning that you can access course materials and participate in class activities on your own schedule. Course materials, such as lectures, discussion boards, and e-mails, are recorded and always available, so if you miss any information or require more explanation, you can survey the material again.

Online learning, however, also comes with challenges. It is easier to procrastinate when your only contact with your classmates and instructor is online. The lack of formal structure can make it hard for undisciplined or unmotivated students to stay on track. And it is definitely harder to develop relationships with others in your classes. To succeed in an online environment, you will need to be very self-directed and disciplined as a learner. You will need to complete and turn in your assignments on time and become accustomed to taking online tests. However, if you are determined to do your best, your online learning experience can be as valuable as learning in a face-to-face setting.

△ **Connect Online**
College isn't just a physical place anymore, as an increasing number of students are choosing to take classes online. While it's true that online students have to work harder to connect with others, it isn't impossible. If you put in a little effort, you will likely meet people with many different perspectives, backgrounds, and goals in your classes, which will make learning online more engaging and enriching.
Hill Street Studios/Getty Images

[1] D. Frank Smith, "Report: One in Four Students Enrolled in Online Courses," *Ed Tech*, February 25, 2016, https://edtechmagazine.com/higher/article/2016/02/report-one-four-students-enrolled-online-courses.
[2] Paul Fain, "Only Sometimes for Online," *Inside Higher Ed*, April 26, 2013, https://www.insidehighered.com/news/2013/04/26/online-courses-are-second-choice-community-college-students-some-subject-areas.

Instructors

An important type of relationship you can develop in college is one with your instructors. Frequent, high-quality interaction with your instructors can have a positive effect on how well you do academically. Your instructors will expect you to be independent and to take the initiative to seek their advice and assistance. In addition, you will enjoy getting to know many of them, especially those who share your interests.

What do instructors expect? Whether you're a nontraditional student adjusting to less freedom than you're used to or a traditional student adjusting to more freedom, you will find that your instructors, whether online or face to face, are not going to tell you what, how, or when to study. In addition, they will rarely monitor your progress. You will, however, have more freedom to express views that are different from theirs.

TRY IT!

FEELING CONNECTED ▷ Get to Know Your Instructors

Developing relationships with your course instructors is important to your college success and to making a successful transition to college. Before your next class, do an Internet search on one of your instructors, and look for him or her on your campus website. Did anything you read pique your interest to learn more by talking with that instructor face to face? Research your other instructors over the course of the week, then make an appointment with an instructor whose background interests you. Get in the habit of visiting your instructors during office hours when you have a question, have a problem with a class assignment, or feel like strengthening these important connections.

To get a clear sense of instructors' expectations, pay close attention to the syllabus for each course. The syllabus, which you will receive on the first day of class, is both a statement of course requirements and a contract between you and the instructor. Whether on paper or online, the syllabus will give you information and dates for exams or presentations, a grading rubric, the course attendance policy, and other class guidelines or rules. Be sure to review and save the syllabus for each of your courses, so you can refer to them often.

In college, it is your responsibility to meet your instructors' expectations. In return, you can expect your instructors to be organized, prepared, and knowledgeable. They should give you thoughtful feedback on your work and grade it fairly.

Maximize learning relationships. You can meet with your instructors anytime during the term to ask questions, seek help, or discuss a problem. Most of your instructors will keep office hours—either virtual (meaning you connect online) or in person—during which they will be available to you. Talking with an instructor may seem a bit scary, but most instructors welcome the opportunity to get to know their students. By taking advantage of instructors' office hours, you are letting them know that you are serious about learning. During office hours, you can ask your instructors for direct help with any question or misunderstanding that you have. You might also want to ask questions about their educational careers and particular research interests, and share your own interests. Instructors who teach part time at your college, often called adjuncts, may not have assigned offices. While adjuncts are not usually required to maintain office hours, they are typically available to meet with you before or after class or by appointment.

The relationships you develop with your instructors can be valuable to you both now and in the future; you may even find that one or more of your instructors become lifelong mentors and friends. They can also write that

all-important letter of recommendation when you are applying for internships, research opportunities, graduate school, or a job during or after college. Many successful college graduates can name a particular instructor who made a positive difference in their lives and influenced their academic and career paths.

If you ever have a problem with an instructor, ask for a meeting to discuss the problem. If the instructor refuses, go to a person in a higher position in the department or college. If the problem is a grade, remember that your instructors have the right to assign grades based on your performance, and no one can force them to change those grades. However, you can always speak with your instructor,

66 Of all the relationships you experience in college, those you have with instructors may be among the most enjoyable and influential. 99

find out what mistakes you made, and determine how you can improve your grade in the future.

Administrators, Advisers, and Other Staff Members

Administrators, academic advisers, and other staff members at your college will provide you with all kinds of assistance and support: advising, tutoring, counseling, career planning, financial advising, and much, much more. They will keep you and other students on track and your college running smoothly.

These people make the most significant policy decisions, determine important financial allocations and priorities, and—along with faculty members—help govern the institution. You will interact with some of these leaders, but because they are so busy, you may have to make the effort to do so. One way to meet administrators and other important staff members is to get a job on campus. Another way is to use the support services available to you. While it is harder to connect with administrators and staff members in an online program, these programs often have robust support services, which allow you to talk with key people in real time over chat or on the phone. ∎

Send Professional E-mails

When you start college, you'll need to activate your college e-mail as soon as possible to receive information regarding class cancellations, weather-related closings, student events, and other types of communication that the college or your instructors may send you. Many colleges require you to use your student e-mail account to send and receive official communications. It is a good idea to get in the habit of checking that account daily or at least every other day. Whether your class meets online or face to face, at some point you will need to communicate with your instructor via e-mail unless he or she gives you another preferred method of communication. Writing e-mails to your instructors is different from writing e-mails or sending texts to your friends. Constructing well-written e-mails demonstrates that you are serious about learning and that you respect your instructor.

the GOAL

Send professional e-mails to your instructor.

how TO DO it

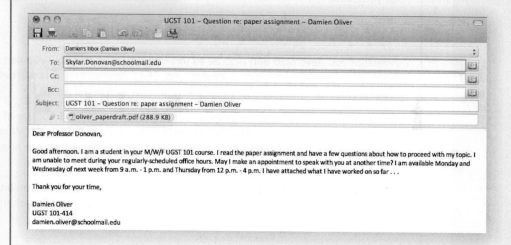

Follow the example here. It's best to use your college e-mail address because it has your name and college e-mail address, which will help your instructor recognize immediately that your message has been sent by a student. If you have to use another e-mail address, use a simple, professional address that includes your name. Here are some tips:

- **Make the subject line informative.** Your instructor might receive hundreds of e-mails every day, and a relevant subject line—such as the name of the course or the assignment—will help him or her respond to your e-mail promptly. A subject line like "Class" or "Question" isn't helpful; a blank subject line usually sends the e-mail to the instructor's spam folder.
- **Address your instructor with respect.** Think about how you address your instructor in class, or look at your syllabus to see his or her proper title. If an instructor uses "Doctor" (or "Dr."), then you should, too. If you don't know your instructor's title, you can never go wrong with "Dear Professor" plus his or her last name.
- **Sign every e-mail with your full name and course number.**
- **When attaching files to your e-mail, use widely accepted file formats, such as .doc, .docx, or .pdf.** Also include your last name as part of the file name.

your TURN

Draft a sample e-mail to one of your instructors asking for clarification on an assignment. Exchange your e-mail with a partner, then provide feedback on each other's e-mails.

Chapter Review

Reflect on Choices

Your decision to go to college is one of the most important decisions you will ever make. Chapter 1 explores how you can make the most of your college experience by connecting with others, thinking about the choices you make every day, and defining your purpose and your goals. Reflect on what you found most useful or meaningful in this chapter. What additional information do you need?

Apply What You've Learned

Now that you have read and discussed this chapter, consider how you can apply what you have learned to your academic and personal lives. The following prompts will help you reflect on the chapter material and its relevance to you both now and in the future.

1. Why are you in college? Reflect on your decision to enter this college at this time in your life. Be honest about who or what influenced you to make this decision. What challenges do you face, and what strategies for success in this chapter can you use to overcome those challenges?

2. What experience do you have in setting and achieving goals? Do you have attitudes or behaviors that get in the way of reaching your goals? How can you change any negative attitudes that tend to obstruct your progress?

Use Your Resources

GO TO ▷ Your college success instructor, check your college's directory or website, or call or visit student services or student affairs: If you need help finding college support services.

GO TO ▷ The academic advisement center or your assigned academic adviser: If you need help choosing courses and understanding degree requirements.

GO TO ▷ The career center: If you are interested in learning more about careers, finding job and internship listings, and evaluating your fit with a particular career.

GO TO ▷ Commuter services: If you need help finding off-campus housing options, information about your community, transportation information, or possible roommates.

GO TO ▷ The computer center: If you are looking for information on campus computer resources; need help using Word, Excel, PowerPoint, or e-mail; or want to improve your computer skills.

GO TO ▷ The counseling center: If you need help dealing with personal problems and stress management.

GO TO ▷ The financial aid and scholarship office: If you want to learn more about financial aid programs, scholarships, and grants.

GO TO ▷ The learning center: If you need help finding tutors and improving your study skills.

GO TO ▷ The veterans' affairs office: If you are a veteran who wants to learn more about opportunities available to you, including financial aid.

LaunchPad Solo
macmillan learning

LaunchPad Solo for *Step by Step* is a great resource. Go online to master concepts using the LearningCurve study tool and much more. **launchpadworks.com**

Cultivating Motivation, Resilience, and Emotional Intelligence

IDesign/Shutterstock

Although your cognitive, or academic, skills are key to doing well in college, much of your college success will also depend on your noncognitive characteristics—that is, your patterns of thought, feelings, and behavior that affect how well you do in your academic work. What if you have to work this afternoon and need to study for a test you have tomorrow? What if you experience car trouble on your way to work? What if your computer crashes and you have a paper due tomorrow? In these tough moments, how you think and feel will make all the difference. If you feel powerless and overwhelmed, you're more likely to give up—to skip studying, miss work entirely, or turn in a late paper. But if you believe you can overcome these challenges, you'll feel energized to keep going and figure out solutions.

One of the most important attributes you can develop is motivation—the ability to consistently and steadily pursue a goal by taking a course of action that you have chosen freely and "own" because you want to do it. Developing motivation also requires resilience—the ability to continue in spite of temporary setbacks. And lastly, it takes emotional intelligence, or the ability to recognize and manage moods, feelings, and attitudes. In this chapter, we'll look at these patterns of thought, feelings, and behavior and how they work together to help you become more successful in college and in life.

LaunchPad Solo
macmillan learning

To access ACES, the LearningCurve study tool, videos, and more, go to LaunchPad Solo for *Step by Step*.
launchpadworks.com

Review Your ACES Score

Take a moment to reflect on your **Motivation, Decision Making, and Personal Responsibility** ACES score, and insert it in the box to the right. Now, let's take action!

Did you score in the high, moderate, or low range? Are you surprised by your score? This score will help you learn more about yourself by measuring your strengths and weaknesses in understanding how to stay motivated, make decisions, and cultivate personal responsibility in college. In this chapter, we will focus on building skills in motivation, resilience, and emotional intelligence. Even if you already feel strong in these areas, be open to learning new strategies to help you improve your score as you move through the chapter. This chapter will further your understanding of why these topics are essential to your success in college.

Score:

○ High
○ Moderate
○ Low

To find your ACES score, log on to LaunchPad Solo for *Step by Step* at **launchpadworks.com**.

Preview the topic headings in this chapter. Then, in a journal or a readily accessible file, reflect on your current skills by answering the following questions:

▶ **What are your current strengths and challenges?**
▶ **What do you hope to learn from this chapter?**

Powering Through Challenges

AVAVA/Shutterstock

It's hard to believe that I, Tiffany, am getting ready to graduate from Wright State University. It hasn't always been easy for me. My first year got off to a great start. I was happy with all my courses, and I was making a lot of friends. However, during the last week of October, my dad called and told me that he had lost his job and probably wouldn't be able to pay my tuition for the spring term or the following year. I thought my life was over, and I couldn't see how I would be able to stay in school. For the next three weeks, I lost all motivation to keep up in my courses, and none of my new "friends" seemed to care about what I was going through.

It began to change for me when my college success instructor noticed that I wasn't paying attention in class and seemed really sad. She pulled me aside and asked what was going on. I told her about my dad's situation, and she shared her personal story with me. I learned that after high school, her family had very little money to support her going to college, and so she received a federally supported Pell grant. She also had to find a job almost immediately and had to balance her work and her studies throughout college. "I also had to send some of the money I was earning back to my family," she added. "It was hard, but I made it through by staying motivated and keeping the right attitude. And you can, too." She advised me to go to the university's counseling center to learn how to bounce back from hard times and also to visit the financial aid office to get help in finding a part-time job. When I discovered these resources, I felt empowered. I learned that there is a lot of help available on my campus. I worked part time throughout my college career, but I made it. Now I try to reach out to other students who seem to be giving up. Sometimes it's about money; other times it's about a romantic breakup or a really tough class. But I want to let students know that no matter what, help is available, and they can make it here at Wright State.

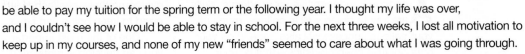

How did Tiffany change her situation? What skills did Tiffany need to learn in order to bounce back from her difficult situation? What can you learn from Tiffany's story that you can apply to your own challenges in college?

Motivation, Attitude, and Mindset

If you're like most students, you will face many challenges every day, from studying for exams to dealing with money troubles to taking care of family members. At some point in your college career, things *will* go wrong. When you're facing such challenges, how you *think* and especially how you *feel* will have a huge effect on your ability to solve problems and keep going.

The good news is that you can learn the skills you need to handle tough moments. And remember, you're not alone. Many of your classmates share your challenges and struggles. In this section, we'll go over important habits of mind and give you strategies that will help you achieve your goals. These goals include staying motivated, keeping a good attitude, and developing a growth mindset, all of which we'll explain in this section.

Motivation

Motivation, your desire to do well, is an essential ingredient of success, whether it is success in the classroom, in the office, or in life. The reasons why some of us are motivated or unmotivated represent a complex mix of our internal characteristics, attitudes, desires, and views on external rewards and punishments. When you are motivated, you have a high level of commitment and energy that you use to stay focused on a goal. You are determined to follow a course of action and do your best. When you hit obstacles, you make adjustments and work around them, or you deal with them head on.

In general, there are two kinds of motivation. *Intrinsic motivation* comes from a desire inside yourself to achieve something, and the reward is the feeling of satisfaction you get from achieving your goal. *Extrinsic motivation* comes from the expectation of an external reward or the fear of an undesirable outcome or punishment. In actual fact, you are motivated by both internal and external factors; there is always a mixture of reasons why you make the decisions you make and do what you do. It is important to note that motivation is not fixed and can change as you evolve, adjust your choices, and make choices throughout. Motivation is also tied to setting and achieving your goals. If your source of motivation is only extrinsic, you may have a tough time persisting to the goal.

TRY IT!

SETTING GOALS ▷ Extrinsic or Intrinsic?

Think about the goals—academic, personal, and career—that you are working toward now, and work through the exercise below. Name a goal in each category; write what is motivating you to work toward each goal; and circle whether your motivation is extrinsic, intrinsic, or both. You can expand on this exercise in a journal entry or in a group discussion.

My goals	My motivation	Extrinsic, intrinsic, or both?
Academic goal: _____	I'm motivated to achieve this goal because _____.	extrinsic intrinsic both
Personal goal: _____	I'm motivated to achieve this goal because _____.	extrinsic intrinsic both
Career goal: _____	I'm motivated to achieve this goal because _____.	extrinsic intrinsic both

Attitude

Attitude is the way you are thinking and feeling in relation to the events around you. Attitude is also an important part of staying motivated because it shapes your behavior and choices, whether it's being motivated to land a better-paying job, work out, or take advantage of all that college has to offer. For instance, if you have a bad attitude about writing, you might try to avoid the kinds of writing-intensive course experiences that are important to your success in and after college.

Whether positive or negative, attitudes often come from our previous environments and experiences with others. Have you ever wondered whether you were "college material"? Perhaps, at some point, someone—a family member or teacher—questioned your innate abilities. How would such a comment affect your attitude about starting college? Or maybe friends or family members told you how proud they are that you are in college, and this made you feel determined to work hard.

Your attitude will affect your success in your courses, your willingness to try out new experiences, and your ability to make and keep new friends. Search the term "self-fulfilling prophecy." This term describes the power of your own predictions about yourself to result in certain outcomes, whether positive or negative. If you have a negative attitude, you will put less energy into your academic work and you will be less willing to seek out new and different experiences. A positive attitude, however, will make a positive difference in the outcomes you experience in college—we guarantee it.

A good starting place in developing a more positive attitude is to think honestly about the attitude you're likely to have in certain situations. How would you handle stressful or surprising situations such as the ones listed below?

Situation	Describe your attitude. How would you react?
Your financial aid check doesn't arrive in time for you to purchase your books.	
You are responsible for taking care of a sick family member.	
As a non-native English speaker, you're struggling in many of your classes.	
You have a fight with your spouse or partner the night before a major exam.	
Your commute to campus is taking twice as long due to major road construction.	
You lose your notes, and your psychology final is next week.	
A group project isn't going well because other members aren't doing their share of the work.	

Any of these things can and do happen to students just like you. Most college students have many responsibilities, which can make it hard to maintain a good attitude and stay motivated. When you face these kinds of frustrations, do you get mad or stress out? Do you expect the worst, or do you stay relaxed, do your best, and keep going?

If you've been told by people who know you well that you're negative or pessimistic, or if you realize that you always expect the worst, maybe it's time for an attitude adjustment:

- Spend time thinking about what you can learn from difficult situations you have faced and overcome.

- Give yourself credit for good choices you have made, and think about how you can build on these successes.

- Seek out individuals, both on and off campus, who are positive. Ask them where their optimism comes from.

- Recall experiences in which things did not work out, and try to think through the mistakes you made and how you could have done better.

- Take advantage of the opportunities you will get in your college success course to explore the effect your attitude has on the outcomes you want.

- Be mindful of your attitude as you move through the weeks of this term.

Mindset

Another way to look at motivation is to examine what are called *mindsets*. Mindsets refer to what you believe about yourself and about your most basic qualities, such as your personality, intelligence, or talents. If you have a *fixed mindset*, you are likely to believe that your characteristics and abilities—whether positive or negative—are not going to change through any effort or adjustments to your behavior. A *growth mindset*, however, means that you are willing to try new approaches and that you believe that you can change.[1]

People with a fixed mindset are often trying to prove themselves, and they're very sensitive about being wrong or making mistakes. They also think that having to make an effort means that they are not smart or talented. People with a growth mindset believe that their abilities can be improved—that there is no harm in

[1] Carol S. Dweck, *Mindset: The New Psychology of Success* (New York: Ballantine Books, 2006), 16.

Mindsets: For each pair of statements, select the one that sounds more like you.

1a. You believe that your efforts won't change your grades.
1b. You believe that with effort, you can improve your grades.

2a. You believe that a good grade means you have learned everything you need to know.
2b. You believe that you can always learn more, even if you have received an A.

3a. You tend to blame the world around you when things go wrong.
3b. You try to solve the problem when things go wrong.

4a. You are often afraid to try new things because you fear you will fail.
4b. You believe that failure is an opportunity to learn more.

5a. You believe that some jobs are for "women only" or for "men only."
5b. You are open to exploring all job opportunities.

6a. You believe that leaders are born, not made.
6b. You believe that leadership can be developed.

7a. You tend to believe negative things that others say about you.
7b. You don't allow others to define who you are.

8a. You would prefer a life partner who will always tell you that you're perfect.
8b. You would prefer a life partner who will be honest with you, even if that means you will have to take occasional criticism.

9a. You tend to pick only those college courses that have a reputation for being easy.
9b. You like to pick some college courses that will challenge you, even if you might not earn an outstanding grade.

10a. You believe that negotiating with others is a sign of weakness.
10b. You believe that negotiating with others can be a sign of strength.

If you selected mostly "a" statements, you likely have a fixed mindset; if you selected mostly "b" statements, you likely have a growth mindset. As mentioned previously, our mindset can change depending on the task. Keep in mind that a mindset that is fixed today might not be fixed tomorrow. With some motivation, you can challenge yourself, take some risks, and develop a positive attitude about your ability to grow and change.

being wrong or making a mistake, and that making an effort is what makes them smart or talented. Some of us have a different mindset for different tasks. For instance, you may find that you have a fixed mindset in terms of your athletic abilities, but a growth mindset when it comes to music. What can you learn about your mindset by completing the following exercise?

Whether you're in your college classes, your job setting, or your home, your

mindset—similar to your attitude—can influence how you think about yourself and others, your opportunities, and your relationships. A fixed mindset will cause you to limit the things you do, the people you meet, and even the classes you take in college. A growth mindset will help you be more willing to explore classes and activities outside of your comfort zone. It will help you stay motivated because you will see disappointments or failures as opportunities to learn. ∎

Succeeding in an Online Class: It Takes Motivation!

If you are taking an online class or considering one for next term, it may be because it's the only way the class is offered, it's less expensive, you can participate on your own time rather than on a fixed schedule, or you don't have to leave home—working in your pajamas does sound appealing! Compared to your traditional courses, which are scheduled on particular days and times, most online courses are less structured and allow you to decide when to complete your coursework within the deadline. Because of this flexibility, many students find it challenging to maintain their motivation to do their best work and stay on top of their workload. As a result, they can fall further and further behind.

Before you dive into online learning, ask yourself the following questions: How can I keep up and do my best without face-to-face class meetings? What will motivate me in an online course? Am I ready to learn on my own without immediate access to other students and my instructor? Have I communicated with my instructor to get

some tips for doing my best? It's important to realize that online learning can be difficult—and sometimes even more difficult than face-to-face courses. Although some students learn just as well or even more effectively in an online environment, others find that it's not the best learning environment for them. If you're having difficulty with online learning, don't give up. Seek out suggestions by doing an Internet search on a broad topic such as "doing well in online courses." Communicate with your instructor and fellow students, and share strategies for being successful with one another.

Online courses require you to be a self-starter, so before you go online, be aware of what motivates you to learn best, and work on developing a positive attitude and mindset for doing well. If you discover that you will benefit more from a face-to-face lecture in terms of paying attention, consider signing up for in-person courses during your first year of college.

Resilience

Motivation requires a clear vision, courage, and persistence. And it takes *resilience*—not giving up or quitting when faced with difficulties and challenges. A resilient person maintains a positive attitude even when faced with difficult situations. Students who are resilient—who bounce back quickly from difficult situations—will be more successful both in college and in life. These students stay focused on achieving their purpose. Learning to keep going when things are hard is one of the most important lessons you'll learn in this class.

Another component of resilience is *grit*, a combination of perseverance, passion, and resilience. Psychologist Angela Duckworth studied grit and found that people who are "gritty" are more likely to be both academically and personally successful.[2] In her research, Duckworth studied cadets at West Point and contestants in the National Spelling Bee and found that those who succeeded in these stressful situations remained committed to their goal and never gave up. Grit refers to the ability to apply a sustained effort toward one's long-term goals. Like running a marathon, grit requires resilience and perseverance, but it also requires an ability to defer short-term gratification in favor of one's future. Being a "gritty" person means working every day on your goals, chipping away little by little, and always keeping the big picture in mind.

Another term that encompasses resilience comes from Finland. *Sisu* is a word that dates back hundreds of years and is described as being central to understanding Finnish culture. It means going beyond one's mental or physical ability, taking action even when things are difficult, and displaying courage and determination in the face of challenges and repeated failures.

Resilience is such an important concept in psychological health that the American Psychological Association has developed a list of resilience strategies: "10 Ways to Build Resilience."[3] These are as follows:

1. **Make connections.** Good relationships with close family members, friends, or others are important. Accepting help and support from those who care about you and who will listen to you helps you become more resilient. Assisting others in their time of need can also benefit the helper.

2. **Avoid seeing crises as problems that can't be overcome.** You can't change the fact that highly stressful events happen, but you can change how you view and respond to these events.

3. **Accept that change is part of living.** Accepting situations that cannot be changed can help you focus on those that can be changed.

4. **Move toward your goals.** Develop some realistic goals. Do something regularly—even if it seems like a small accomplishment—that enables you to move toward your goals.

5. **Take decisive actions.** Take decisive actions, rather than just wishing that problems and stresses would go away.

6. **Look for opportunities for self-discovery.** Struggles often make people stronger. Consider what you have learned about yourself from going through tough times.

7. **Develop a positive view of yourself.** Developing confidence in your ability to solve problems and trusting your instincts help build resilience.

8. **Keep things in perspective.** Even when facing a very painful event, try to consider the big picture and avoid blowing the event out of proportion.

9. **Maintain a hopeful outlook.** Try visualizing what you want, rather than worrying about what you fear.

10. **Take care of yourself.** Pay attention to your own needs and feelings. Engage in activities that you enjoy and find relaxing. Taking care of yourself helps keep your mind and body ready to deal with situations that require resilience.

[2] E. Packard, "Grit: It's What Separates the Best from the Merely Good," *Monitor on Psychology* 38, no. 10 (2007): 10, www.apa.org/monitor/nov07/grit.aspx.
[3] "The Road to Resilience," American Psychological Association, accessed September 4, 2015, www.apa.org/helpcenter/road-resilience.aspx.

In addition to these strategies, there are other ways to deal with challenges and stressful situations. For example, some people write about their thoughts and feelings related to trauma or other stressful events in their life. Meditation and spiritual practices help some people build connections and restore hope.

Think about your own reactions to frustration and stress. Do you often give up because something is just too hard or because you can't figure something out? Do you take responsibility for what you do, or do you blame others if you fail? For example, how have you reacted to receiving a D or an F on a paper or getting rejected for a job? Do you have trouble making connections with others in class?

Negative experiences might cause you to question whether you should even be in college.

△ **Don't Let Anything Stop You**
Show your grit. Have sisu. Be resilient. Succeeding in college can sometimes feel like making your way up a mountain. You will likely face lots of ups, downs, and rocky obstacles, but just imagine how great you'll feel when you reach the top. Whatever your goal, overcome the obstacles that get in your way, no matter what they are, and take in the views. Buena Vista Images/Getty Images

TRY IT!

FEELING CONNECTED ▷ **Share Your Story**
Think about a challenge you faced in the past. How did you feel at the time, and how did you respond to the challenge? In class, share your story with a partner, and reflect on each other's experiences. Have you ever experienced a challenge similar to your partner's? What do you admire about how your partner responded to that challenge? What can you learn from your partner's reaction and apply to your own challenges?

Resilient and "gritty" students, though, look past negative experiences, learn from them, and try again. For instance, what could you do to improve your grade on your next paper? Perhaps you didn't allow yourself enough time to do the necessary research. Why did you get rejected for the job you wanted? It's possible that you need to work on your interview skills. How can you feel more comfortable in your classes? Maybe it would help to join a study group or go to the academic learning center. You were born with the ability to be resilient. Many successful people have overcome tough circumstances and failure. For instance, J. K. Rowling, the author of the Harry Potter series, was divorced and penniless when she wrote the first Harry Potter book, which was rejected by twelve publishers before finally being accepted. Think of other examples of people who didn't let rejection stop them from working toward their goals. What about innovations ranging from vaccinations to spacecraft? Consider all the "failures" that scientists and engineers experience as they work toward their goals.

So far in this chapter we have asked you to consider how thoughts and feelings affect behavior. We've discussed motivation, attitude, mindset, and resilience, and we've asked you to explore what motivates you, to think about your own attitude and how it helps or hurts you, to examine your particular mindset, and to reflect on whether you are able to bounce back from difficulty. These topics are part of a broader discussion of emotions, which we examine next. ■

Understanding Emotional Intelligence

Emotional intelligence (EI) is the ability to recognize, understand, use, and manage your emotions—moods, feelings, and attitudes. Your emotional intelligence is related to how resilient you are, and it affects your ability to stay motivated and committed to your goals. As we noted earlier in this chapter, how you think and feel makes all the difference in whether you succeed or give up. Developing an awareness of emotions allows you to use your feelings to improve your thinking. If you are feeling sad, for instance, you might view the world in a negative way; if you are feeling happy, you are likely to view the same events differently. Once you start paying attention to emotions, you can learn not only how to cope with life's pressures and demands but also how to use your knowledge of the way you feel for more effective problem solving, decision making, and creativity.

Particularly in the first year of college, many students have difficulty establishing positive relationships with others, dealing with pressure, or making wise decisions. Other students are optimistic and happy and seem to adapt to their new environment without any trouble. Being optimistic doesn't mean that you ignore your problems or pretend that they will just go away, but optimistic people believe in their own abilities to address problems successfully as they arise. As you recall from the discussion earlier in this chapter, attitude has a big impact on success in college and in life.

Emotions, for better or worse, are a big part of who you are. Being aware of your own and others' feelings helps you gather correct information about the world around you and allows you to respond in appropriate ways. If you are a returning student, you probably have a great deal of life experience in dealing with tough times, and you can draw on this experience in college. The better the emotional awareness you have about a situation, the more appropriately you can respond to it.

Think about the behaviors that help people, including yourself, do well and the behaviors that interfere with success. Get to know yourself better, and take the time to examine your feelings and the impact they have on the way you act. You can't always control the challenges of life, but with practice you *can* control how you respond to them. Remember that emotions are real, can be changed for the better, and significantly affect whether a person is successful.

Perceiving and Managing Emotions

Perceiving emotions involves the ability to monitor and identify feelings correctly (nervous, happy, angry, relieved, and so on). This can be used to determine why you feel the way you do and predict how others might feel in a given situation. Emotions contain information, and the ability to understand and think about that information plays an important role in behavior.

Managing emotions is based on the belief that feelings can be modified, even improved. Sometimes you need to stay open to your feelings, learn from them, and use them to take appropriate action. At other times, it is better to disengage from an emotion and return to it later.

The Role of Emotional Intelligence in Everyday Life

Emotional intelligence may be a new term for you, but your emotions guide your behavior throughout your life, even if you do not realize it. Naming and labeling emotions, in addition to focusing on related experiences, improves emotional intelligence. As you work to develop your emotional intelligence, consider how to use logic rather than your own emotional reactions to evaluate a situation and be helpful to yourself and others.

Managing anger. Anger management is an EI skill that is important to develop. Anger can hurt others and can harm your mental and physical health. You may even know people who use their anger to manipulate and control those around them. In spite of the problems it creates, anger does not always result in negative outcomes. Psychologists see anger as a primary and natural emotion that has value for human survival. If you have a good reason to be angry, your anger can help you take a stand against injustice.

Managing priorities. Using healthy emotional intelligence to prioritize involves deciding what's most important to you and then allocating your time and energy according to those priorities. For example, if exercise, a healthy diet, friends, and studying are most important to you, then you must make time for them all. When you successfully make time for what is most important to you, your emotional health benefits: you feel more confident, more in control, and more capable of living your life with a positive attitude and handling others with patience. On the other hand, if you cannot keep what is most important to you at the top of your list of priorities, your attitude becomes negative, you feel stressed out, and you have less patience for other people. Part of developing strong emotional intelligence involves paying attention to your priorities and making adjustments when needed.

Emotional Intelligence Questionnaire

Your daily life gives you many opportunities to take a hard look at how you handle emotions. Here are some questions that can help you start thinking about your own EI:

1. What do you do when you are under stress?
   a. I tend to deal with it calmly and rationally.
   b. I get upset, but it usually blows over quickly.
   c. I get upset but keep it to myself.

2. My friends would say that:
   a. I play, but only after I get my work done.
   b. I am ready for fun anytime.
   c. I hardly ever go out.

3. When something changes at the last minute, I:
   a. easily adapt.
   b. get frustrated.
   c. don't care, since I don't really expect things to happen according to plan.

4. My friends would say that:
   a. I am sensitive to their concerns.
   b. I spend too much time worrying about other people's needs.
   c. I don't like to deal with other people's petty problems.

5. When I have a problem to solve, such as having too many assignments due at the end of the week, I:
   a. make a list of the tasks I must complete, come up with a plan indicating specifically what I can accomplish and what I cannot, and follow my plan.
   b. am very optimistic about getting things done and just dig right in and get to work.
   c. get a little overwhelmed. Usually I get a number of things done and then push aside the things I can't do.

Review your responses: "a" responses indicate that you have a good basis for strong emotional intelligence; "b" responses indicate that you have some strengths as well as some challenges in your EI; "c" responses indicate that your EI could negatively affect your future success in school and in life.

MANAGING TIME ▷ **Don't Waste Time Fussing and Fuming**

How much time do you spend on unnecessary drama, whether arguing over a text message with a friend or family member or obsessing about the bad way you were treated years ago by someone you thought you could trust? Time wasted on engaging in an ongoing battle with someone in your life or fuming about things that happened to you in the past is time you will never recover. Recapture your time and let it go.

Improving Emotional Intelligence

As you reflect more on your attitudes and behavior and learn why you have the emotions you do, you'll improve your emotional intelligence. Interacting with new and diverse people in the first year of college will challenge your EI skills and force you to step outside your comfort zone. Your first year will give you a significant opportunity to grow emotionally as well as intellectually.

Daniel Goleman, a well-known psychologist and journalist who has studied and written about emotional intelligence, offers two primary strategies for improving your EI. First, he says you should commit to improving your EI.[4] Goleman suggests that you get "360-degree feedback" from those around you—especially your friends and instructors. With this feedback, you can then work to strengthen specific areas of your personality. Goleman's second strategy is to "get practical." Instead of trying to change everything

[4] Daniel Goleman, "Emotional Intelligence," April 3, 2013, http://www.danielgoleman.info/developing-emotional-intelligence/.

> " Your first year will give you a significant opportunity to grow emotionally as well as intellectually. "

△ **Don't Boil Over**
If you leave negative emotions unchecked, they can boil over and affect other areas of your life. By learning to identify and manage your emotions, you can respond to the challenges of everyday life and establish positive relationships with others. PhotoAlto/Laurence Mouton/Getty Images

at once, you should focus on specific behaviors that need improvement. Goleman believes that behaviors change through practice over time, so be patient and devote three to six months to changing the "default" behavior into a new one. If you are struggling to get started, make an appointment with a counselor, who can provide you with support and guidance as you work to improve your EI.

A second EI expert, Reuven Bar-On, developed a helpful EI model,[5] which is adapted in Table 2.1. This model shows how categories of emotional intelligence directly affect general mood and lead to effective performance.

> **Motivation, attitude, mindset, and resilience are all linked to emotional intelligence.**

Identifying Your EI Skills and Competencies

Table 2.1, based on Bar-On's work, lists skills that influence a person's ability to cope with life's pressures and demands. Which skills do you think you already have? Which ones do you need to improve? Which ones do you lack? Consider the emotional intelligence skills and competencies listed in

[5] Reuven Bar-On, "What Is Emotional Intelligence?" in *Bar-On EQ-i Technical Manual* (Toronto, Canada: Multi-Health Systems, 1997). Reproduced with permission from Multi-Health Systems, Inc.

Table 2.1, and rank them accordingly: A = skills I already have; B = skills I need to improve; C = skills I lack. Then go back and rank each one in terms of its usefulness in addressing the challenges of being a successful college student.

Motivation, attitude, mindset, and resilience are all linked to emotional intelligence. Students with healthy emotional intelligence are more assertive—they are more likely to ask instructors for feedback on projects, papers, and tests; participate in classroom discussions; and join study groups. Students with unhealthy EI are more likely to struggle academically, panic before taking tests, have trouble concentrating on coursework, and engage in risky behaviors—such as alcohol and drug abuse—in an effort to cope.

You can do well enough to get by in college without strong EI. However, you might miss out on the full range and depth of skills and competencies that can help you succeed in your chosen field and have a fulfilling and meaningful life. ∎

TRY IT!

MAKING GOOD CHOICES ▷
Improve Your EI

Review how you ranked the EI skills and competencies in Table 2.1. What did you learn about yourself? Which skills do you have? Which ones do you need to improve? Which ones do you lack? Explore the resources available at your institution's learning and counseling centers to help you make the improvements in your emotional intelligence that will propel you forward in college and in your career. Doing so could be one of the best decisions of your life.

Table 2.1 ▽ **EI Skills and Competencies**

Skills	Competencies	Rank
Intrapersonal	**Emotional self-awareness.** Knowing how and why you feel the way you do.	
	Assertiveness. Standing up for yourself when you need to without being too aggressive.	
	Independence. Making important decisions on your own without having to get everyone's opinion.	
	Self-regard. Liking yourself in spite of your flaws (and we all have them).	
	Self-actualization. Being satisfied and comfortable with what you have achieved in school, work, and your personal life.	
Interpersonal	**Empathy.** Making an effort to understand another person's situation or point of view.	
	Social responsibility. Establishing a personal link with a group or community, and cooperating with other members in working toward shared goals.	
	Interpersonal relationships. Seeking out healthy and mutually beneficial relationships—such as friendships, professional networks, family connections, mentoring, and romantic partnerships—and making a persistent effort to maintain them.	
Stress management	**Stress tolerance.** Recognizing the causes of stress, responding in appropriate ways, and staying strong under pressure.	
	Impulse control. Thinking carefully about potential consequences before you act, and delaying gratification for the sake of achieving long-term goals.	
Adaptability	**Reality testing.** Ensuring that your feelings are appropriate by checking them against external, objective criteria.	
	Flexibility. Adapting and adjusting your emotions, viewpoints, and actions as situations change.	
	Problem solving. Approaching challenges step by step, and not giving up in the face of obstacles.	
	Resilience. Having the ability to bounce back after a setback.	
General mood	**Optimism.** Looking for the bright side of any problem or difficulty, and being confident that things will work out for the best.	
	Happiness. Being satisfied with yourself, with others, and with your situation in general.	

El = College and Career Success

Emotions are strongly tied to physical and psychological well-being. For example, some studies have suggested that cancer patients with strong EI live longer than those with weak EI. People who are aware of the needs of others tend to be happier than people who are not. An extensive study done at the University of Pennsylvania found that the best athletes succeed, in part, because they're extremely optimistic. A number of studies link strong EI skills to college success in particular. Here are a few highlights of those studies:

"Any other people skills, besides 400 Facebook friends?"

© Randy Glasbergen

- **Emotionally intelligent students get higher grades.** Researchers looked at students' grade point averages at the end of their first year of college. Students who had tested high for intrapersonal skills, stress tolerance, and adaptability when they entered in the fall did better academically than those who had lower overall EI test scores.
- **Students who can't manage their emotions struggle academically.** Some students have experienced full-blown panic attacks before tests. Others, who are depressed, can't concentrate on coursework. And far too many students turn to risky behaviors (drug and alcohol abuse, eating disorders, and worse) in an effort to cope. Dr. Richard Kadison, a former director of mental health services at Harvard University, noted that "the emotional well-being of students goes hand-in-hand with their academic development. If they're not doing well emotionally, they are not going to reach their academic potential."[6]
- **Students who can delay gratification tend to do better overall.** Impulse control leads to achievement. In the famous "marshmallow test" performed at Stanford University, researchers examined the long-term behaviors of individuals who, as four-year-olds,

were tested to see whether they would practice delayed gratification. The children were each given one marshmallow and told that if they didn't eat it right away, they could have another. Fourteen years later, the children who had immediately eaten their marshmallow were more likely to experience significant stress, irritability, and an inability to focus on goals. The children who had waited to eat their marshmallow scored an average of 210 points higher on the SAT; had better confidence, concentration, and reliability; held better-paying jobs; and reported being more satisfied with their lives.

- **El skills can be enhanced in a college success course.** Because these skills can be learned, infusing them in a college success course can improve first-year students' emotional intelligence and thus their ultimate success.[7]

Increasingly, employers are looking for strong interpersonal skills in job applicants. So, in addition to the greater personal success you'll find by developing strong EI skills, more career opportunities await as well!

[6] Richard Kadison and Theresa Foy DiGeronimo, *College of the Overwhelmed: The Campus Mental Health Crisis and What to Do about It* (San Francisco: Jossey-Bass, 2004), 156.

[7] Nicola S. Schutte and John M. Malouff, "Incorporating Emotional Skills Content in a College Transition Course Enhances Student Retention," *Journal of the First-Year Experience and Students in Transition* 14, no. 1 (2002): 7–21.

Monitor Your Online Image

You're open and honest with just about everyone on your social media accounts. Why is this a problem? It's not that you can't be yourself, but your online presence should be something that you can be proud of. Remember, once you put something online, it is public forever, regardless of your privacy settings. You have very little control over what happens to material after you make it public.

▶ the GOAL

Manage your online image to ensure that it sends the appropriate message to the world.

▶ how TO DO it

Allard Schager/Alamy

- **Honesty is the best policy, but oversharing is not, especially in the digital age.** This goes double for students, since colleges and employers—both present and future—can look you up online.

- **Manage your online image by being proactive and aware.** Make sure your privacy settings on Facebook are updated. Be careful about expressing controversial opinions online that could work against you. Encourage your friends not to share photos or videos that might be harmful to someone's reputation. If you are tagged in a picture that makes you look irresponsible, ask that the photo be removed immediately. The guiding rule should be to never assume that something that seems to have vanished from online sites, such as Snapchat or Facebook, is truly gone.

- **Delete old accounts.** If you have an old Twitter, Instagram, or WordPress/Blogger account—or another out-of-date account that is still open to the public—delete it. Old accounts can include incorrect information, and it is possible for your account to be hacked without your noticing.

- **Stay one step ahead.** Do an Internet search on yourself regularly, especially when applying for jobs. Make sure you know what potential employers can see.

▶ your TURN

Do an Internet search on yourself. What did you find? Is there anything that you don't want your instructor, family, or employer to see? If in doubt, ask a friend or classmate to give you feedback on your digital persona. Then take action!

Chapter Review

Reflect on Choices

This chapter offers several opportunities for self-reflection and writing in an effort to encourage you to develop an awareness of your noncognitive characteristics—those personal thoughts, feelings, and behaviors that can affect your college success. You can improve your motivation, attitude, mindset, resilience, and overall emotional intelligence; you just have to choose to do so. What strategies did you learn from this chapter that can help you when times get tough? What choices can you make that involve these noncognitive characteristics? Reflect on these strategies and choices in a journal entry or readily accessible file.

Apply What You've Learned

Now that you have read and discussed this chapter, consider how you can apply what you have learned to your academic and personal lives. The following prompts will help you reflect on the chapter material and its relevance to you both now and in the future.

1. Developing resilience is an important part of overcoming the challenges inherent in life and reaching your goals. Think about a time when you wanted to give up on a goal. What did you do? How does this event relate to earning a college degree? After reading this chapter, what strategies will you adopt to develop more resilience?

2. No one has the same mindset in all situations. For instance, you may be willing to challenge yourself at your job but not in the classroom. In what areas are you the most "fixed" in your self-assessment, and where do you welcome opportunities for challenge and growth?

3. Managing stress is an important skill in college, and balancing priorities is a component of emotional intelligence. Look through your course syllabi to identify upcoming assignments, exams, and other important dates. Can you anticipate times when you might be especially likely to become stressed? What can you do in advance to avoid becoming overwhelmed and overstressed?

Use Your Resources

GO TO ▷ The learning center: If you need help developing strategies for learning and good study skills. Students at all levels use campus learning centers to improve on the particular skills discussed in this chapter.

GO TO ▷ The counseling center: If you need help talking about problems you are having with motivation or managing your emotions. It is normal to seek such assistance. This kind of counseling is strictly confidential (unless you are a threat to yourself or others) and is usually provided free of charge, which is a great benefit.

GO TO ▷ The library: If you need help finding books and articles about motivation, resilience, or emotional intelligence.

GO ONLINE TO ▷ TED Talks: If you need help getting motivated and you enjoy inspiring talks. Search TED Talks for topics on motivation, failure, and resilience—for example, Dan Pink's "The Puzzle of Motivation" or Angela Duckworth's "Grit: The Power of Passion and Perseverance."

GO ONLINE TO ▷ Mind Tools: If you need help testing your emotional intelligence skills.

GO ONLINE TO ▷ Derek Sivers's website: If you need help finding additional perspectives on mindset; search "Derek Sivers mindset." Or search "psychology theories of motivation" to explore theories of motivation.

 **LaunchPad Solo** macmillan learning LaunchPad Solo for *Step by Step* is a great resource. Go online to master concepts using the LearningCurve study tool and much more. **launchpadworks.com**

03

Managing Your Time

Alexandr III/Shutterstock

How often do you find yourself saying "I don't have time"? Once a week? Once a day? Several times a day? The next time you find yourself saying it, stop and ask yourself whether it is really true. Do you really not have time, or have you made a choice, consciously or unconsciously, not to make time for that particular task or activity? Once you recognize that you can control and change how you use your time, you'll want to assess your time-management strengths and then set time-management goals and priorities.

The first step in this assessment is to acknowledge that you have control over how you use your time and many of the commitments you choose to make. Every day you make many small decisions that affect your time-management success, such as what time you get up in the morning, how much sleep you get, how much time you spend studying, and whether you allocate any time to exercise. All these small decisions have a big effect on your success in college and in life.

Being in control means that you make your own decisions and take responsibility for your actions. If you're a recent high school graduate, you'll find that two ways in which college differs significantly from high school are students' increased autonomy, or independence, and greater responsibility. If you're a returning student, you most likely have a high level of independence, but coming back to college creates responsibilities above and beyond those you already have, whether they be employment, family, community service, or other commitments. Whichever type of student you are, making the transition to college will create some unanticipated demands on your time, demands that will require new time-management strategies. You'll find these strategies in this chapter along with tools to help you set time-management goals, get organized, recognize and avoid common time-management problems, and make your schedule work for you.

Review Your ACES Score

Take a moment to reflect on your **Organization and Time Management** ACES score, and insert it in the box to the right. Now let's take action!

Score:

○ High
○ Moderate
○ Low

Did you score in the high, moderate, or low range? Are you surprised by your score? This score will help you learn more about your strengths and weaknesses in understanding how well you are able to stay organized and manage your time. Even if you already feel strong in this area, be open to learning new strategies to help you improve your score as you move through the chapter. This chapter will further your understanding of why these topics are essential to your success in college.

To find your ACES score, log on to LaunchPad Solo for *Step by Step* at **launchpadworks.com**.

Preview the topic headings in this chapter. Then, in a journal or a readily accessible file, reflect on your current skills by answering the following questions:

▶ **What are your current strengths and challenges?**

▶ **What do you hope to learn from this chapter?**

Getting Out of a Jam

On the first day of my English class, my instructor spent a lot of time talking about deadlines. "Review the syllabus, and enter all your upcoming tests and papers in your planner," Professor Hughes advised. So, I began typing everything into my phone's calendar. But once I opened my calendar, I got sidetracked thinking about my busy week, with all my shifts at the restaurant, the assignments for my upcoming classes, and my one-woman show, "Alyssa's Jam." It's sort of hard for me to think about the future when I'm not even sure when I'll be able to complete the assignment for the next class!

"Your final research paper should be at least fifteen pages long and will count for 25 percent of your final grade," Professor Hughes added. "Find a topic, and start gathering research materials now." I jotted down a couple of ideas during class and figured I'd go to the library later in the week to get help. As the term went on, I did a pretty good job of keeping up with assignments and tests that were coming up in the immediate future, but I kept putting off working on my final paper.

Cut to two weeks before the deadline: I still hadn't made it to the library, and panic was starting to set in. I decided to ask Professor Hughes for some help. He referred me to the chapter in my college success textbook on information literacy, and we walked over to the library together so that I could connect with a librarian. I knew that I would have to spend the weekend in the library in order to get the paper done and would have to manage my time very carefully for the next two weeks. I also realized I needed to make some tough choices about my priorities for the rest of the term, but I felt determined not to get myself into this kind of time jam again!

We often put off long-term projects in favor of what needs to get done in the moment, but this isn't a good time-management strategy, as shown by Alyssa's story. What could Alyssa have done differently to stay out of this jam? Have you ever found yourself in similar situation? What did you do? What time-management techniques do you hope to get from this chapter that you could apply to a situation like this?

Time: Your Most Valuable Resource

The way you spend your time should align with your most important values. To begin connecting your use of time with your values, first set some goals for the future. What are your goals for the coming decade? If you're like most students reading this book, one of your goals is probably to earn a degree. Maybe you've already decided on the career that you want to pursue. Or perhaps you plan to go on to graduate or professional school. As you look ahead to the future, you may see yourself buying a new car, owning a home, starting a family, owning a business, or retiring early. Achieving these goals will take a lot of your *time*, and time management is one of the most effective tools to assist you.

When considering all the things you'll need to do and the limited time you have, start with this question: How do you approach time? Because people are innately different and come from many different cultures, they tend to view time in different ways. For example, if you're a natural organizer, you probably enter all dates for assignments, quizzes, and exams on your calendar as soon as you receive each course syllabus, and you may be good at adhering to a strict schedule. On the other hand, if you are more laid-back, you may prefer to be more flexible, or to just go with the flow, rather than follow a daily or weekly schedule. You may excel at dealing with the unexpected, but you may also be a procrastinator. If this sounds like you, find time-management techniques that feel comfortable but that still help you keep on track. You may have to stretch a bit, but your efforts can have a significant payoff.

Setting Goals

More than likely, one goal you will set is to find a good job when you complete your degree, or a job that is significantly better than the one you have now. You might be working on identifying just what that "good job"

△ **Sold!**
Many people dream of owning their own home. How you spend your time is directly related to how you intend to spend your money. When planning a significant purchase, carefully consider how much money you need to earn and save before you can make the purchase. How much time will it take to make this happen?
© Ariel Skelley/Getty Images

looks like—what it pays, where the best opportunities to get that job are, what the hours are likely to be, and so on. You might even be taking steps to make yourself a competitive candidate in a job search.

In a job search, good grades and a college degree may not be enough to distinguish you. When setting goals and objectives for allocating your time, consider the importance of having a well-rounded résumé when you graduate. What would such a résumé look like? It might show that you participated in extracurricular activities, gained leadership experience, engaged in community service, took advantage of internship or co-op opportunities, developed job-related skills, kept up-to-date on technological advances, or pursued relevant part- or full-time employment while attending classes.

When it is time to look for a full-time job, you want to demonstrate that you have used your college years wisely. Doing so will require planning and effective time-management skills, which are highly valued by employers. Your college or university career center can help you arrange for an internship, a co-op program, or community service that will give you valuable experience and strengthen your résumé.

Prioritizing

Once you have established goals and objectives, your next step is to prioritize your time. Which goals and objectives are the most important to you? For example, is it more important to study for a test tomorrow or to attend a job fair today? Keep in mind that ignoring long-term goals in order to meet short-term goals isn't always a good idea. In fact, the more time and thought you devote to setting your long-term goals, the easier it becomes to know how to spend your time in the short term. With good time management, you can study during the week before a test so that you can attend a job fair the day before the test. One way that skilled time managers establish priorities is to create a to-do list (discussed in more detail later in this chapter), rank the items on the list, and then determine a schedule and deadline for each task. These tasks can be related to both long- or short-term planning.

TRY IT!

SETTING GOALS ▷ "I've Got to Get My Priorities in Order!"

How many times have you heard or said this? It's very common to find yourself spending time on the wrong things. Commit to making a list of your priorities for the week. Knowing which obligations and activities are most important helps you manage your time properly. If you are determined to get all the "have-tos" out of the way, you'll have more time to invest in "want-tos" and have more balance in your life. Balance helps you maintain your overall motivation for college.

Finding Balance

Another aspect of setting priorities in college is finding an appropriate way to balance your academic schedule, your social life, family and work responsibilities, and time for yourself. Social activities are an important part of the college experience. Being involved in campus life or the local community can increase your satisfaction with college and thus boost your achievement level and your determination to stay in college. However, if you never have time alone or time to study and think, you might feel overwhelmed. Plus, employment and family obligations are often time-consuming and usually aren't optional. For many students, the greatest challenge of prioritizing is to balance college with these other valuable dimensions of life.

Time in College and in Career

If you have a job, you have already learned your supervisor's expectations about time. If you need to start work at 8:00 a.m., it's not OK to come in at 8:15. If you work on projects, you likely have to meet deadlines. You cannot ignore them or make excuses for missing them. If you haven't had a job, you have probably observed someone in your family who works on a set schedule. Unless you work for yourself, you'll find punctuality to be a standard workplace rule, and even if you are self-employed, your clients will expect you to maintain schedules and do the work you promise. How likely are you to keep your job or earn a promotion if you cannot be depended on to do work on time? College is a lot like the workplace. While no one will "fire" you for being late to class or turning in a paper late, such behavior will have a negative effect on how others, especially instructors, view you, and it will also result in lower grades.

Many decisions you make today are reversible. You may later decide to change your major, and your career and life goals may shift as well. But the decision to take control of your life—to establish your own goals for the future, to set your priorities, and to manage your time accordingly—is important for both the present and the future.

Successful people frequently say that staying focused is a key to their success. To help you stay focused, make a plan. Begin with your priorities, and then think about the necessities of life. Finish what needs to be done before you move from work to pleasure. ■

R-E-S-P-E-C-T

How does time management relate to respect? Think of a time you had an appointment with someone who either arrived very late or forgot the appointment entirely. Were you upset or disappointed with the person for wasting your time? In college, if you repeatedly arrive late for class, you are showing a lack of respect for your instructors and your classmates, whether your actions are intentional or unintentional.

At times, what instructors perceive as inappropriate or disrespectful behavior may result from a cultural misunderstanding. All cultures view time differently. In American academic culture, punctuality is a virtue. Being strictly on time may be a difficult adjustment for you if you grew up in a culture that is more flexible in its approach to time, but it is important to recognize the values of the new culture you are encountering.

Here are a few basic guidelines for respectful behavior in class and in other interactions with instructors:

- Be in class on time. Arrive early enough to get settled and ready for class.
- Avoid behavior in class that is disrespectful to the instructor and other students. This includes answering your cell phone, texting, or checking Facebook; doing homework for another class; falling asleep; and whispering or talking.
- Don't "hog the floor" when participating in class discussion; give others the opportunity and time to express their ideas as well.
- Be on time for scheduled appointments with your instructors and advisers, and be prepared with good questions. This will show how much you appreciate their time and the help they can give you.

Time management is a lifelong skill. To secure and succeed at a good job after college, you will have to manage your own time and possibly that of the people you supervise. If you go to graduate or professional school, time management will continue to be essential to your success. Time management is also important as a way in which you show respect for others—your friends, your family, and your college instructors.

Managing Your Energy

Your best plans will not work if you do not have the energy to make them happen. You may plan to spend a couple of hours on your math homework at the end of a busy day before you go to bed. However, you may find that you are too tired to concentrate and solve the math problems. While learning to manage your time effectively, you must also learn to manage your energy, so that you have more control over your life and can achieve success in college.

Along with time, energy is an essential resource, and we have a choice about how we use it. Although energy is renewable, each of us has a limited amount of it in a twenty-four-hour period. Individuals have a daily pattern of physical, emotional, and mental activity. For instance, some people are early risers and have a lot of energy in the morning; others feel the least productive in the morning and can accomplish tasks at the end of the day more effectively, especially tasks that require mental energy and concentration.

The first step to managing your energy is to recognize your daily energy pattern and establish a routine around it. Use Table 3.1 to record your high, average, and low energy levels every day for a week. Use H for high, A for average, and L for low to identify which times of day you feel more or less energetic.

What did you learn about yourself by completing Table 3.1? What are the best and worst times for you to study? Determine whether you are capable of getting up very early in the morning to study or whether you can stay up late at night and still get to morning classes on time.

Table 3.1 ▽ **Monitoring Your Energy Level**

Time	Energy						
	Mon.	Tues.	Wed.	Thurs.	Fri.	Sat.	Sun.
Early morning							
Late morning							
Early afternoon							
Late afternoon							
Early evening							
Late Evening							

Establishing a study routine based on your daily energy pattern will help you develop a schedule that you can maintain and use to your advantage. If you have more energy on the weekend, for example, take advantage of that time to review or catch up on major projects, such as term papers, that can't be completed effectively in short blocks of time.

Schedule some downtime for yourself to regain your energy. Different activities work for different people. For example, you may stream Netflix or use Instagram for an hour or take a nap before you start doing your homework. Just make sure that you do not go over the amount of time you set aside as your downtime.

Your energy level also depends on your diet and other habits, such as exercise or lack of it. If you are juggling many responsibilities across several locations, you can use some very simple strategies to take care of yourself:

- Carry healthy snacks with you, such as fruit, nuts, or yogurt. You'll save time and money by avoiding trips to snack bars and convenience stores, and you'll keep your energy up by eating better.

- Drink plenty of water.

- Take brief naps when possible. Research shows that naps are more effective for regaining your energy than caffeine.[1]

- Try meditation. While meditation takes some time, it will increase your energy level so that you can accomplish more in fewer hours. ∎

[1] Sara C. Mednick, Denise J. Cai, Jennifer Kanady, and Sean P. A. Drummond, "Comparing the Benefits of Caffeine, Naps and Placebo on Verbal, Motor and Perceptual Memory," *Behavioural Brain Research* 193, no. 1 (2008): 79–86v.

△ **Stay Awake**
Like this student, you probably have a lot of demands on your time. Make sure to effectively manage your energy by getting enough rest, eating properly, and pacing yourself, or you might find yourself falling asleep while studying. OJO Images/Getty Images

Time-Management Pitfalls

Because you are human, you likely procrastinate at least occasionally, which makes it harder to manage your time. In fact, procrastination is one of the biggest challenges for college students; therefore, we're going to tackle it right away, along with the other most common time-management pitfalls.

Procrastination

To procrastinate means to put off doing something or to be slow or late about doing a task that should be done. Dr. Piers Steel, a leading researcher and speaker on the science of motivation and procrastination, writes that

---

Is Procrastination a Problem for You?

Take the following procrastination self-assessment to get a sense of whether procrastination is a problem for you. Place a number from 1 to 5 before each statement. (For example, if you "Agree" with a statement, place a 4 before the statement.)

1 = Strongly Disagree
2 = Disagree
3 = Mildly Disagree
4 = Agree
5 = Strongly Agree

____ I have a habit of putting off important tasks that I don't enjoy doing.
____ My standards are so high that I'm usually not satisfied enough with my work to turn it in on time.
____ I spend more time planning what I'm going to do than actually doing it.
____ The chaos in my study space makes it hard for me to get started.
____ The people I live with distract me from doing my classwork.
____ I have more energy for a task if I wait until the last minute to do it.
____ I enjoy the excitement of living on the edge.
____ I have trouble prioritizing all my responsibilities.
____ Having to meet a deadline makes me very nervous.
____ My biggest problem is that I just don't know how to get started.

If you responded that you "Agree" or "Strongly Agree" with two statements or fewer, you procrastinate from time to time, but it may not be a major problem for you. Reading this chapter will help you continue to stay focused and avoid procrastination in the future.

If you responded that you "Agree" or "Strongly Agree" with three to five statements, you are having difficulties with procrastination. Revisit the statements with which you "Agree" or "Strongly Agree," and look in the chapter for strategies that specifically address these issues to help you overcome obstacles. You *can* get a handle on your procrastination!

If you responded that you "Agree" or "Strongly Agree" with six or more statements, you may be having a significant problem with procrastination, and it could interfere with your success in college if you do not make a change. Revisit the statements with which you "Agree" or "Strongly Agree," and look in the chapter for strategies that specifically address these issues. Also, if you are concerned about your pattern of procrastination and you aren't having success in dealing with it yourself, consider talking to a professional counselor in your campus counseling center. It's free and confidential, and counselors have extensive experience working with students who have problems with procrastination.

procrastination is on the rise, with 80 to 95 percent of college students spending time procrastinating.[2] According to Steel, half of all college students report that they procrastinate on a daily basis, spending as much as one-third of their time in activities solely related to procrastination. These numbers, plus widespread acknowledgment of the negative effects of procrastination, provide evidence of a serious issue that trips up many otherwise capable people.

The good news is that of all the people who procrastinate on a regular basis, 95 percent say they want to change their behavior.[3] An important first step toward change is to understand why you procrastinate. According to Steel, people who are highly motivated often fear failure—and some people even fear success. Consequently, some students procrastinate because they are perfectionists; not doing a task might be easier than having to live up to their own very high expectations or those of their parents, teachers, or peers. Many procrastinate because they are easily distracted, have difficulty organizing and regulating their lives, or have difficulty following through on long-term goals. These students might find an assigned task boring or irrelevant or consider it unimportant busywork.

Changing how you approach less enjoyable assignments is key to overcoming procrastination and increasing your success in college. For instance, simply disliking an assignment is an *excuse* for putting it off, not a valid *reason*. Life is full of tasks you won't find interesting, and, in many cases, you won't have the option to ignore them. Whether it is cleaning your house, filing your taxes, completing paperwork, or responding to hundreds of e-mails, tedious tasks will always be there, and you will have to figure out strategies for completing them. Remind yourself of the possible consequences if you do not begin your work. Then get started. When you're in college, procrastinating can signal that it's time to reevaluate your goals and objectives and your readiness for academic work at this point in your life. A counselor or an academic adviser can help you sort this out.

[2] Piers Steel, "The Nature of Procrastination: A Meta-Analytic and Theoretical Review of Quintessential Self-Regulatory Failure," *Psychological Bulletin* 133, no. 1 (2007): 65–94.
[3] Ibid.

> ❝ Being overextended is a primary source of stress for college students. ❞

Being Spread Too Thin

Being overextended is a primary source of stress for college students and another pitfall to managing time. Often, students underestimate how much time it will take to do well in college and overschedule themselves with work and other commitments. The best advice is to prioritize—focus on what you *can* manage.

If you do not have enough time to carry your full course load and meet your commitments, drop a course before the deadline so that you don't end up with a low grade on your permanent record. Keep in mind, however, that if you receive financial aid, you must be registered for a minimum number of credit hours to maintain your current level of aid. If dropping a course is not feasible, let go of one or more of your least important nonacademic commitments. Learn to say no. Saying no can be

△ **Just Give Mommy a Minute . . .**
Anyone who has tried to get work done at home with children around knows that it doesn't usually work out very well. Trying to focus on kids and work at the same time results in neither getting enough attention. Try to set aside time in your day for uninterrupted studying. Sometimes this will mean hitting the books after the kids have gone to bed. © JDC/Getty Images

difficult, especially if you think that you are letting other people down. However, it is far more preferable to respectfully excuse yourself from an activity than to fail to come through at the last minute.

Distractions

Distractions are another common pitfall when it comes to time management. Some students use distractions as excuses to procrastinate. Others don't want to be distracted, and they need coping strategies to help them focus on the tasks at hand.

Consider the types of distractions you encounter, and when and where you are most often distracted. For instance, where should you study? Some students find it best to avoid studying in places associated with leisure, such as at the kitchen table, in the living room, or in front of the TV. Similarly, it might not be wise to study on your bed because you might drift off to sleep. Instead, find quiet places—both on campus and at home—where you can concentrate without interruption each time you sit down to do your work. Also, it is

TRY IT!

MANAGING TIME ▷ **Are You about to Lose It?**

Are you trying to do too much, and is your crazy schedule reducing your motivation for college? Are you working too many hours? Are you feeling extremely stressed out? In a small group, brainstorm strategies for reducing your stress level and maintaining your motivation for being successful in your academic work.

important to stay offline and off your mobile device during planned study sessions.

Accurately predicting the distractions you will face is especially important. For instance, if you have children at home, assume that they will always want your attention no matter how much others try to help out. It's a good idea to develop strategies for minimizing distractions while you study. To get started, take a look at the examples and activity in Table 3.2.

Table 3.2 ▽ Strategies for Minimizing Distractions

Distraction	Solution
You're tempted to message your friends or check social media.	Turn off the sound and vibration on all devices; put them in another room or leave them at another location.
Your children want your attention.	If possible, study away from home or after the children have gone to bed.
You keep falling asleep during studying.	Sit upright at your desk or worktable; avoid studying in bed or on the couch; try to get more rest. Use Table 3.1 to build a new study schedule.

List some distractions that you face, and come up with solutions to avoid them.

Distraction	Solution
_____	_____
_____	_____
_____	_____
_____	_____
_____	_____

Motivation Problems

Motivation is an essential component of setting and achieving your academic and life goals, and the absence of motivation is a major pitfall. Forcing yourself to do something in which you have no interest is almost impossible. If you have lost interest in your academic or career path—if you feel unmotivated—it may be time to consider a change. Talk with an academic adviser or counselor about how to refocus your purpose for being in college and regain your motivation.

Many students of all ages question their decision to attend college and sometimes feel overwhelmed by the additional responsibilities that being in college brings. Prioritizing, rethinking some commitments and letting some things go, and weighing the advantages and disadvantages of attending college part time versus full time can help you work through this adjustment period. Make a plan that begins with your priorities: attending classes, studying, working, and spending time with the people who are important to you. Then think about the necessities of life: sleeping, eating, exercising, and relaxing. Leave time for fun things—such as talking with friends, tweeting, streaming your favorite show, and going out—but finish what *needs* to be done before you move from work to pleasure. Also, don't forget about personal time. If you live in a residence hall or share an apartment with other students, talk with your roommates about how to coordinate your class schedules so that each of you has some privacy. If you live with your family, particularly if you are a parent, work with family members to create special family times as well as quiet study times. If you're taking courses online, finding ways to stay engaged and organized can be more difficult. Time management in online courses that have few or no weekly meetings is challenging. Connecting with another student in your courses can help both of you stay on track with deadlines for submitting assignments, completing projects, and posting comments.

Don't let the challenges of this early adjustment period into college kill your motivation. Take control of this transition by developing a plan to manage your time. ∎

Ask Yourself the Tough Questions

If you are having trouble with one or more of these time-management pitfalls, it's time to get honest: Why are you in college here and now? Why are you taking the courses you have chosen? What is really important to you? Is what you value important enough to forgo some short-term fun or laziness and get down to work? Are your academic goals really your own, or were they imposed on you by family members, your employer, or society? Think about your answers to these tough questions. Then consider this: Why aren't you motivated to get busy?

Once you are able to get at the heart of why you are struggling to get down to work, you'll be able to better tailor your strategy for combating it. Did you discover that you struggle with perfectionism, and starting an assignment feels too overwhelming? Begin by breaking down an assignment into manageable pieces, then tackle those steps that you can easily finish to begin building your confidence. If you are still struggling, talk to a counselor about strategies to shift your mindset to embrace mistakes and imperfections as part of the learning process. Or maybe you realized that you're not motivated to work because you aren't excited about your major. If that is the case, take some time to discover what you might be interested in studying, and talk with an academic adviser about switching your major. There is always a solution if you are willing to dig deep. Consider the strategies mentioned throughout this chapter to remain focused and motivated on your goals, and seek support from instructors, fellow students, and college staff.

Get Smart about Organizing Your Days, Weeks, Tasks, and More

As you begin your first year of college, how far ahead are you in making plans and developing a schedule? Your academic year will be divided into chunks of time, or terms—either semesters, which are fourteen to sixteen weeks long, or quarters, which are about twelve weeks long. You will quickly discover the temptation to plan for only today or tomorrow, but begin by taking a long view. Think of the time between now and when you plan to graduate. Do you have a good idea of which courses you will have to take and when? Work with your academic adviser to make sure that you stay on track and get in all your requirements for graduation. If you plan to transfer, make sure that the new institution will accept the credits for the courses you are taking now or are planning to take. Seek help from your academic adviser and from an adviser at the college or university to which you plan to transfer.

If you are a parent or are working off campus, the whole idea of planning ahead may seem futile. We all know how often life gets in the way, and the best-laid plans may have to be adjusted to meet last-minute emergencies. You'll be more likely to manage your life and juggle your responsibilities, though, if you create a term-length calendar as you begin your college experience. Many techniques and tools, both paper and digital, are available to help you manage your time. Which system you choose doesn't really matter; what *does* matter is that you select a tool and use it every day.

Using a Daily or Weekly Planner

In college, as in life, you will quickly learn that managing your time is a key not only to survival but also to success. Consider buying a week-at-a-glance organizer for the current year. Your campus bookstore may sell one specifically designed for your college or university, with important dates and deadlines already provided. Many students today prefer to use an electronic planner; that's fine—your computer, smartphone, or tablet comes equipped with a calendar.

Carry your planner with you at all times, and enter all due dates as soon as you know them. Write in meeting times and locations, scheduled social events, study time for each class, and so on. Add phone numbers and e-mail addresses, too, in case something comes up and you need to cancel plans with someone. Get into the habit of using a planner to help you keep track of commitments and maintain control of your schedule. Choose a specific time each day to check your notes for the current and coming weeks. Making certain that you aren't forgetting something important takes just a moment— and helps relieve stress!

Scheduling Your Time Week by Week

Use the following steps to schedule your time for each coming week:

- Begin by entering all your commitments for the week—classes, work hours, family commitments, and so on—on your schedule.

- Track your activities for a full week by entering into your schedule everything you do and how much time each task requires (see Figure 3.1). Use this record to help you estimate the time you will need for similar activities in the future.

- Try to reserve at least two hours of study time for each hour spent in class. This 2-for-1 rule reflects many faculty members' expectations for how much work their students should do to master the material in their classes. So, for example, if you are taking a typical full-time class load of fifteen credits, you should plan to study an additional thirty hours each week. Think of this forty-five hour per week commitment as comparable to a full-time job.

- Establish a study routine that is based on your daily energy pattern (see Table 3.1), obligations, and potential distractions.

Figure 3.1 ▽ Weekly Timetable

Using your class schedule for the term and adding other obligations, create your own weekly timetable using an app like iCal or LifeTopix. At the beginning of the term, track all of your activities for a full week by entering into your schedule everything you do and how much time each task requires. Use this record to help you estimate the time you will need for similar activities in the future.

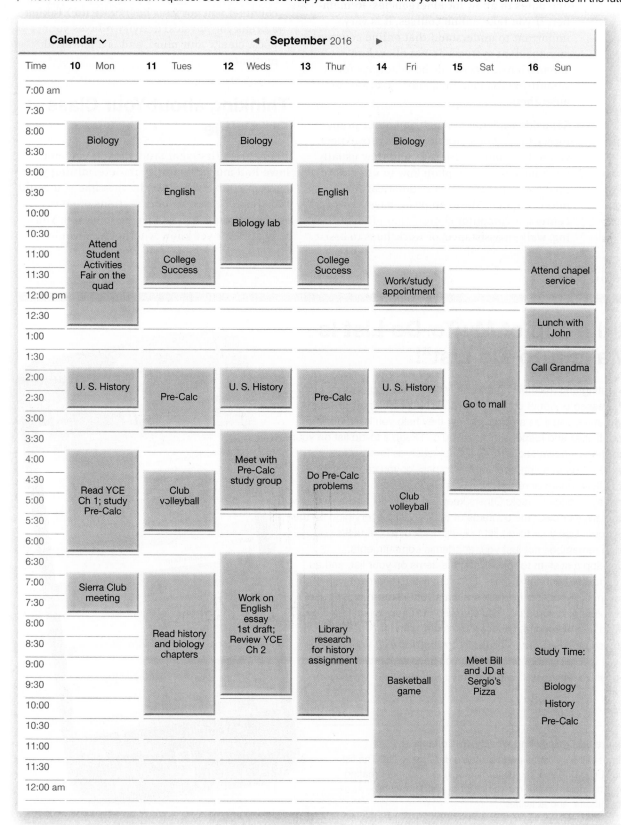

- Estimate how much time you will need for each assignment, and plan to begin your work early. A good time manager frequently plans to finish assignments before the actual due dates to allow for emergencies. Remember: If you take online courses, it is very important to understand that online course management systems do not allow late submissions. Record all the deadlines for submitting assignments, and make sure to meet them.

- Set aside time for research and other preparatory tasks. For example, instructors expect you to be computer literate, and they usually don't have time to explain how to use a word processor, spreadsheet, or statistical computer program. Most campuses have learning centers or computer centers that offer tutoring, walk-in assistance, or workshops to assist you with computer programs, e-mail, and Internet searches.

- Schedule at least three aerobic workouts per week. (Walking to and from classes only counts if you get your heart rate up.) Taking a break for physical activity relaxes your body, clears your mind, and is a powerful motivator.

Thinking about Your Class Schedule

If you are a first-year student, you may not have had much flexibility in determining your current course schedule; by the time you could register for classes, some sections of your required courses may have been closed. You may also not yet know whether you would

At the Top of My To-Do List Is "Make a To-Do List"!

Creating and maintaining a to-do list can help you avoid feeling stressed or out of control. If to-do lists become part of your daily routine, you'll be amazed at how they help you keep up with your activities and responsibilities. You can keep a to-do list on your smartphone—download a to-do list app such as Errands (see Figure 3.2)—or in a notebook or memo pad, or you can post it on your bulletin board or refrigerator. Some people start a new list every day or once a week. Others keep a running list and only throw a page away or clear the contents of the list when everything on the list is done. Use your to-do list to keep track of all the tasks you need to remember, not just your academic commitments.

Develop a system for prioritizing the items on your list, and as you complete each task, cross it off your list. Experiment with color—make your lists in black and cross out items in red, or use highlighters or colored ink. You can also rank your to-do items by marking them with one, two, or three stars; with the letters A, B, or C; and so on. Use your to-do list in conjunction with your planner. You will feel good about how much you have accomplished, and this positive feeling will help you stay motivated.

Figure 3.2 ▷ Daily and Weekly To-Do Lists
Almost all successful people keep a daily to-do list. The list may be in paper or digital form. Get in the habit of creating and maintaining your own daily list of appointments, obligations, and activities.

prefer taking classes back-to-back or having a break between classes.

In building a schedule that is right for you, you have to consider many factors. How early in the morning are you willing to start classes, and how late would you want to be in class? What impact will work or family commitments have on your scheduling decisions? What times of day are you more alert? Less alert? How many days a week do you want to attend classes? Over time, have you found that you prefer spreading your classes over four or five days of the week? Or have you discovered that you like to go to class just two or three days a week, or only once a week for a longer class period? Your attention span as well as your other commitments may influence your decisions about your class schedule.

It is also important to factor your travel time into your schedule, whether going from class to class or commuting to and from your college. If you live on campus, you may want to create a schedule that situates you near a dining hall at mealtimes or allows you to spend breaks between classes at the library. Or you may need breaks in your schedule for relaxation. You may want to avoid returning to your residence hall to take a nap between classes if a nap will make you feel lethargic or cause you to oversleep and miss later classes. Also, if you attend a large

> ❝ It is also important to factor your travel time into your schedule, whether going from class to class or commuting to and from your college. ❞

TRY IT!

FEELING CONNECTED ▷ Compare Your Class Schedules

Are you happy or unhappy with your class schedule? Do you have enough time to get from one class to another? Are any classes too early or too late for your preference? In a small group, share your current class schedules, and exchange ideas on how to handle time-management problems and the challenges you see in your schedules. Discuss how you would arrange your schedule differently for the next term. Go online and check the days and times of the classes you'd like to take next term. See if it's possible for you to get the courses you want within the schedule that you prefer.

△ **Getting from Here to There**
College students have the responsibility to get themselves to class on time and must plan transportation carefully, whether walking, driving, bicycling, ride sharing, taking public transportation, or using another method of getting from place to place. If you have an emergency situation that causes you to run late, talk to your instructor. He or she will understand a real emergency and help you make up any work you missed. wong yu liang/Shutterstock

college or university, be sure that you allow adequate time to get from building to building.

If you are a commuting student or you work off campus, you may prefer scheduling your classes together in blocks without breaks. *Block scheduling*, which means enrolling in back-to-back classes, allows you to cut travel time by attending classes one or two days a week, and it may provide more flexibility for scheduling employment or family commitments.

In spite of its advantages, block scheduling also has its drawbacks. If you become ill on a class day, you could fall behind in all your classes. You might also become fatigued from sitting in class after class. Also consider that, for back-to-back classes, several exams might be held on the same day. Scheduling classes in blocks might work better if you have the option of attending lectures at alternative times in case you are absent, if you alternate classes with free periods, and if you seek out instructors who are flexible about due dates for assignments. ∎

Use Digital Tools to Control Your Time

Whether or not you're taking an online class, you probably spend a great deal of time each day using various forms of technology. In today's world, the ability to use technology is essential to many aspects of daily life; almost everything you do—applying for a job, making a doctor's appointment, purchasing the things you need—can be done online. Technology can help you save time, but you must be in control of the way you use it. Even if you start out with the best intentions to go online for one specific purpose, you may find yourself scrolling through interesting websites or checking social media while the hours fly by.

▶ the GOAL

Explore new tech tools to take control of how you spend your time.

▶ how TO DO it

One way to make technology work for you is to explore the variety of apps that help you organize your time and your life. Here are a few for you to explore:

- **Focus@Will.** This app provides you with music that has been scientifically optimized to increase concentration. It allows you to customize the intensity of the music to fit your mood, and to track your productivity over time to better personalize the app for your biorhythms.
- **iStudiezPro.** This electronic planner allows you to track your course load, lectures, grades, and GPA, as well as organize your assignments based on due date and priority.

◁ iStudiezPro App for Android Devices
Courtesy of iStudiez Team

- **Remember the Milk.** This task-management and reminder app lets you create to-do lists.
- **Trello.** Trello will help you keep track of projects from the big picture to the small details. And, with its collaborative features, it will help you manage your group projects as well.
- **Toggl.** Toggl is a time-tracking app that allows you to measure how long you spend on your projects in order to use your time in the best way possible.

▶ your TURN

Do any of these tools interest you? Download one of these tools to your smartphone or computer, and try it out for a week.

Maximizing Study and Review Time

Studying effectively means that you need to consider the time of day or night when you study best, where you can study with the least distractions, and how to actually learn while you study. Here are some strategies you can use to get the most benefit from your study time:

- **Find your space.** Use the same study area regularly, and make sure it is free of distractions and quiet enough that you can focus. The library is usually the best choice. Try empty classrooms and study halls on campus, too. Bring essential supplies to your study area. Make sure you have everything you need.

- **Stick to a study routine.** The more firmly you have established a specific time and a quiet place to study, the more effective you will be in keeping with your schedule.

- **Break down large tasks.** Tackle short, easy-to-accomplish tasks first. By taking small steps, you will make steady progress toward your academic goals.

- **Set realistic goals for your study time.** Assess how long it takes to read a chapter in different types of textbooks and to review notes in your courses, and then schedule your time accordingly. Allow adequate time to both review and test your knowledge when preparing for exams. Online classes often require online discussions and activities that take the place of face-to-face classroom instruction, so be prepared to spend additional time on these tasks.

- **Review when the material is fresh.** Schedule time to review your notes immediately after class or as soon as possible; this will help you remember more of what you learned in class. Invest in tools (note cards, digital recorders, flash-card apps) to convert less productive time into study time.

- **Time and attention.** Know your best times of day to study, and routinely assess your attention level. Schedule activities such as doing laundry, checking Facebook or Instagram, and seeing friends or family for those times of day when you have difficulty concentrating. Also, use waiting time (on the bus, before class, before appointments) to review.

- **Study difficult or uninteresting subjects first, when you are fresh.** (Exception: If you are having trouble getting started, it might be easier to begin with your favorite subject.)

- **Divide study time into fifty-minute blocks.** Study for fifty minutes, take a ten- or fifteen-minute break, then study for another fifty-minute block. Try not to study for more than three fifty-minute blocks in a row, or you will find that you are not accomplishing fifty minutes' worth of work in each block. (In economics, this drop-off in productivity is known as the "law of diminishing returns.") If you have larger blocks of time available on the weekend, take advantage of them to review or to catch up on major projects.

- **Script your study sessions.** Break extended study sessions into a variety of activities, each with a specific objective. For example, begin by reading, then develop flash cards by writing key terms and their definitions or key formulas on note cards, and finally test yourself on what you have read.

- **Avoid multitasking.** Although you may be good at juggling many tasks at once, or at least you *think* that you are, the reality is (and research shows) that you will study more effectively and retain more if you concentrate on one task at a time.

- **Limit distracting and time-consuming communications.** Check your phone, tablet, or computer for messages or updates at a set time, not whenever you think of it. Constant texting, browsing, or posting can keep you from achieving your academic goals. Particularly if you are taking online courses and need to be connected when studying, turn off all the notifications on your device. The notifications may tempt you to check messages or posts and thus waste valuable study time. Remember: When time has passed, you cannot get it back.

- **Let others help.** Find an accountability partner to help keep you on track. If you struggle with keeping a regular study schedule, find a friend, relative, or classmate to keep you motivated and on course. If you have children, plan daily family homework times, and encourage family members to help you study by taking flash cards wherever you go.

- **Be flexible.** You cannot anticipate every disruption to your plans. Build extra time into your study schedule so that unexpected interruptions do not prevent you from meeting your goals.

- **Reward yourself!** Develop a system of short- and long-term study goals, as well as rewards for meeting those goals. Doing so will keep your motivation high. ■

Chapter Review

Reflect on Choices

College presents you with choices. One of them is whether you are going to pay close attention to how you spend your time. If you choose to neglect the issue of time management, you will risk both losing a resource that you can never recover and sabotaging your chances for success in college. Did any of the time-management tips in this chapter appeal to you? If so, which ones? Do you still have questions about time management? If so, what are they? Write about your preferred tips and any questions that remain in a journal entry or readily accessible file. Revisit these questions throughout your first-year experience.

Apply What You've Learned

Now that you have read and discussed this chapter, consider how you can apply what you have learned to your academic and personal lives. The following prompts will help you reflect on the chapter material and its relevance to you, both now and in the future.

1. Review the "Time-Management Pitfalls" section in this chapter. Think of an upcoming assignment in one of your current classes, and describe how you can avoid waiting until the last minute to get it done. Break down the assignment, and list each step that you will take to complete the assignment. Give yourself a due date for each step and for completing the assignment.

2. Now that you've read about effective time-management strategies, consider the ways in which you manage your own time. If you were grading your current set of time-management skills, what grade (A, B, C, or lower) would you give yourself? Why? Have you overloaded your schedule? Are you working too many hours off campus? Are you being distracted by your roommate, family, or friends? What is your biggest challenge to becoming a more effective time manager?

Use Your Resources

GO TO ▷ The academic skills center: If you need time-management advice that is specific to you, whether it is help studying for exams, reading textbooks, or taking notes. If you are an online student, communicate with your instructor or other online students about how to manage time in an online environment.

GO TO ▷ The counseling center: If you need help with difficult emotional issues related to time management.

GO TO ▷ Your academic adviser/counselor: If you need help in finding another person on campus to help you with time-management issues.

GO TO ▷ The office for commuter students: If you commute back and forth and need help finding the quickest ways to get to and from campus.

GO TO ▷ Your peer leader: If you want to discuss the time-management strategies he or she has developed.

GO TO ▷ Fellow students: If you need to commiserate with others who know what it feels like to try to make time for everything a college student needs to do.

LaunchPad Solo
macmillan learning

LaunchPad Solo for *Step by Step* is a great resource. Go online to master concepts using the LearningCurve study tool and much more. **launchpadworks.com**

Learning and Thinking in College

IDesign/Shutterstock

Learning and thinking are intertwined concepts. In order to learn in college and in life, you will need to go beyond just accepting what others say; you will also need to be a strong thinker, able to solve problems, analyze and synthesize different ideas, and make decisions. Your thinking skills will help you gain knowledge about the subjects you are studying, learn more about yourself, and feel empowered to make the academic and personal decisions that are best for you. In this chapter, we'll look at what science tells us about how we learn, then help you explore your own style of thinking and learning. We'll also discuss what constitutes college-level thinking—the type of thinking that will help you excel.

Nobel Prize-winning economist Daniel Kahneman describes two types of thinking: "fast thinking" and "slow thinking."

He characterizes fast thinking as something you do when you are facing a crisis and need to make an immediate decision. Slow thinking, however, is more deliberate and logical and is very similar to critical thinking.[1]

You may have heard the term *critical thinking* before without knowing precisely what it means. The term refers to thoughtful consideration of the information, ideas, and arguments we encounter in order to guide belief and action. By improving your slower and critical-thinking abilities, you will become a better learner and problem solver. In this chapter, we will provide you with strategies for developing your thinking skills, and we will explain how developing and applying these skills can make the search for answers an exciting adventure.

[1] Daniel Kahneman, *Thinking, Fast and Slow* (New York: Farrar, Straus and Giroux, 2013).

Review Your ACES Score

Take a moment to reflect on your **Learning Preferences** and **Thinking Critically and Setting Goals** ACES scores, and insert them in the boxes to the right. Now let's take action!

Score:

○ High
○ Moderate
○ Low

Did you score in the high, moderate, or low range? Are you surprised by your scores? These scores will help you learn more about your strengths and weaknesses in understanding how you learn, think critically, and set goals. In this chapter, we will be focusing on learning and thinking. Even if you already believe that you are strong in these areas, be open to learning new strategies to help you improve your scores as you move through the chapter. This chapter will further your understanding of why these topics are essential to your success in college.

To find your ACES score, log onto LaunchPad Solo for *Step by Step* at **launchpadworks.com**.

Preview the topic headings in this chapter. Then, in a journal or a readily accessible file, reflect on your current skills by answering the following questions:

▶ **What are your current strengths and challenges?**
▶ **What do you hope to learn from this chapter?**

Seeing Things in New Ways

sirtravelalot/Shutterstock

For a week before our first college debate team meeting, I had nightmares about being thrown in the deep end with some horrendous topic, like whether terrorism can be justified. When the day arrived, our team adviser, Mr. Randall, gave us a subject I could really work with: capital punishment. Even better, he put me in the "pro" camp. I mean, how can you argue against executing violent murderers?

"Be sure to set aside your opinions on the subject, learn about different views, and use your critical-thinking skills to help develop your argument," Mr. Randall said. "Remember: You'll be arguing only one side of the issue. But you'll need to understand both sides if you want to outthink your opponent."

Fast-forward to the next debate meeting: "So I've been learning about both sides of the issue," I told Mr. Randall. "It turns out that it's more expensive to put people to death in the United States than it is to keep them locked up. Also, many studies show that the death penalty doesn't prevent murders from happening. What's worse, a lot of people who've been put to death turned out to be innocent. So now I don't know what to think."

"Don't worry, Tamara," said Mr. Randall. "That just means that you've learned why this is such a tough issue. Your mind is working—and that's a good thing. It sounds like it's going to be a great debate."

Can you think of a time when learning more about an issue caused you to question your prior opinions? Did you, like Tamara, feel confused about "what to think"?

How People Learn

You may not realize it, but you have been learning your whole life. Your formal educational experience has been part of that learning, but you have also learned a great deal from your life experiences and interactions with people outside of class. During your lifetime, research on the brain and the way we learn has exploded. We know far more today about how the brain works and how it can adapt to different stimuli over a life span. In this section, we'll explore how you can use these findings while you're in college, and introduce a tool that will help you identify your particular learning preferences.

Get Ready for Learning

All people have the ability to learn, but *how* exactly do we learn? It may not surprise you to hear that learning begins with the brain. In fact, researchers and academics have applied themselves to studying the brain and how it relates to learning through a field called *learning science*. The following list summarizes what we currently know about learning from researchers, psychologists, and scientists. As you read through this list, think about ways you can apply these findings to your own success in college.

- **You will learn best when your basic needs are met.** Psychologist Abraham Maslow argued that in order for students to learn, their needs must be met—basic needs such as food, water, and shelter; safety and security needs such as employment and property; needs for love and belonging; needs for self-esteem that comes from achievement; and needs for self-actualization that can be reached through having purpose and meeting your potential.[2]

- **Your emotions can affect your ability to learn.** Emotions can have a huge impact on our lives, including our ability to learn.[3]

If you are feeling anxious, stressed, or upset, you won't be able to learn. There are different strategies you can use to alleviate some of these negative emotions before you get to class or sit down to study. Some people find exercise to be a good way to process difficult emotions. Others use personal journals to get their thoughts out on paper, or speak with a counselor or professional who can offer guidance and support.

- **You will learn more effectively with others than alone.** Albert Bandura, a psychology researcher, developed a theory of social learning that suggests that people learn from each other by observing others' actions and the results of those actions.[4] While in college, you will observe and interact with many other students—those who are successful and those who are not. If you pay attention, you can figure out what behaviors actually lead to success. Later in this chapter, we will look at the benefits of collaborative learning.

- **Your brain can change.** Recent research has found that the human brain can change over time to compensate for disabilities or even to revise fixed ways of thinking.[5] As we learn, our brains can literally rewire themselves and create new pathways and connections. The scientific term for the ways the brain can change is *neuroplasticity*. Through repeated practice, you will continue to strengthen these new connections.

> " Our brains can literally rewire themselves and create new pathways and connections. "

[2] Abraham H. Maslow, *Motivation and Personality*, 2nd ed. (New York: Harper & Row, 1970).

[3] Jean-Didier Vincent, *The Biology of Emotions* (Cambridge, MA: Basil Blackwell, 1990).

[4] Albert Bandura, *Social Learning Theory* (Englewood Cliffs, NJ: Prentice Hall, 1977).

[5] Sara Bernard, "Neuroplasticity: Learning Physically Changes the Brain," Edutopia, December 1, 2010, https://www.edutopia.org/neuroscience-brain-based-learning-neuroplasticity.

Making a transition to college is a learning opportunity, and seeking assistance during your first year will increase your chances for success. Discuss with a partner your past learning experiences, whether in high school, in your personal life, or at work. Have you experienced any difficulties adapting to learning in college? Are there any obstacles you need to overcome before you can learn effectively? Share your thoughts with each other, and together identify places or people at your college or university to whom you might turn for assistance.

- **You learn based on your previous experiences.** The impact of prior experiences on learning is part of a learning theory called "constructivism."[6] Researchers have found that when we encounter something new, one of three things happens: We reconcile it with our previous ideas and experience, change what we believe, or consider the new information to be irrelevant. In other words, we are active creators of our own knowledge.

- **You will continue to learn throughout your life.** In your life, you will undergo many transitions, which will require you to learn new skills and knowledge. In her work on how adult students learn, counseling psychologist Nancy Schlossberg found that adults learn new roles when they go through change (or transition) in their lives, and this change helps adult grow and learn new ways of thinking and behaving.[7] Becoming a college student and then moving from being a college student to being an employee are significant transitions that will require you to continue learning long after you graduate.

[6] "Constructivism," Learning Theories and Transfer of Learning, accessed October 13, 2017, http://otec.uoregon.edu/learning_theory.htm#Constructivism.

[7] Mary L. Anderson, Jane Goodman, and Nancy K. Schlossberg, *Counseling Adults in Transition: Linking Schlossberg's Theory with Practice in a Diverse World*, 4th ed. (New York: Springer, 2012).

Personalize Your Learning: The VARK and Other Tools

In addition to looking at research-based strategies for effective learning, we can think about how people learn by focusing on personal learning preferences. Simply put, learning preferences are ways of learning. Through work and other experiences, you may have some sense of how you like or don't like to learn. Researchers have developed formal methods and tools—both simple and complex—to identify, describe, and understand different learning preferences. These tools help students learn to adapt the way they prefer to learn to different classroom situations. Remember: It is your responsibility to take charge of your learning in order to be successful in college, and you will be more likely to succeed in college if you know and use your most effective learning preference.

There are many models for thinking about and describing learning preferences, such as the VARK Learning Styles Inventory, the Kolb Learning Styles Inventory, and the Myers-Briggs Type Indicator (MBTI). The VARK inventory investigates how learners prefer to use their senses in learning, while the Kolb inventory focuses on abilities we need to develop in order to learn. The MBTI investigates basic personality characteristics and how they relate to human interaction and learning. You can read more about these tools online and take online assessments.

In this section, we will look more closely at the VARK inventory to help you determine your best mode of learning. The VARK inventory includes a questionnaire that focuses on how learners prefer to use their senses (seeing, hearing, reading and writing, or experiencing) to learn. The letters in VARK stand for *visual, aural, read/write,* and *kinesthetic.*

- **Visual learners** prefer to learn information through charts, graphs, symbols, and other visual means.

- **Aural learners** prefer to hear information.

- **Read/write learners** prefer to learn information that is displayed as words.

- **Kinesthetic learners** prefer to learn through experience and practice, whether simulated or real.

To determine your learning preference(s) according to the VARK Inventory, enter "VARK questionnaire" in any search engine and complete the inventory online. Keep in mind that your learning preference cannot be reduced to one or two defining characteristics. Learning preferences are complex and can vary based on what and where you are learning. But the knowledge you will gain about yourself from working through the VARK inventory is a tremendous step in taking responsibility for your learning.

Use VARK Results for Success

Knowing your VARK results can help you do better in your college classes. Here are ways of using learning preferences to develop your own study strategies:

- If you have a visual learning preference, underline or highlight your notes; use symbols, charts, or graphs to display your notes; use different arrangements of words on the page; redraw your pages from memory.

△ **How Do You Learn?**
This electrical engineering student values kinesthetic learning in order to test her ideas through experimentation, experience, and learning from her mistakes. Use your own learning preference(s) to help you personalize your academic path, but be open to embracing new ways to learn as you encounter different learning environments. Huntstock/Brand X Pictures/Getty Images

- If you are an aural learner, talk with others to verify the accuracy of your lecture notes; record your notes and listen to them, or record class lectures; read your notes out loud; ask yourself questions and speak your answers.

- If you have a read/write learning preference, write and rewrite your notes; read your notes silently; organize diagrams or flowcharts into statements; write imaginary exam questions, and respond in writing.

- If you are a kinesthetic learner, you'll need to use all your senses in learning—sight, touch, taste, smell, and hearing. Supplement your notes with real-world examples; move and gesture while you are reading or speaking your notes. ■

Adapting to Different Learning Environments

In college, you are responsible for your own learning. In the previous section, we looked at some of the conditions necessary for learning and allowed you to explore your own learning preferences. However, during college, you will be exposed to different teaching styles and learning environments, whether a hands-on lab, a lecture, or an online course. Don't depend on the instructor or the learning environment to give you everything you need to make the most of your learning. Instead, take control; use your preferences, talents, and abilities to develop many different ways to learn, stay engaged during class, and learn how to retain information. In this section, we'll consider some of the challenges you may face and how to adapt.

Become a Multimodal Learner

During college, you will be expected to adapt to many different learning environments, regardless of your learning preference. You could be a kinesthetic learner taking a lecture class, or a read/write learner who is required to do hands-on lab work. As a college student, you will want to develop learning strategies that allow you to excel in whatever environment you are in. In order to do this, you must become a *multimodal learner*—someone who is able to use different learning strategies to match different learning environments.

By becoming multimodal, not only will you do better in all your classes—regardless of how they are taught—but you will take control of your own learning and success. Learning in different ways may be uncomfortable or even hard at first, but the payoff for becoming a multimodal learner will be huge. There are many ways for you to develop new learning strategies that may not come naturally. A good place to start is with your peers. Model the strategies of students who have different learning preferences from you. For example, if you are in a lecture class, seek out students who have a preference for aural learning. What are some of their strategies for doing well in that class? Try out what they recommend. Your instructors and tutors are also available to discuss strategies for developing new ways of learning.

> " By becoming multimodal, not only will you do better in all your classes—regardless of how they are taught—but you will take control of your own learning and success. "

TRY IT!

SETTING GOALS ▷ Adapt to Different Teaching Styles

Instructors tend to teach in ways that fit their own particular preferences for learning. An instructor who learns best in a read/write mode or an aural mode will probably just lecture, but an instructor who prefers a more interactive, hands-on environment will likely involve students in discussion and hands-on activities. Because these are all essential components of your college education, it's important for you to make the most of each situation. Think about one class in which you are struggling with your instructor's method of teaching. Set a goal to generate a list of strategies you can use to help you retain information and stay engaged in class. Try them out over the next week. Which ones were successful?

◁ **Learn to Adapt**
In college, you will find that some instructors may have teaching styles that are challenging for you. Seek out the kinds of classes that conform to the way you like to learn, but also develop your adaptive strategies to make the most of any classroom setting. William G. Browning, Minneapolis, MN

"As we start a new school year, Mr. Smith, I just want you to know that I'm an Abstract-Sequential learner and trust that you'll conduct yourself accordingly!"

Think about Your Thinking: Metacognition

The term *metacognition* means "thinking about thinking." When you use metacognitive thinking, you become aware of how you learn and think; with this self-knowledge, you can take more ownership over your learning. If you pay attention, you may notice how your instructors use metacognitive strategies to help you learn as well. For instance, biology instructor Kimberly Tanner helps students evaluate what they already know before class through a preassessment; helps them identify their "muddiest point," or area of most confusion; and prompts students to consider how they performed on the last exam and why.[8] To develop your metacognitive skills, consider the following strategies developed by instructional designer Connie Malamed:

1. **Identify the ways you learn, and be able to describe them to others.** Self-assessment tools, such as the VARK Inventory, MTBI, or ACES (available with this book), will help you learn more about how you prefer to learn.

2. **Know the limits of your memory, and develop supplemental ways to remember information.** Use memory tools, such as rhymes and acronyms, to increase your recall abilities. Search "memory strategies" online to learn more about how to improve your memory.

3. **Be aware of your ability to comprehend what you're learning.** This will allow you to target where you need help. For example, if you read a paragraph and don't understand what you've just read, visit your campus learning center for help with reading comprehension.

4. **Test yourself occasionally to see how well you have learned something.** Or work with a small group of students and test one another.

5. **Reflect on your mistakes.** Mistakes are a natural part of learning, so instead of viewing them as failures, reflect on why you made them. Getting into this habit of self-reflection will help you identify your strengths as well as areas for improvement.[9]

[8] Kimberly Tanner, "Promoting Student Metacognition," *CBE—Life Sciences Education* 11 (2012):113–20.

[9] Connie Malamed, "Metacognition and Learning: Strategies for Instructional Design," The eLearningCoach, accessed October 3, 2017, http://theelearningcoach.com/learning/metacognition-and-learning/.

△ **Many Heads Are Better Than One**
Each person brings his or her own perspective and life experiences to a project—whether it's answering an essay question in an English class, doing experiments in a chemistry lab, framing a roof in a carpentry class, or making a dress in a fashion design class. By taking a team approach to learning, you will not only learn better but also have more fun doing it. When you're in a group, you benefit from companionship and are more likely to be challenged by new techniques and ideas. ©Zero Creatives/Getty Images

In addition to these strategies, the activities throughout this book are designed to help you tap into your metacognitive processes by asking you to reflect and learn more about yourself—so take advantage of them! The self-knowledge you will gain is a powerful tool for making sure you are a successful learner in college and throughout your life.

Learn to Collaborate

In college, you will likely find that instructors will incorporate collaborative learning opportunities into their courses. This is for good reason: Research shows that students who engage in learning through a team approach not only learn better but also enjoy their learning experiences more. Working in a group, you will be more likely to try new

ideas and discover new knowledge by exploring different viewpoints instead of just memorizing facts. And, as you leave college and enter the working world, you will find that collaboration—not only with people in your work setting but also with those around the globe—is essential to almost any career you pursue.

This doesn't mean, however, that collaboration always goes smoothly. Sometimes, not all members of a group contribute, and tensions can arise when group members have different visions for how to complete an assignment. Therefore, it is important to find a way to communicate effectively so that all team members are heard and held accountable for contributing to the learning of their teammates. Make it clear at the outset that every member will be expected to take an occasional leadership role in group meetings to ensure that all members are invested in the success of the group. Also, be sure to learn about how your team members prefer to learn and think. Understanding how others see the world and approach a problem will not only enhance your ability to be more flexible in different learning situations but also help your group use one another's strengths to reach your goal. ■

Learning with a Learning Disability

Learning disability is a general term that covers a wide variety of specific learning problems that can make it difficult to acquire certain academic and social skills. According to national data, between 15 and 20 percent of Americans have a learning disability, making it a very common challenge for students at any age. Learning disabilities, which are the result of neurological disorders, are usually recognized and diagnosed in grade school, but some students can enter college without having been properly diagnosed or assisted. The types of learning disabilities that most commonly affect college students are *attention disorders*, such as ADD and ADHD, which affect the ability to focus and concentrate; and *cognitive disorders*, such as dyslexia, which affect the development of academic skills, including reading, writing, and mathematics. You might know someone who has been diagnosed with a learning disability; it is also possible that you have a special learning need that you are not yet aware of. Therefore, it is important to increase your self-awareness and your knowledge about such challenges to learning. The earlier you address any learning challenges you might have, the better you will perform.

A learning disability is a learning difference, and it is in no way related to intelligence. In fact, some of the most intelligent individuals in history—such as Benjamin Franklin, George Washington, Alexander Graham Bell, and Woodrow Wilson—had a learning disability. If you have a documented learning disability, make sure to notify the office for students with disabilities at your college or university to receive reasonable accommodations as required by law. Reasonable accommodations might include the use of a computer during certain exams, readers for tests, in-class note takers, extra time for assignments and tests, and the use of audio textbooks, depending on the need and the type of disability.

If you think you might have a learning disability but it has not yet been documented, the office for students with disabilities would be a good place to start. You could also discuss this issue with your academic adviser, a learning center professional, or a counselor in your college counseling center. Any one of them can get you to the right resource for evaluation and assistance.

Developing Strong Thinking Skills

Being a strong learner also means being a strong thinker, someone who is able to think logically and rationally about abstract concepts. Most of us have learned something without really thinking about it, such as understanding not to touch a hot stove, but the kind of learning you will do in college requires you to think—to use your mind to produce ideas, opinions, decisions, and memories. During college, courses in every discipline will require you to learn and think by asking questions, sorting through information and ideas, creating connections between what you learn and what you experience, and forming and defending your own opinions.

College-Level Thinking Is Critical Thinking

The level of thinking that your college instructors expect from you will probably exceed the kind of thinking you did in high school, both in terms of the questions that are asked and the answers that are expected. If a high school teacher asked, "What are the three branches of the U.S. government?" there was only one acceptable answer: "legislative, executive, and judicial." A college instructor, on the other hand, might ask, "Under what circumstances might conflicts arise among the three branches of government, and what does this tell you about the democratic process?" There is no simple, quick, or single acceptable answer to the second question—that's the point of higher education. The shift to this higher level of thinking can be an adjustment—it might even catch you off guard and cause you some stress (see Figure 4.1). This kind of thinking can also be referred to as critical thinking.

One step toward deep and critical thinking is becoming comfortable with uncertainty.

Figure 4.1 ▽ **Rate Your Thinking Skills**

Use Figure 4.1 to rate your thinking skills. What do you need to work on improving?

Situations	Never				Sometimes					Always
I ask a lot of questions in class when I don't understand.	1	2	3	4	5	6	7	8	9	10
If I disagree with what the group decides is the correct answer, I challenge the group opinion.	1	2	3	4	5	6	7	8	9	10
I believe that there are many solutions to a problem.	1	2	3	4	5	6	7	8	9	10
I admire those people in history who challenged what was believed at the time, such as the idea that the earth is flat.	1	2	3	4	5	6	7	8	9	10
I make an effort to listen to both sides of an argument before deciding which side I will support.	1	2	3	4	5	6	7	8	9	10
I ask many people for their opinion about a political candidate before I make up my mind.	1	2	3	4	5	6	7	8	9	10
I am not afraid to change my belief if I learn something new.	1	2	3	4	5	6	7	8	9	10
Authority figures do not intimidate me.	1	2	3	4	5	6	7	8	9	10

The more 7–10 scores you have circled, the more you use your thinking skills. The lower scores indicate that you may not be using your thinking skills very often or may be using them only during certain activities. As you read this section, pay attention to ways that you can strengthen your thinking skills.

Rather than just taking in information, studying it, and then recalling it for a test, you'll gain the ability and the confidence to arrive at your own conclusions—to think for yourself.

At the start of this chapter, we described critical thinking as the thoughtful consideration of the information, ideas, and arguments that you encounter in order to guide belief and action. We can also define critical thinking as the search for truth—evaluating information to guide belief and action. This is the kind of thinking you will do in college.

Challenge Assumptions and Beliefs

We develop an understanding of situations and issues we encounter based on our values, worldviews, and family backgrounds; then we form opinions and perspectives. Many of our beliefs are based on gut feelings or blind acceptance of things we have heard, read, or been told, and to some extent, this is unavoidable. Some assumptions, or beliefs we accept as true, should be examined more thoughtfully, especially if they will influence an important

decision. College is a time to challenge and to think critically about the ideas we have always held.

Ask Questions

An important step in learning to think critically is to ask questions. You can begin by asking yourself about the beliefs and assumptions you hold and why you hold them. Instead of accepting ideas, statements, or claims made by others at face value, question them. Here are a few suggestions:

- What approach should you take when you come across an idea, a statement, or a claim that you consider interesting, confusing, or suspicious?

- Do you fully understand what is being said, or do you need to pause and think about what it means?

- Do you agree with the statement? Why or why not?

- Can the idea or claim be interpreted in more than one way?

Don't stop there.

- Ask whether you can trust the person or group making a particular claim.

- Ask how the new idea relates to what you already know.

- Think about where you might find more information about the subject.

- Ask yourself about the effects of accepting a new idea as truth.
  - Will you have to change or give up what you have believed in for a long time?
  - Will you need to do something differently or influence others to a new way of thinking?

Consider Multiple Points of View, and Draw Conclusions

Before you draw any conclusions about the validity of information or opinions, it's important to consider more than one point of view. You might encounter differences of opinion in college reading assignments or as you do research for a project. Your own belief system will influence how you interpret information. For example, consider your own ideas about the cost of college in the United States. American citizens, politicians, and others often voice their opinions on private versus public institutions. What kind of higher education do *you* think is best, and why do you hold this viewpoint? The more ideas you consider about this or any other issue, the better your thinking will become. Ultimately, you will not only discover that it is OK to change your mind but also recognize that a willingness to do so is the mark of a reasonable, educated person.

Develop an Argument

When you think about the word *argument*, the first image that comes to mind might be of an ugly fight you had with a friend, a yelling match you witnessed on the street, or a heated disagreement between family members. While these unpleasant confrontations do qualify as arguments, the term also refers to a calm, reasoned effort to persuade someone of the value of an idea.

Arguments are central to academic study, work, and life in general. Scholarly articles, business memos, and requests for spending money all have something in common: they make a general claim, provide reasons to support it, and back up those reasons with evidence.

It's important to consider multiple arguments in tackling new ideas and complex questions, but remember that all arguments are not equally valid. Whether examining an argument or making one, a good critical thinker is careful to ensure that ideas are presented in an understandable, logical way and to assess whether those making the arguments have presented enough information to justify their positions.

TRY IT!

MAKING GOOD CHOICES ▷
Make Up Your Own Mind

What would motivate you to draw your own conclusions based on evidence rather than to blindly follow others? What if you were faced with a decision that could affect your health? For instance, suppose you were out with friends who were trying e-cigarettes, and they were attempting to persuade you that e-cigarettes aren't dangerous like conventional cigarettes are. Would you risk believing them without checking into it further? Be motivated to develop an attitude of healthy skepticism. This doesn't mean you have to be rude or combative. Rather, you can request more time to ask questions, do research, or think carefully about a decision before following the crowd.

Examine Evidence

Another important part of thinking critically is checking that the evidence supporting an argument—whether someone else's or your own—is of the highest possible quality. To do that, simply ask a few questions about the argument:

- What is the general idea behind the argument?

- Are good and sufficient reasons given to support the overall claim?

- Are those reasons backed up with evidence in the form of facts, statistics, and quotations?

- Does the evidence support the conclusions?

- Is the argument based on logical reasoning, or does it appeal mainly to emotions?

- Do I recognize any questionable assumptions?

- Can I think of any counterarguments, and if so, what facts can I muster as proof of one position or the other?

- If other people or organizations are making the argument, what do I know about them?

- What credible sources can I find to support the information?

If you have evaluated the evidence used in support of a claim and are still uncertain of its quality, it's best to keep looking for more evidence. Drawing on questionable evidence for an argument has a tendency to backfire. In most cases, a little persistence will help you find better sources.

Logic: another thing that penguins aren't very good at.

△ **Logic That Just Doesn't Fly**
This cartoon is an obvious example of faulty reasoning. Some conversations or arguments tend to include reasoning like this. Can you think of a time when someone used an illogical leap like this one on you? How did you use critical thinking to counter it? Or did your emotions get the best of you?
© Randy Glasbergen

Recognize and Avoid Faulty Reasoning

Although logical reasoning is essential to solving any problem, you need to go one step further to make sure that an argument hasn't been compromised by faulty reasoning. Here are some of the most common missteps—logical fallacies or flaws in reasoning—that people make in their use of logic:

- **Attacking the person.** Arguing against other people's positions or attacking their arguments is perfectly acceptable. Going after their personalities, however, is not OK.

- **Begging.** "Please, officer, don't give me a ticket! If you do, I'll lose my license, and I have five little children to feed, and I won't be able to feed them if I can't drive my truck." None of the driver's statements offer any evidence, in any legal sense, as to why this person shouldn't be given a ticket. An appeal to facts and reason would be more effective: "I fed the meter, but it didn't register the coins. Since the machine is broken, I'm sure you'll agree that I don't deserve a ticket."

- **Appealing to false authority.** Citing true authorities can offer valuable support for an argument. However, we see examples of false authority all the time in advertising: sports stars who are not doctors, dieticians, or nutritionists urge us to eat a certain brand of food; famous actors and singers who are not dermatologists extol the medical benefits of a costly remedy for acne.

- **Jumping on a bandwagon.** Sometimes we are more likely to believe something that many others also believe. Even accepted truths can turn out to be wrong, however. At one time, nearly everyone believed that the earth was flat, until someone came up with evidence that it was round.

- **Assuming that something is true because it hasn't been proven false.** If you go to a library or look online, you'll find dozens of books detailing close encounters with flying

© Randy Glasbergen.
www.glasbergen.com

GLASBERGEN

saucers or ghosts. These books describe the people who had such encounters as honest and trustworthy. Because no one could disprove the claims of the witnesses, the events are said to have actually occurred. Even in science, few things are ever proved completely false—but evidence *can* be discredited.

- **Falling victim to false cause.** A basis for many superstitions is that just because one event followed another, the first event must have caused the second. The ancient Chinese once believed that they could make the sun reappear after an eclipse by striking a large gong, because it had happened once before. Most effects, however, are usually the result of several causes. Don't be satisfied with easy cause-and-effect claims; they are rarely correct.

- **Making hasty generalizations.** If someone selected a green marble from a barrel containing a hundred marbles, you wouldn't assume that the next marble drawn from the barrel would also be green. However, if you were given fifty draws from the barrel and you drew only green marbles, you would be more willing to conclude that the next marble drawn would be green, too. Reaching a conclusion based on the opinion of one source is like assuming that all the marbles in the barrel are green after pulling out only one marble.

- **Accepting a slippery slope argument.** "If we allow tuition to increase, the next thing we know, it will be $40,000 per term." Such an argument is an example of slippery slope thinking.

Fallacies like these can slip into even the most careful reasoning. One false claim can derail an entire argument, so be on the lookout for weak logic in what you read and write. Never forget that accurate reasoning is a key factor in succeeding in college and in life. ■

Applying Your Thinking Skills

As is true for any skill that you want to develop, you need to practice thinking critically in order to get good at it. Now that you are aware of what good thinking is (and isn't), you can look for opportunities to improve.

Collaborate

As we discussed earlier in this chapter, collaboration is an important part of learning. Researchers who investigate student thinking across grade levels find that critical thinking and collaboration go hand and hand. By getting feedback from others, you can see the possible flaws in your own position or approach. Whether debating an issue in a political science class or making a dress in a fashion design class, learn to appreciate how fellow students and instructors bring their own life experiences, personal taste, knowledge, and expertise to the table. Having more than one student involved in the learning process generates a greater number of ideas and discussions, which can challenge your thinking and assumptions. Creative brainstorming and group discussion encourage original thought. These habits also teach participants to consider alternative points of view carefully and to express and defend their ideas clearly.

Be Creative

Another way to develop strong thinking skills is to take advantage of opportunities to be creative. Our society is full of creative individuals who think outside the box or simply ask questions that others are not asking. Many have achieved

fame by using their thinking skills and actions to change the world. As you move through your other first-year courses, such as sociology, psychology, history, or math, you will encounter assignments that will encourage you to be creative. You will also learn about people who have used their creative-thinking abilities to find a sense of purpose and to become world changers in both academic and nonacademic areas.

Learn to Problem-Solve

Your success both in college and in your future life will depend on how well you make decisions and solve problems. Making decisions and solving problems involve thinking logically, weighing evidence, and formulating conclusions. Here are some examples of situations you might experience in college that will require these skills:

- Deciding which sources are most important to include in your research paper

- Finding a way to negotiate a problem situation with your roommate

- Determining the kinds of exercise you need to maintain a healthy fitness level and avoid weight gain

- Understanding the advantages and disadvantages of accessing information sources, including Facebook, Twitter feeds, CNN, *USA Today*, *The New York Times*, the *Onion,* and your school newspaper

In addition to these situations, the college years represent a time in your life when you get to know yourself and what you believe. You will begin to develop your own positions on societal and political issues, learn more about what is important to you, and develop into a contributing citizen of your country and also the world.

In college, you'll be exposed to ideas and often conflicting opinions about contemporary issues, such as same-sex marriage, military operations, immigration, global human rights, public education in the United States, and student loan debt and forgiveness. Before accepting any opinion on any issue as "the truth," be sure to look for evidence that supports different positions on these debates. In fact, look for opportunities to participate in such debates. ∎

TRY IT!

MAKING GOOD CHOICES ▷ Study Groups: Pros and Cons

Decide whether you will join a study group. Make a list of the ways you think you could benefit from joining a study group. Make another list of the reasons you might decide not to join one. Compare your lists with those of a few classmates. What insights into the arguments for or against joining a study group did you gain? If you have decided to join a study group, how will you proceed?

Bloom's Taxonomy and Your First Year of College

Benjamin Bloom, a professor of education at the University of Chicago, worked with a group of researchers to design a system of classifying goals for the learning process. This system is known as Bloom's taxonomy, and it is now used at all levels of education to define and describe the process that students use to understand and think critically about what they are learning.

Bloom identified six levels of learning (see Figure 4.2). The higher the level, the more critical thinking it requires.

If you pay close attention, you will discover that Bloom's taxonomy is often the framework that college instructors use to design classroom activities and out-of-class assignments. As you work through the courses in your first year of college, you will recognize material you've learned before, and you will practice your skills of defining and remembering. Be aware of how you use each of these levels to build your critical-thinking skills. No matter what the topic is, this framework will help move you towards a deeper understanding and an ability to apply what you learn to other situations and concepts.

To retain new information, you'll need to move to level 2, understanding the information clearly enough so that you can describe the concepts to someone else. Many of your classes will require you to apply what you've learned to new situations (level 3). As you engage with material in this way, your comprehension grows, as does your ability to retain new knowledge. Next you'll move on to level 4 to analyze—break down information into parts—and level 5 to evaluate new ideas, making decisions about them, and judging them. As you reach the sixth (and highest) level, you'll create something new by combining information, concepts, and theories.

Let's take a closer look at Bloom's taxonomy by taking a concept you're likely to encounter in your first year of college—diversity—and matching your cognitive development of the concept to Bloom's taxonomy.

Level 1 (Remember): Read a dictionary definition of the word *diversity*.

Level 2 (Understand): Explain the concept of diversity to another student without reading the dictionary definition.

Level 3 (Apply): Write about all the types of human diversity that exist within the student body at your college or university and possible categories of human diversity that are not represented there.

Level 4 (Analyze): Conduct two separate analyses to break down the issue into components or questions. The first analysis will look at why your institution has large numbers of certain types of students. The second analysis will consider why your institution has small numbers of other types of students.

Level 5 (Evaluate): Write a paper that combines your findings in level 4 and hypothesizes what components of your college or university culture either attract or repel certain students.

Level 6 (Create): In your paper, describe your institution's "diversity profile," and suggest new ways for your campus to support diversity.

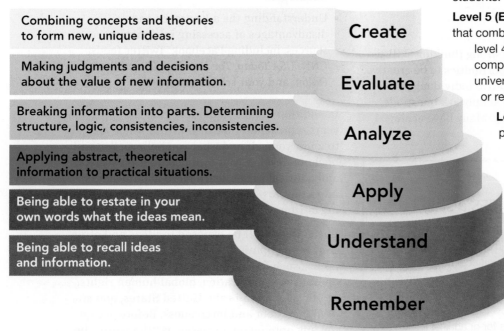

Combining concepts and theories to form new, unique ideas. — **Create**

Making judgments and decisions about the value of new information. — **Evaluate**

Breaking information into parts. Determining structure, logic, consistencies, inconsistencies. — **Analyze**

Applying abstract, theoretical information to practical situations. — **Apply**

Being able to restate in your own words what the ideas mean. — **Understand**

Being able to recall ideas and information. — **Remember**

Figure 4.2 △ The Six Levels of Learning of Bloom's Taxonomy

What Is Real and What Is Fake?

If we want to learn about something, many of us automatically say "Let me Google that." With the Internet and search engines such as Google and Yahoo, we have access to information at the click of a button. However, with all this information, we have to sift through sources spreading inaccurate information, otherwise known as fake news. When completing your coursework as well as educating yourself, it is important to be able to distinguish sources that are credible versus those that are not.

▶ the GOAL

Use critical thinking skills to avoid fake news.

▶ how TO DO it

alvarez/Getty Images

- **Are they yelling, selling, or telling?** Remember: Anybody can post on the Internet. Use your critical-thinking skills to determine whether somebody is trying to communicate a biased viewpoint, promote a product or service, or provide credible information.

- **Be wary of any information shared only through social media.** Be sure to validate information you receive through Facebook or other sources, and don't share unless you can confirm the accuracy of the information.

- **Use a variety of news outlets to confirm information.** When you see the same information in a variety of credible sources, you can begin to trust its accuracy.

- **Be particularly alert to "anonymous" information sources.** Named sources are more likely to be accurate.

- **Consider the quality of the information, and evaluate the sources.** Ask yourself: Where did it come from? Who said it, and why? When was it published? Is this information up-to-date?

- **Be aware of your biases.** When developing your thinking skills, it is important to check your own biases. While it can be uncomfortable to challenge yourself, be sure to seek out different opinions and sources before drawing any conclusions.

▶ your TURN

As you conduct Internet searches on different topics, use the steps above to develop strong thinking skills to scrutinize the yellers, sellers, and tellers. Bring a sample of a fake news source and a credible news source to class. In small groups, share your findings, and discuss how you were able to make your determinations. Be sure to apply these skills whenever you need to conduct solid research.

Chapter Review

Reflect on Choices

This chapter has introduced you to strategies for maximizing your learning and developing strong thinking skills. The choice of what to do with that information is up to you. Successful college students learn *how* to learn and adapt to learning environments that they may not prefer. They also challenge themselves to think critically. In a journal entry or a readily accessible file, reflect on what you have learned about how you learn and think, and discuss how you can apply the information and strategies from the chapter to college and your future career. Revisit and build on these observations throughout your first-year experience.

Apply What You've Learned

Now that you have read and discussed this chapter, consider how you can apply what you have learned to your academic and personal lives. The following prompts will help you reflect on the chapter material and its relevance to you, both now and in the future.

1. It is important to understand how you learn and to be aware of how your particular learning preferences can affect your experience in the classroom. Considering your learning preference(s), what kinds of teaching and learning methods do you think will work best for you? What teaching and learning methods will be especially challenging? How can you compensate for courses that don't match your learning preference(s)?

2. In your opinion, is it harder to think critically than to base your arguments on how you feel about a topic? Why or why not? What are the advantages of finding answers based on your feelings? Based on critical thinking? How might you use both approaches in seeking answers?

Use Your Resources

GO TO ▷ The library or the Internet: If you want general information about learning styles and learning disabilities. LD Pride and the National Center for Learning Disabilities are both good places to start. Some valuable online resources are also available through the Foundation for Critical Thinking. Be sure to evaluate your search results!

GO TO ▷ The learning center: If you want to take an inventory that reveals your learning preferences.

GO TO ▷ The career center: If you need guidance in applying information about how you learn to career planning.

GO TO ▷ A counselor in the office for students with disabilities: If you need advice on learning disability testing, diagnosis, and accommodations.

GO TO ▷ Your first-year seminar instructor: If you want to find out more about learning styles and learning disabilities.

GO TO ▷ Logic courses listed in your course catalog: If you need help developing your critical-thinking skills.

GO TO ▷ The English department: If you need help formulating arguments. Investigate courses that will help you develop the ability to formulate logical arguments and to avoid such pitfalls as logical fallacies.

GO TO ▷ Your student activities office or the speech or drama department: If you need help practicing your debate skills. Find out if your campus has a debate club/society or a debate team.

 **LaunchPad Solo** macmillan learning   LaunchPad Solo for *Step by Step* is a great resource. Go online to master concepts using the LearningCurve study tool and much more. launchpadworks.com

Getting the Most Out of Class

Martial Red/Shutterstock

LaunchPad Solo
macmillan learning

To access ACES, the LearningCurve study tool, videos, and more, go to LaunchPad Solo for *Step by Step*. launchpadworks.com

In order to earn high grades in any college class you take, you'll need to master certain skills, such as listening, taking notes, and being engaged in learning. Engagement in learning means that you take an active role in your classes by attending, listening critically, asking questions, contributing to discussions, and providing answers. These active-learning behaviors will enhance your ability to understand abstract ideas, find new possibilities, organize those ideas, and recall the material once the class is over, resulting in strong performance on exams.

By taking an active role in your classes, you will listen better and take more meaningful notes. In this chapter, we'll show you several note-taking methods; choose the one that works best for you. With thorough notes, you can connect your understanding of what went on in class with your understanding of the reading assignments. This increased capacity to analyze and understand complex material will result in better academic performance while you are in college and will also be valued by a wide range of employers.

This chapter provides valuable suggestions for becoming a skilled listener, class participant, and note taker. After you decide which techniques work best for you, practice them regularly until they become part of your study routine.

Review Your ACES Score

Take a moment to reflect on your **Taking Effective Notes** ACES score, and insert it in the box to the right. Now let's take action!

Did you score in the high, moderate, or low range? Are you surprised by your score? This score will help you learn more about your strengths and weaknesses in understanding how well you are able to engage during class and take effective notes. Even if you already feel strong in this area, be open to learning new strategies to help you improve your score as you move through the chapter. This chapter will further your understanding of why these topics are essential to your success in college.

Score:

○ High
○ Moderate
○ Low

To find your ACES score, log on to LaunchPad Solo for *Step by Step* at **launchpadworks.com**.

Preview the topic headings in this chapter. Then, in a journal or a readily accessible file, reflect on your current skills by answering the following questions:

▶ **What are your current strengths and challenges?**

▶ **What do you hope to learn from this chapter?**

Tongue-Tied

© Matelly/Getty Images

"So, Amy, why do you think Harper Lee chose to give *To Kill a Mockingbird* a child narrator?" my professor asked me at our second literature class. Minutes earlier, I'd been tapping my pencil on my notebook, feeling happy as we discussed my favorite book. Suddenly, I was grasping for something to say.

"Er," I managed. Thirty-two twenty-something-year-old faces were looking at me. I felt my face go beet red. They didn't want to hear from the "old lady" in the class, twice their age.

"Anyone else?" he asked, looking around. "Speak up."

"Scout has an innocent perspective," said the girl sitting next to me.

"Exactly," said Professor Kelso. "And why is that such an effective device here?"

Because the difference between what the reader sees happening in the book and what Scout perceives generates a lot of irony, I thought to myself. Because we see her learn something important. Because her childlike tone disguises the serious purpose of the plot.

"Because we see her start to understand how her world works—in good and bad ways," said a student across the room.

The professor crossed his arms and nodded. "Good job, Aziz. That's a point toward your class participation grade." Then he caught a glance at my stricken face. "Amy, did you have something to add?"

"Uh, well . . . I, um," I said. Yep, it looked like being back in college was going to be rough.

How is Amy's reticence about speaking in front of her younger classmates affecting her performance in college? What kind of preparation before class would have helped Amy? Flip through the chapter. What other suggestions can you find that would have helped her speak up?

Preparing for Class

Imagine you're a track star. Would you come to a meet without having trained really hard? Of course not. Think of each class as an important event, like a track meet. To do your best, you'll need to prepare ahead of time. Here are some strategies that will help you begin listening, learning, and remembering before each class session, whether the course is face to face or online:

1. **Pay attention to your course syllabus.** A syllabus is not something you ignore or discard. It is an important, formal statement of course expectations, requirements, and procedures.

2. **Do the assigned reading.** Instructors expect you to have a basic understanding of the material before they expand on it during class. If you have done the reading, you will find that the lecture means more to you and class participation is a lot easier.

3. **Use additional materials provided by the instructor.** Many professors post lecture outlines or notes online. Download and print these materials to provide an organizational structure for note taking.

4. **Warm up for class.** Before class begins, review your textbook's chapter introductions and summaries as well as your notes. This review will put you in tune with the

TRY IT!

FEELING CONNECTED ▷ **Prepare Better by Working Together**

A great way to prepare for class is to discuss readings, lectures, and other course materials with your classmates. Some of them are sure to know the material, and they may understand concepts that you find challenging. At the same time, explaining concepts to your classmates will help you solidify your own understanding. In small groups, go over your notes from the previous class with your classmates, then reflect on how discussing the course material benefited you.

lecture that is about to begin and prompt you to ask questions about material from the previous lecture that might not have been clear to you.

5. **Get organized.** Decide whether a three-ring binder, a spiral notebook, a digital device, or some combination of the three will work best for you. You might also want to create a folder for each course. If you use a laptop or tablet, create a "Documents" folder for each course, and carefully label the notes for each class meeting. ■

Why Be an Engaged Learner?

Engaged students are those who are fully involved with the college experience and spend the time and energy necessary to learn, both in and outside of class. Engaged learners who have good listening and note-taking skills get the most out of college. Practice the techniques of active learning by talking with others, asking questions in class, studying in groups, and seeking out information beyond the lecture material and required reading. Explore information sources in the library or on the Internet. Think about how the material relates to your own life. For instance, what you learn in a psychology class might help you recognize patterns of behavior in your own family, or the material presented in a sociology class may shed light on the group dynamics of a team you have joined. When you are actively engaged in learning, you will not only learn the material in your notes and textbook but also

build valuable skills that you can apply to college, work, and your personal life:

- working with others
- improving your thinking, listening, writing, and speaking skills
- functioning independently and teaching yourself
- managing your time
- gaining sensitivity to cultural differences

Engagement in learning requires your full and active participation in the learning process. Your instructors will set the stage and provide valuable information, but it's up to you to do the rest. For instance, if you disagree with what your instructor says, politely share your opinion. Most instructors will listen. They might still disagree with you, but they will almost always appreciate your efforts to think independently.

Pay Attention! Listening, Participating, and Taking Notes

Think about your conversations with friends and family members. When you listen carefully to what the other person says, you can communicate effectively. But if you tune out, you won't have much to contribute, and you might get caught off guard if you are asked a direct question. The same is true in class; there is a give-and-take between students and the instructor, especially in classes where the instructor emphasizes interactive discussion, calls on students by name, shows students signs of approval and interest, and avoids criticizing anyone for an incorrect answer.

> " Listening carefully in class—really paying attention—is one of the most important skills you can develop. "

Listening carefully in class—really paying attention—is one of the most important skills you can develop. If you don't listen, you won't know which concepts your instructor identifies as the most important—concepts that are likely to show up on tests. And, of course, paying attention will help you understand and remember what you've heard, which will make you more likely to participate in class—especially when you are prepared.

Listening Critically

If you are taking classes in which instructors lecture all or part of the time, then aural learning (learning by listening) is a skill you will need to develop to be academically successful, whether or not learning by listening is your preference. Critical listening, however, goes one step further; it involves examining how we listen and evaluating what is said so that we can form our own ideas and opinions.

Here are some suggestions for being a critical listener:

1. **Be ready for the message.** Prepare yourself to hear, listen, and receive the message. If you have done the assigned reading, you will know the details in the text, so you can focus your notes on key concepts during the lecture.

2. **Listen for the main concepts and central ideas, not just facts and figures.** Facts will be easier to remember when you can place them in the context of a broader theme.

◁ **Hands Up!**
Participating in class not only helps you learn but also shows your instructor that you're interested and engaged. You may be anxious the first time you raise your hand, but after that first time, you'll find that participating in class raises your interest and enjoyment. PeopleImages/Getty Images

3. **Listen for new ideas.** Even if you know a lot about a topic, you can still learn something new.

4. **Repeat what you hear mentally.** Think about what you hear, and restate it silently in your own words. If you don't understand a concept, ask for clarification.

5. **Decide whether what you are hearing is not important, very important, or somewhat important.** If a point in the lecture is not important, let it go. If it is very important, highlight or underline the point in your notes. If it is somewhat important, relate it to a very important topic.

6. **Keep an open mind.** Your classes will expose you to new ideas and different perspectives. But instructors want you to think for yourself, and they do not expect you to agree with everything they or your classmates say.

7. **Listen to the entire message.** Concentrate on the big picture, but also pay attention to specific details and examples that can assist you in understanding and retaining the information.

8. **Sort, organize, and categorize.** While you listen, try to match what you are hearing with what you already know. Take an active role in deciding how best to recall what you are learning.

Becoming an Active Class Participant

In all your classes, try using the following techniques to ramp up your participation:

1. **Sit as close to the front as possible.** If students are seated by name, and your name begins with a letter that comes toward the end of the alphabet, request to be moved up front.

2. **Keep your eyes on the instructor.** Sitting close to the front of the classroom will make this easier for you to do.

3. **Focus on the lecture.** Do not let yourself be distracted by other students. If you are taking the class online, be sure to watch the lecture and do your coursework in a place where you will be able to concentrate.

TRY IT!

SETTING GOALS ▷ Do You Ask Questions in Class?

How many times during the past week have you raised your hand in class to ask a question? Do you ask questions frequently, or is this something you avoid? Make a list of reasons you either do or don't ask questions in class. Would asking more questions help you earn better grades? Set a goal to participate during the next class.

4. **Raise your hand when you don't understand something.** But don't overdo it—the instructor and your peers will tire of too many questions that disrupt the class.

5. **Speak up in class.** It becomes easier every time you do so. If you are an online learner, participate in chats and discussion groups.

6. **Never feel that you're asking a "stupid" question.** You have a right to ask for an explanation.

7. **When the instructor calls on you to answer a question, don't bluff.** If you know the answer, give it. If not, just say so.

8. **If you've recently read a book or an article that is relevant to the class, bring it in.** You can provide additional information that was not covered in class.

Taking Notes

Listening and taking notes go hand in hand. Some students find it difficult to take notes while they are listening. As you gain experience, you will improve your ability to do these things simultaneously. If you find that your notes are missing a lot of important details, you may want to record the lecture (with the instructor's permission) using one of the many apps available, such as QuickVoice Recorder, Smart Voice Recorder, or Audio Class Notes. Listening to the recording will actually improve your aural learning abilities, but you should continue to take notes regardless.

> **Listening and note-taking skills are especially important in college because your instructors are likely to introduce material that your texts don't cover.**

Listening and note-taking skills are especially important in college because your instructors are likely to introduce material that your texts don't cover. College and university professors often integrate their own ideas into their lectures, which expand on—or even differ from—what you read in your textbooks. Be aware that instructors often think that what is discussed in class is more important than what is in the text. Chances are very good that your instructors will include much of the material they introduce in class on weekly quizzes and major exams.

While you are listening and taking notes, be sure to participate in class discussions when you have something important to say or a question to ask. If you have questions about your notes, you might choose to approach the instructor after class or go over your notes with a classmate. Learning how to balance these three aspects of being in class—listening, participating, and taking notes—will help you get the most out of each class meeting. ■

Engage in Online Learning

If you are currently taking an online course, you'll find that the online format presents some unique challenges to class participation. Some online courses are synchronous, meaning you are required to log in and participate on a specific day and time. More often, however, they are asynchronous, meaning you are in control of when you watch lectures, respond to group discussions, and complete other required coursework. The online environment can make it more difficult to get questions answered and interact with your peers, but if you put in a little effort, you can get just as much out of your online courses as those that are face to face. Here are a few strategies to keep in mind in order to stay actively engaged in your online courses:

- **Log on every day.** Even if you spend just ten minutes checking for updates from your instructor or reading the discussion board, this simple action will become part of your daily routine and will help you stay engaged in the course and aware of upcoming assignments.

- **Get involved.** Be sure to take advantage of all available opportunities to become involved in the class—joining chat groups, contributing to discussion boards, and getting to know other students and the instructor. Some online courses even require this as part of a participation grade. Also take advantage of scheduled meetings with your instructor over video or chat.

- **Apply the same active learning strategies that you would for a traditional class.** As you watch course lectures, take notes on what you are hearing using the strategies described in this chapter. Follow up with your instructors over e-mail (or their preferred method of communication) regarding any questions you have about the course material or assignments.

Note-Taking Systems and Strategies

Taking notes in college classes isn't optional. You must take notes in order to make the best use of your class time, but first you have to decide on a note-taking system that works best for you.

Cornell Format

In the Cornell format, you create a "recall" column on each page by placing a vertical line a few inches from the left border (see Figure 5.1). As you take notes during the lecture—whether writing down ideas, making lists, or using an outline or a paragraph format—write only in the wider column on the right; leave the recall column blank. Then, as soon as you can after class, sift through your notes and write down the main ideas and important details in the recall column. Many students find that the recall column is an important study device for tests and exams.

Figure 5.1 ▽ Note Taking in the Cornell Format

	Psychology 101 **1/29/19** **Theories of Personality**
Personality trait: define	Personality trait = "durable disposition to behave in a particular way in a variety of situations"
Big 5: Name + describe them	Big 5—McCrae + Costa–(1) extroversion, (or positive emotionality) = outgoing, sociable, friendly, upbeat, assertive; (2) neuroticism = anxious, hostile, self-conscious, insecure, vulnerable; (3) openness to experience = curiosity, flexibility, imaginative; (4) agreeableness = sympathetic, trusting, cooperative, modest; (5) conscientiousness = diligent, disciplined, well organized, punctual, dependable
Psychodynamic Theories: Who?	Psychodynamic Theories–focus on unconscious forces
3 components of personality: name and describe	Freud—psychoanalysis—3 components of personality–(1)id = primitive, instinctive, operates according to pleasure principle (immediate gratification); (2) ego = decision-making component, operates according to reality principle (delay gratification until appropriate); (3) superego = moral component, social standards, right + wrong
3 levels of awareness: name and describe	3 levels of awareness—(1) conscious = what one is aware of at a particular moment; (2) preconscious = material just below surface, easily retrieved; (3) unconscious = thoughts, memories, + desires well below surface, but have great influence on behavior

Outline Format

Some students find that an outline is the best way for them to organize their notes. In a formal outline, Roman numerals (I, II, III) mark the main ideas. Ideas relating to each main idea are marked by uppercase letters (A, B, C). Arabic numerals (1, 2, 3) and lowercase letters (a, b, c) mark related ideas in descending order of importance or detail. Using the outline format allows you to add details, definitions, examples, applications, and explanations (see Figure 5.2).

Figure 5.2 ▽ Note Taking in the Outline Format

Psychology 101
1/29/19
Theories of Personality

I. Personality trait = "durable disposition to behave in a particular way in a variety of situations"

II. Big 5—McCrae + Costa

    A. Extroversion (or positive emotionality) = outgoing, sociable, friendly, upbeat, assertive

    B. Neuroticism = anxious, hostile, self-conscious, insecure, vulnerable

    C. Openness to experience = curiosity, flexibility, imaginative

    D. Agreeableness = sympathetic, trusting, cooperative, modest

    E. Conscientiousness = diligent, disciplined, well organized, punctual, dependable

III. Psychodynamic Theories—focus on unconscious forces—Freud —psychoanalysis

    A. 3 components of personality

        1. Id = primitive, instinctive, operates according to pleasure principle (immediate gratification)

        2. Ego = decision-making component, operates according to reality principle (delay gratification until appropriate)

        3. Superego = moral component, social standards, right + wrong

    B. 3 levels of awareness

        1. Conscious = what one is aware of at a particular moment

        2. Preconscious = material just below surface, easily retrieved

        3. Unconscious = thoughts, memories, + desires well below surface, but have great influence on behavior

Paragraph Format

When you take notes while you read, you might decide to write summary paragraphs—two or three sentences that sum up a larger section of material (see Figure 5.3).

This method might not work well for class notes because it's difficult to summarize a topic until your instructor has covered it completely. By the end of the lecture, you might have forgotten critical information.

Figure 5.3 ▽ **Note Taking in the Paragraph Format**

> **Psychology 101**
> **1/29/19**
> **Theories of Personality**
>
> A personality trait is a "durable disposition to behave in a particular way in a variety of situations"
>
> Big 5: According to McCrae + Costa most personality traits derive from just 5 higher-order traits: extroversion (or positive emotionality), which is outgoing, sociable, friendly, upbeat, assertive; neuroticism, which means anxious, hostile, self-conscious, insecure, vulnerable; openness to experience characterized by curiosity, flexibility, imaginative; agreeableness, which is sympathetic, trusting, cooperative, modest; and conscientiousness, which means diligent, disciplined, well organized, punctual, dependable
>
> Psychodynamic Theories: Focus on unconscious forces
>
> Freud, father of psychoanalysis, believed in 3 components of personality: id, the primitive, instinctive, operates according to pleasure principle (immediate gratification); ego, the decision-making component, operates according to reality principle (delay gratification until appropriate); and superego, the moral component, social standards, right + wrong
>
> Freud also thought there are 3 levels of awareness: conscious, what one is aware of at a particular moment; preconscious, the material just below surface, easily retrieved; and unconscious, the thoughts, memories, + desires well below surface, but have great influence on behavior

List Format

The list format can be effective when taking notes on terms and definitions, sequences, or facts (see Figure 5.4). It's easy to use lists in combination with the Cornell format, with key terms on the left and their definitions and explanations on the right.

Figure 5.4 ▽ Note Taking in the List Format

Psychology 101
1/29/19
Theories of Personality

- A personality trait is a "durable disposition to behave in a particular way in a variety of situations"
- Big 5: According to McCrae + Costa most personality traits derive from just 5 higher-order traits
    - extroversion (or positive emotionality), which is outgoing, sociable, friendly, upbeat, assertive
    - neuroticism, which means anxious, hostile, self-conscious, insecure, vulnerable
    - openness to experience characterized by curiosity, flexibility, imaginative
    - agreeableness, which is sympathetic, trusting, cooperative, modest
    - conscientiousness, which means diligent, disciplined, well organized, punctual, dependable
- Psychodynamic Theories: Focus on unconscious forces
- Freud, father of psychoanalysis, believed in 3 components of personality
    - id, the primitive, instinctive, operates according to pleasure principle (immediate gratification)
    - ego, the decision-making component, operates according to reality principle (delay gratification until appropriate)
    - superego, the moral component, social standards, right + wrong
- Freud also thought there are 3 levels of awareness
    - conscious, what one is aware of at a particular moment
    - preconscious, the material just below surface, easily retrieved
    - unconscious, the thoughts, memories, + desires well below surface, but have great influence on behavior

Taking Notes in Class

Once you've decided on an approach to note taking, you'll need to actually use it in class. To do so effectively, try these techniques:

1. **Identify the main ideas.** Well-organized lectures always contain key points. The first principle of effective note taking is to write down the main ideas around which the lecture is built. Some instructors announce the purpose of a lecture or offer an outline, thus providing the class with the skeleton of main ideas, followed by the details. Others develop overhead transparencies or PowerPoint presentations and may make these materials available on a class website before the lecture.

2. **Don't try to write down everything.** Attempting to record every word from a class lecture or discussion will distract you from an essential activity: thinking. If you're an active listener, you will ultimately have shorter but more useful notes.

3. **Don't be thrown by a disorganized lecturer.** When a lecturer is disorganized, it's your job to organize what he or she says into general and specific frameworks. When the order is not apparent, indicate the gaps in your notes. After the lecture, consult your reading material, your study team, or a classmate to fill in these gaps, or visit the instructor during office hours with your questions.

Make Adjustments for Different Classes

As you become comfortable with the different systems for note taking, you will learn to adjust your approach depending on the kind of class you're in. Nonlecture courses might pose special challenges because they tend to be less organized and more free-flowing. Be ready to adapt your note-taking methods to match the situation. Group discussion has become a popular way to teach in college because it involves active learning. Your campus may also have Supplemental Instruction (SI) classes, which provide further opportunity to discuss the information presented in lectures. Take advantage of this option if it's available and be sure to attend all the sessions.

Imagine that you are taking notes in a problem-solving group assignment. You would begin your notes by asking, What is the problem? and writing the problem down. As the discussion progresses, you would list the solutions offered. These solutions would be your main ideas. The important details might include the positive and negative aspects of each view or solution. The important thing to remember when taking notes in nonlecture courses is that you need to record the information presented by your classmates as well as by the instructor and to consider all reasonable ideas, even though they may differ from your own.

How to organize the notes you take in a class discussion depends on the purpose or form of the discussion. It usually makes good sense to begin with the list of issues or topics that the discussion leader announces. Another approach is to list the questions that the participants raise for discussion. If the discussion is an exploration of the reasons for and against a particular argument, it's reasonable to divide your notes into columns or sections for pros and cons. When conflicting views arise in the discussion, record the different perspectives and the rationales behind them.

Use Specific Strategies for Note Taking in Quantitative Courses

Taking notes in math and science courses can be different from taking notes in other types of courses, where it may not be a good idea to try to write down every word the instructor says. In a quantitative course, quote the instructor's words as precisely as possible. Technical terms often have exact meanings and cannot be paraphrased.

Quantitative courses such as mathematics, chemistry, and physics often build on each other from term to term and from year to year. Thus, you will likely need to refer to notes you take now in future terms. For example, when taking organic chemistry, you may need to go back to notes taken in earlier chemistry courses. This review process can be particularly important when a lot of time has passed since your last course, such as after a summer break. Here are some ideas for getting organized:

1. **Create separate binders or digital folders for each course.** Keep your notes and supplementary materials (such as instructors' handouts) for each course in a separate three-ring binder or computer folder labeled with the course number and name.

2. **Download materials from your instructor *before* class.** Your instructor may post a broad range of materials on a class website, such as notes, outlines, diagrams, charts, graphs, and other visual explanations. Be sure to download these materials before class and bring them with you. You can save yourself considerable time and distraction during a lecture if you do not have to copy complicated graphs and diagrams while the instructor is talking.

3. **Leave space to add comments, questions, or further details.** If you are using pen and paper, take notes only on the front of each piece of loose-leaf paper. Later, you can use the back of each sheet to add further details, annotations, corrections, comments, questions, and a summary of each lecture. Alternatively, once you've placed what have now become the left-hand pages in the binder, you can use them the same way you would use the recall column in the Cornell format, noting key ideas to be used for testing yourself when preparing for exams.

4. **Listen carefully to other students' questions and the instructor's answers.** Take notes on the discussion and during question-and-answer periods.

5. **Use asterisks, exclamation points, question marks, or your own symbols** to highlight important points or questions in your notes.

6. **Consider taking notes in pencil or erasable pen.** In science and math classes, it can be hard to create diagrams on a screen, even if you would otherwise prefer to type your notes. If you use pencil or erasable pen on paper, it will be easier and faster to re-create formulas and diagrams.

7. **Refer to the textbook after class.** The text may contain diagrams and other visual representations that are more accurate than those you are able to draw while taking notes in class.

8. **Write down any equations, formulas, diagrams, charts, graphs, and definitions that the instructor puts on the board or screen.** You want to keep your notes as neat as possible.

9. **Use standard symbols, abbreviations, and scientific notation.**

10. **Write down all worked problems and examples, step by step.** These often provide the format for exam questions. Actively try to solve each problem yourself as it is solved at the front of the class. Be sure that you can follow the logic and understand the sequence of steps.

11. **Organize your notes in your binder chronologically.** Then create separate tabbed sections for homework, lab assignments, returned tests, and other materials.

12. **Label and store handouts immediately.** If the instructor distributes handouts in class, label them and place them in your binder either immediately before or immediately after the notes for that day.

13. **Keep your binders for math and science courses until you graduate** (or even longer if there is any chance that you will attend graduate school in the future). They will serve as beneficial review materials for later classes in math and science sequences and for preparing for standardized tests, such as the Graduate Record Examinations (GRE) or the Medical College Admission Test (MCAT). ■

Use Technology to Power Your Note Taking

Studies have shown that people remember only half of what they hear, which is a major reason to take notes during lectures. Solid note taking will help you distill key concepts and make it easier to study for tests. Note taking also engages the brain in a process known as rehearsal. Writing things down is important for you to start the process of creating your own way of understanding the materials. Along with making use of the note-taking formats that will be presented in this section, use your smartphone, tablet, or laptop to save information and create tools that will help you study.

the GOAL

Use technology to take effective notes.

how TO DO it

1. **Microsoft Word is great for most classes.** To highlight main ideas, you can bold or underline text, change the size and color, highlight whole sections, or insert comments. You can organize information with bullet points and tables. As you review your notes, you can cut and paste to make things more coherent.

benis arapovic/Alamy

2. **Microsoft Excel works well for any class that involves calculations or financial statements.** You can embed messages in the cells of a spreadsheet to explain calculations. (The notes will appear whenever you hover your cursor over that cell.)

3. **Microsoft PowerPoint can be invaluable for visual learners.** Some instructors also post the slides that they plan to use in class before each session. You can write notes on printouts of the slides, or download them and add your notes in PowerPoint.

Some Cool Apps for Note Taking and Reviewing

- **Pocket (iOS and Android)** allows you to store and review written content from your phone.
- **Evernote (iOS and Android)** lets you take a picture of handwritten or printed notes—or anything else you want to recall—and then you can file content and search it by keyword later.
- **CamScanner (iOS and Android)** allows you to scan and store notes, and convert and share documents in PDF or JPEG formats.
- **StudyBlue (iOS, Android, and Web)** allows you to make flash cards.

Whatever program or app you use, be sure to use the note-taking strategies described in this chapter. Stay organized by dating your notes and saving files using file names with the course number, name, and date of the class. And be sure to back up everything! If you find it hard to keep up, practice your listening and typing skills, and consider a typing class, program, or app to learn how to type properly. If you prefer a spiral notebook and a ballpoint pen, that's OK, too; these formats are tried and true.

your TURN

Do you use technology to take your notes? Why or why not? In small groups, discuss your experiences with note taking using technology, and troubleshoot any difficulties. Then share your strategies for using technology as a study aid.

Keep It Fresh by Reviewing Your Notes

We forget much of the information we receive within the first twenty-four hours of encountering it, a phenomenon known as "the forgetting curve." If you do not review your notes almost immediately after class, it can be difficult to retrieve the material later. In two weeks, you will have forgotten up to 70 percent of the material or information. Don't let the forgetting curve take its toll on you.

> " We forget much of the information we receive within the first twenty-four hours of encountering it. "

For interactive learners, the best way to learn something might be to teach it to someone else. You will understand something better and remember it longer if you try to explain it. Explaining material to someone else helps you discover your own reactions and uncover gaps in your comprehension. (Asking and answering questions in class can also provide you with the feedback you need to make certain your understanding is accurate.) Now you're ready to embed the major points from your notes into your memory. Follow these important steps to remember the key points from the lecture:

1. **Write down the main ideas.** For five or ten minutes, quickly review your notes and select key words or phrases that will act as labels or tags for main ideas and key information in your notes.

2. **Recite your ideas aloud.** Recite a brief version of what you understand from the class. If you don't have a few minutes after class to concentrate on reviewing your notes, find some other time during that same day to review what you have written. You might also want to ask your instructor to glance at your notes to determine whether you have identified the major ideas.

3. **Prepare to use your notes as a study tool.** As soon as you can after class, preferably within an hour or two, sift through your notes and create a recall column to identify the main ideas and important details for tests and examinations. In anticipation of using your notes later, treat your notes as part of an exam-preparation system.

Compare Notes

Comparing notes with other students in a study group, SI session, or test review session has a number of benefits: You will most likely take better notes when you know that someone else will be seeing them, you will discover whether your notes are as clear and organized as those of other students, and you will see whether you agree with other students on what the most important points are.

Take turns testing each other on what you have learned. This will help you predict exam questions and find out if you can answer them. In addition to sharing specific information from the class, you can share tips on how to take and organize your notes. You might get new ideas that will help your overall learning.

Be aware, however, that merely copying another student's notes, no matter how good those notes are, does not benefit you as much as comparing notes does. If you had to be absent from a class because of illness or a family emergency, it's fine to look at another student's notes to see what you missed, but just rewriting those notes might not help you learn the material. Instead, summarize the other student's notes in your own words to enhance your understanding of the important points.

Class Notes and Homework

Good class notes can help you complete homework assignments, too. Follow these steps:

1. **Do a warm-up for your homework.** Before starting the assignment, look through your notes again. Use a separate sheet of paper to rework examples, problems, or exercises. Go over any related assigned material in the textbook. Look at the text examples. Cover the solutions, and attempt to answer each question or complete each problem.

2. **Do assigned problems, and answer assigned questions.** When you start your homework, read each question or problem and ask, What am I supposed to find or find out? What is essential, and what is extraneous? Read each problem several times, and restate it in your own words. Work each problem without referring to your notes or the text.

3. **Don't give up.** When you encounter a problem or question that you cannot readily handle, move on only after a reasonable effort. After you have reached the end of the assignment, return to the items that stumped you. Try once more, and then take a break. You may need to mull over a particularly difficult problem for several days.

4. **Complete your work.** When you finish an assignment, consider what you learned from it. Think about how the problems and questions were different from one another, which strategies you used to solve them, and what form the answers took. Ask the professor, a classmate, your study group, someone in the campus learning center, or a tutor to help you with difficult problems and any remaining questions. ▪

TRY IT!

MAKING GOOD CHOICES ▷ **Making Your Classes Count**

However you're paying for college—through loans, grants, work, money from your parents—college costs a lot of money. Take your overall tuition payment for this term and divide it by the number of classes you are taking. What you're actually paying for each class may shock you.

But you have a choice—to make your classes count, or to waste the money you are spending. And that big choice is made up of lots of little choices. Think about all the choices that will affect how well you do in your classes. Will you choose to become actively engaged by listening critically, speaking up when you have a comment or question, taking good notes using one of the methods suggested in this chapter, and reviewing your notes before each class period? No one can make you do these things. The choice of what kind of student you want to be is up to you.

Chapter Review

Reflect on Choices

This chapter offers several options for effective note taking. Before you make a choice to try a new note-taking format, think back on those we suggested: Cornell, outline, paragraph, and list. Which one is most similar to the method you currently use, and which is most different? Reread the material, and do a brief written comparison of the recommended formats. Which do you think is most complex, which would be the easiest to use, and—given your learning style—which would help you best understand and remember the material?

Apply What You've Learned

Now that you have read and discussed this chapter, consider how you can apply what you have learned to your academic and personal lives. The following prompts will help you reflect on the chapter material and its relevance to you, both now and in the future.

1. How would you rate your current level of participation in the classes you are taking this term? Do you speak up, contribute to discussions, and ask questions, or do you daydream or sit silently? Do your instructors encourage you to participate, or do they seem to intentionally discourage your involvement? Research finds that students learn more when they contribute to class discussions and feel comfortable asking and responding to questions. Think about how your own level of participation—whether it's high or low—relates to learning and enjoyment in the classes you're currently taking.

2. This chapter makes the point that it is easier to learn and remember new material when you can connect it to something you already know or have experienced. Which of your first-year classes connects most directly to something you learned in the past or something that happened to you? Write a brief paper in which you describe these connections.

Use Your Resources

GO TO ▷ The learning assistance center: If you need help with developing strategies for learning and good study skills. Students at all levels use campus learning centers to improve in the skills discussed in this chapter.

GO TO ▷ Fellow college students: If you need help finding a tutor or joining a study group. Often the best help you can get is from your fellow students; look for the most serious, purposeful, and directed students.

GO TO ▷ The computer center: If you need help using Word, Excel, PowerPoint, or electronic note-taking systems.

GO TO ▷ The math center: If you are having difficulty figuring out what kind of notes to take in math classes.

GO TO ▷ The office for students with disabilities: If you cannot take notes because of a documented disability and need help arranging for a note taker.

 **LaunchPad Solo**
macmillan learning

LaunchPad Solo for *Step by Step* is a great resource. Go online to master concepts using the LearningCurve study tool and much more. **launchpadworks.com**

06

Reading to Learn

WunderfulPixel/Shutterstock

LaunchPad Solo
macmillan learning

To access ACES, the LearningCurve study tool, videos, and more, go to LaunchPad Solo for *Step by Step*. launchpadworks.com

Why is reading a college textbook more challenging than reading a high school textbook or reading for pleasure? The answer is that college textbooks are loaded with terms, concepts, and complex information that you will be expected to learn on your own in a short time. The amount of material that instructors will expect you to read, especially for courses like English literature, history, psychology, and sociology, may come as a surprise. To accomplish this, you will find it helpful and worthwhile to learn and use the active reading strategies outlined in this chapter. Together, these strategies form a textbook reading plan that will help you get the most out of your college reading.

How much reading did you do in high school? Many college students tell us that they did very little reading—only what they were required to do. Today, many readers opt for online sources, which tend to be shorter and often use more informal language. But whatever your previous reading habits might have been, college will require a higher level of focus and attention. Some students may be able to read quickly but find that their comprehension level is low. In college, you may occasionally need to reread a particularly difficult set of pages more than once in order to fully understand the concepts. Depending on how much reading you did before coming to college—reading for pleasure, reading for classes, reading for work—you may find that reading is your favorite way to learn, or it may be your least favorite. Either way, however, reading is absolutely essential for doing well both in college and in life. Any professional career that you might choose—such as medicine, engineering, law, accounting, or teaching—will require you to do lots of reading.

Review Your ACES Score

Take a moment to reflect on your **Reading for College Success** ACES score, and insert it in the box to the right. Now let's take action!

Did you score in the high, moderate, or low range? Are you surprised by your score? This score will help you learn more about your strengths and weaknesses in understanding how to develop active reading skills. Even if you already feel strong in this area, be open to learning new strategies to help you improve your score as you move through the chapter. This chapter will further your understanding of why this topic is essential to your success in college.

Score:

○ High
○ Moderate
○ Low

To find your ACES score, log on to LaunchPad Solo for *Step by Step* at **launchpadworks.com**.

Preview the topic headings in this chapter. Then, in a journal or a readily accessible file, reflect on your current skills by answering the following questions:

▶ **What are your current strengths? Where do you feel challenged?**
▶ **What do you hope to learn from this chapter?**

You Can't Put a Price on Knowledge

Kreativ Kolors/Shutterstock

The day after I registered for classes and got my list of assigned textbooks, I looked up the books on the campus online bookstore. My biology textbook alone was $200. I figured borrowing the textbook from a classmate or from the library would be OK. I could even photocopy a few sections if necessary, or I could order an old edition online. We'd probably cover most chapters in class anyway.

That was the plan, but because we had a ton of assigned reading, nobody wanted to share a book with their new pal Titus. Most of my classmates were pre-med and studied nonstop. My lab partner said that I could borrow his book on Saturday nights if I returned it by 8:00 a.m. each Sunday. The four-hundred-page beast was as thick as a toaster, and photocopying was a pain.

I realized three things: (1) the lone library copy would never be available; (2) old editions were marked up and lacked important updates; and (3) a huge part of learning in college involves teaching yourself. I went to see my instructor during her office hours. She suggested I buy an e-book version from the publisher's website. I took her advice, and it saved me a lot of money. It felt good to have the book on my laptop, so I could stay on pace with the syllabus.

The price tag of course materials can be tough to swallow, but as Titus discovered, obtaining those materials is an essential part of learning and being successful in your coursework. Why is it so important to keep up with your outside reading assignments in college?

Four-Step Plan for Active Reading

A textbook reading plan can pay off by increasing your focus and concentration, promoting greater understanding of what you read, and preparing you to study for tests and exams. The plan you'll learn in this section is based on four main steps: previewing, marking, reading with concentration, and reviewing.

Step 1: Previewing

When you read actively, you use strategies that help you stay focused. The first strategy, previewing, will give you an idea, or overview, of what is to come in the chapter. By previewing, you get the big picture—you see what you are about to read, and you can begin to consider how it's connected to what you already know and to the material the instructor is covering in class. Begin your preview by reading the title of the chapter. Next, skim the learning objectives (if they appear at the beginning of the chapter) and the introductory paragraphs, and then scan the list of key terms and read the summary at the end of the chapter (if the chapter includes either of these features). Skim the chapter headings and subheadings. Finally, look for any study exercises at the end of the chapter.

As part of your preview, check the number of pages in the chapter. Estimate how many pages you can reasonably expect to cover in your first fifty-minute study period. You may require more or less time to read different types of textbooks. For example, depending on your interests and previous knowledge, you may be able to read a psychology text more quickly than a foreign language text that presents an entirely new system of words and meanings.

As you preview the text, look for connections between the text material and the related lecture material. Call to mind the terms and concepts that you remember from the lecture. Use these strategies to warm up. Ask yourself: Why am I reading this? What do I need to learn? You'll find that if you have previewed a chapter, you will be able to read it more quickly and with greater comprehension.

△ **Be Prepared**
Go through the textbook before class, and try to identify the main points. Later you'll be able to compare your thoughts on the main points with what your instructor emphasized. Was there any overlap, and if so, where? What did you miss? track5/Getty Images

TRY IT!

SETTING GOALS ▷ **Stay Motivated to Tackle Your Required Reading**

Some first-year students, especially those who have trouble managing their time, think they can skip some required reading and still get good grades on tests and exams. The best students, however, will tell you that this isn't a smart strategy. Instructors assign readings that are important to your understanding, and include concepts and details from readings on tests. Set a goal to finish the required reading assigned for this week. Ask yourself these questions: Do I need to manage my time better to make sure I can finish the reading? When I finished the reading, did I feel more confident participating in class or completing assignments?

Use Visual Tools

Mapping or outlining a chapter as you preview provides a visual guide for how different chapter ideas fit together. Because about 75 percent of students identify themselves as visual learners, mapping and outlining are excellent learning tools.

To map a chapter while you are previewing, draw either a wheel structure or a branching structure (see Figure 6.1). For a wheel structure, place the central idea of the chapter in the circle. You should find the central idea in the chapter introduction; it may also be apparent from the chapter title. For example, the central idea of this chapter is "learning through reading." Place secondary ideas on the spokes radiating from the circle, and draw offshoots of those ideas on the lines attached to the spokes. For a branching structure, put the main idea (most likely the chapter title) at the top, followed by supporting ideas on the second tier,

and so forth. If you prefer a more step-by-step visual image, make an outline of the headings and subheadings of the chapter (see Figure 6.2). You can usually identify main topics, subtopics, and specific terms within each subtopic by the size of the print. To save time when you are outlining, don't write full sentences. Rather, include clear explanations of new technical terms and symbols, and pay special attention to the topics that the instructor covers in class.

Wheel Map

Branching Map

Figure 6.1 △ Wheel and Branching Maps
Practice using one of these maps by taking the content of the sample outline in Figure 6.2 and writing it where it belongs on the map.

Figure 6.2 ▽ Sample Outline
Figure 6.2 shows how a student might have outlined the first section of this chapter.

I. Active Reading
    A. Previewing—Get lay of the land, skim
        1. Mapping
        2. Alternatives to Mapping
            a. Outlines
            b. Lists
            c. Chunking
            d. Flash cards
    B. Marking textbooks—Read and think BEFORE
        1. Underlining
        2. Highlighting
        3. Annotating (Margin notes)
    C. Reading with concentration—Use suggestions like
        1. Find proper location
        2. Turn off electronic devices
        3. Set aside blocks of time with breaks
        4. Set study goals
    D. Reviewing—Each week, review
        1. Notes
        2. Study questions
        3. Annotations
        4. Flash cards
        5. Visual maps
        6. Outlines

Step 2: Marking What You Read

Marking your textbooks is another active reading strategy that will help you concentrate on the material as you read. Marking means underlining, highlighting, or using margin notes or annotations. Figure 6.3 provides an example of many of these methods. No matter which method you prefer, remember these important guidelines:

1. **Read and think before you mark**. Finish reading a section before you try to determine the most important ideas and concepts. When you read a text for the first time, everything can seem important.

Figure 6.3 ▽ Examples of Marking and Taking Notes

Using a combination of highlighting and margin notes, the reader has made the content of this page easy to review. Without reading the text, note the highlighted words and phrases and the margin notes, and see how much information you can gather from them. Then read the text itself. Does the markup serve as a study aid? Does it cover the essential points? Would you have marked this page any differently? Why or why not?

Source: "The Stress of Adapting to a New Culture." Adapted from *Psychology*, 8th ed., by Sandra Hockenbury et al. © 2018 by Worth Publishers. All rights reserved. Used by permission of the publisher Macmillan Learning.

CULTURE AND HUMAN BEHAVIOR

The Stress of Adapting to a New Culture

differences affecting cultural stress

Refugees, immigrants, and even international students are often unprepared for the dramatically different values, language, food, customs, and climate that await them in their new land. The process of changing one's values and customs as a result of contact with another culture is referred to as *acculturation*. **Acculturative stress** is the stress that results from the pressure of adapting to a new culture (Sam & Berry, 2010).

how attitudes affect stress

Cross-cultural psychologist John Berry (2003, 2006) has found that a person's attitudes are important in determining how much acculturative stress is experienced (Sam & Berry, 2010). When people encounter a new cultural environment, they are faced with two questions: (1) Should I seek positive relations with the dominant society? (2) Is my original cultural identity of value to me, and should I try to maintain it?

4 patterns of acculturation

The answers produce one of four possible patterns of acculturation: integration, assimilation, separation, or marginalization (see the diagram). Each pattern represents a different way of coping with the stress of adapting to a new culture (Berry, 1994, 2003).

1* *Integrated* individuals continue to value their original cultural customs but also seek to become part of the dominant society. They embrace a *bicultural* identity (Huynh & others, 2011). Biculturalism is associated with higher self-esteem and lower levels of depression, anxiety, and stress, suggesting that the bicultural identity may be the most adaptive acculturation pattern (Schwartz & others, 2010). In fact, a meta-analysis of 83 studies showed that biculturalism had the strongest association with psychological and social adjustment (Nguyen & Benet-Martínez, 2013). The successfully integrated individual's level of acculturative stress will be low (Lee, 2010).

2* *Assimilated* individuals give up their old cultural identity and try to become part of the new society. They adopt the customs and social values of the new environment, and abandon their original cultural traditions.

possible rejection by both cultures

Assimilation usually involves a moderate level of stress, partly because it involves a psychological loss—one's previous cultural identity. People who follow this pattern also face the possibility of being rejected either by members of the majority culture or by members of their original culture (Schwartz & others, 2010). The process of learning new behaviors and suppressing old behaviors can also be moderately stressful.

Acculturative Stress Acculturative stress can be reduced when immigrants learn the language and customs of their newly adopted home. Here, students from countries as diverse as Afghanistan, Iran, Chechnya, and Somalia attend government-sponsored language classes in Potsdam, Germany.

3* Individuals who follow the pattern of *separation* maintain their cultural identity and avoid contact with the new culture. They may refuse to learn the new language, live in a neighborhood that is primarily populated by others of the same ethnic background, and socialize only with members of their own ethnic group.

*separation may be self-imposed or discriminating

In some cases, separation is not voluntary but is due to the dominant society's unwillingness to accept the new immigrants. Thus, it can be the result of discrimination. Whether voluntary or involuntary, the level of acculturative stress associated with separation tends to be high.

higher stress with separation

4* Finally, *marginalized* people lack cultural and psychological contact with *both* their traditional cultural group and the culture of their new society. By taking the path of marginalization, they lost the important features of their traditional culture but have not replaced them with a new cultural identity.

Although rare, the path of marginalization is associated with the greatest degree of acculturative stress. Marginalized individuals are stuck in an unresolved conflict between their traditional culture and the new society, and may feel as if they don't really belong anywhere. Fortunately, only a small percentage of immigrants fall into this category (Schwartz & others, 2010).

*marginalized = higher level of stress

	Question 1: Should I seek positive relations with the dominant society?	
	Yes	No
Question 2: Is my original cultural identity of value to me, and should I try to maintain it?　Yes	Integration	Separation
No	Assimilation	Marginalization

Patterns of Adapting to a New Culture According to cross-cultural psychologist John Berry, there are four basic patterns of adapting to a new culture (Sam & Berry, 2010). Which pattern is followed depends on how the person responds to the two key questions shown.

Source: Research from Sam & Berry (2010).

After you complete a section, reflect on it to identify the key ideas. Ask yourself: What are the most important ideas? What will I see on the test? This step can help you avoid marking too much material. On a practical note, if you find that you have made mistakes in how you have highlighted, or if another student has already highlighted your textbook, use a different color highlighter.

2. **Take notes while you read and mark.** Think about it: If you rely on marking alone, you will have to read all the pages again. But if you take notes while you preview in addition to making a map, an outline, a list, or flash cards (see Figure 6.4), you are actively learning and also creating tools you can use to review, whether on your own or with a friend or study group.

3. **Avoid developing bad habits with marking.** Highlights and underlines are intended to pull your eye only to important terms and facts. For some, highlighting or underlining is actually a form of procrastination. If you are reading through the material but aren't planning to learn it until sometime later, you might be giving yourself a false sense of security and thus doing yourself more harm than good. Don't highlight or underline nearly everything you read; you won't be able to identify important concepts quickly if

TRY IT!

SETTING GOALS ▷ **Practice Marking a Chapter**

Have you been marking your assigned chapters to identify the most important points? If so, have you been following the suggestions in the preceding list? If marking chapters is not something you do when you study, set a goal for this week to mark every chapter you are assigned. You can underline, add margin notes, or use a light-colored highlighter. Try using a different method in each chapter to see which approach works best for you. As your understanding of the material grows and your performance on tests improves, you will be motivated to maintain your new good habits.

they're lost in a sea of color or underlines. Ask yourself whether your highlighting or underlining is helping you be more active in your learning process. If it is not, you might want to try a different technique, such as making margin notes or annotations. When you force yourself to put something in your own words while taking notes, you are not only predicting exam questions but also evaluating whether you can answer them.

❝ When you force yourself to put something in your own words while taking notes, you are not only predicting exam questions but also evaluating whether you can answer them. ❞

Step 3: Reading with Concentration

You cannot learn everything you need to know about an academic topic through an instructor's lectures alone. Learning in any class will also depend on your doing the assigned textbook reading. Reading a college textbook, especially if the material is completely unfamiliar or highly technical, is a challenge for most new college students, but using tested strategies such as those outlined here will make you a more effective reader.

Focus, focus, focus. Like many students, you may have trouble concentrating or understanding the content when reading textbooks. Many factors may affect your ability to concentrate and to understand texts: the time of day, your energy level, your interest in the material, and your study location.

Consider the following suggestions, and decide which would be most helpful in improving your reading ability.

- **Find a quiet study location.** If you are on campus, the library is your best option. Set your mobile phone to mute with vibrate off, and store it where you can't see it. If you are reading an electronic document, download the information and disconnect from the network to reduce online distractions.

- **Read in blocks of time, with short breaks in between.** Reading in small blocks of time throughout the day instead of cramming in all your reading at the end of the day should help you understand and retain the material more easily.

- **Set goals for your study period,** such as "I will read twenty pages of my psychology text in the next fifty minutes." Reward yourself with a ten-minute break after each fifty-minute study period.

- **If you're having trouble concentrating or staying awake, do something about it.** Take a quick walk around the library or down the hall. Stretch, take some deep breaths, and think positively about your study goals. Then resume studying.

- **Jot down study questions in the margins, take notes, or recite key ideas.** Reread confusing parts of the text, and make a note to ask your instructor for clarification.

- **Focus on the important portions of the text.** Pay particular attention to the first and last sentences of paragraphs and to words in italics or bold print.

- **Define unfamiliar terms** by using the glossary in the text or a dictionary.

Monitor your comprehension. An important aspect of textbook reading is monitoring your comprehension. As you read, ask yourself whether you understand the material, and check your understanding with a study partner. If you don't understand it, stop and reread the material. Look up words that you don't know. Try to clarify the main points and their relationship to one another.

After you have read the first section of a chapter and marked or taken notes on its key ideas, proceed to each subsequent section until you have finished the chapter. After you have completed each section—and before you move on to the next section—ask yourself again: What are the key ideas? What will I see on the test? At the end of each section, try to guess what information the author will present in the following section. Effective reading should lead you from one section to the next, with each new section adding to your understanding.

Step 4: Reviewing

The final step in effective textbook reading is reviewing. Reviewing involves looking through your assigned reading again. Many students expect that they will read the text material once and be able to remember the ideas at exam time, which may be four, six, or even twelve weeks later. Realistically, however, you will need to include regular reviews in your study process. This is where your notes, study questions, annotations, flash cards, visual maps, or outlines will be most useful. See Figure 6.4 for an example of how to prepare flash cards. Be sure to review the material from each chapter every week.

Consider ways to use your many senses to review. Recite aloud. Tick off each item in a list on each of your fingertips. Post diagrams, maps, or outlines around your living space so that you will see them often and likely be able to visualize them while taking a test. ∎

Figure 6.4 ▽ Examples of Flash Cards

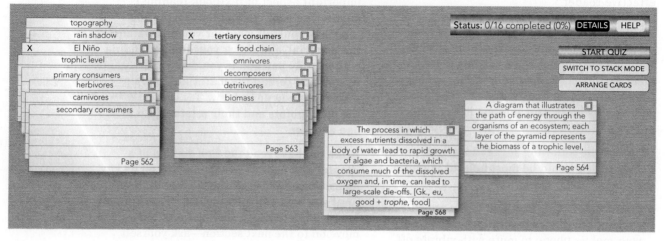

Status: 0/16 completed (0%) DETAILS HELP

START QUIZ
SWITCH TO STACK MODE
ARRANGE CARDS

topography
rain shadow
X El Niño
trophic level
primary consumers
herbivores
carnivores
secondary consumers

Page 562

X tertiary consumers
food chain
omnivores
decomposers
detritivores
biomass

Page 563

The process in which excess nutrients dissolved in a body of water lead to rapid growth of algae and bacteria, which consume much of the dissolved oxygen and, in time, can lead to large-scale die-offs. [Gk., *eu*, good + *trophe*, food]

Page 568

A diagram that illustrates the path of energy through the organisms of an ecosystem; each layer of the pyramid represents the biomass of a trophic level,

Page 564

Reading Online

Are you taking an online class or reading course material online? If so, your reading experience may be different from reading a print book. Educational researchers are just beginning to study how online reading changes the way people comprehend material. In an article in *The New Yorker,* "Being a Better Online Reader," Maria Konnikova cites the research of Ziming Kiu, a professor at San Jose State University and Mary Dyson, a psychologist at the University of Reading in England. Professor Kiu found that while some students comprehend more from reading a print book or article, just the opposite is true for other students. In general, however, people tend to read more quickly online, performing an action that Kiu calls "skimming." Skimming is very different from reading deeply—the type of reading that you'll need to do when reading college texts. Professor Dyson has found that when we read online, we experience more distractions—not only from e-mails or pop-up websites but also from differences in layout and even color of the online material. She adds that these distractions can be exhausting.

College publishers are intentionally developing online learning environments to reduce distractions and to keep students grounded in the content. For instance, many digital textbooks do not contain live links because they might interrupt a student's concentration. In addition, note-taking and highlighting tools are available. So if you are reading textbooks online, practice ways to stay focused. Keep tempting messaging apps and web browsers closed so that you aren't lured away from your assignments, and discipline yourself to use the four-step active reading plan.

Improving Your Reading

With effort, you can improve your reading dramatically. Remember to be flexible. How you read should depend on the material. Evaluate the relative importance and difficulty of the assigned reading, and then adjust your reading style and the time you allot. Connect one important idea to another by asking yourself: Why am I reading this? Where does this fit in? Reading textbooks and other assignments with good understanding and recall takes planning.

Developing Your Vocabulary

When reading textbooks and articles for your college classes, you will inevitably encounter new words and terms. A vocabulary is a set of words in a particular language or field of knowledge. As you become familiar with the vocabulary of an academic field, reading the texts related to that field becomes easier.

If words are such a basic and essential component of our knowledge, what is the best way to learn them? The following are some basic vocabulary-building strategies:

- **Notice and write down unfamiliar terms while you preview a text.** Consider making a flash card for each term or making a list of terms.

- **Think about the context when you come across challenging words.** See whether you can guess the meaning of an unfamiliar term by using the words around it.

- **Consider a word's parts.** If context by itself is not enough, try analyzing the term to discover its root (or base part) and any prefixes (parts that come before the root) or suffixes (parts that follow the root). For example, *transport* has the root *port*, which means "carry," and the prefix *trans*, which means "across." Together the word means "carry across" or "carry from one place to another." Knowing the meaning of prefixes and suffixes can be very helpful. For example, *anti* means "against," and *pro* means "for."

- **Use the glossary of the text or a dictionary.** Textbook publishers carefully compile glossaries to help students learn the vocabulary of a given discipline. If the text has no glossary, have a dictionary on hand. If a given word has more than one definition, search for the meaning that fits your text. *Merriam-Webster Online* is especially helpful for college students.

- **Use new words in your writing and speaking.** If you use a new word a few times, you'll soon know it. In addition, any flash cards you have created will come in handy for reviewing the definitions of new words at exam time.

TRY IT!

SETTING GOALS ▷ Building Your Vocabulary

Choose a chapter in this or another textbook. As you read it, list the words that are new to you or that you don't understand. Using a dictionary, write out the definition of each word. Then write a short sentence using the word in an appropriate context. Set a goal to add at least one new word per week to your personal vocabulary.

What to Do When You Fall Behind in Your Reading

Occasionally, life might get in the way of doing your assigned readings on time. You may become ill or have to take care of a sick family member for a few days, you may have to work extra hours, or you may have a personal problem that prevents you from concentrating on your courses for a short time. While there are valid reasons for getting behind, some students simply procrastinate and think that they can catch up. This is a myth. The less you read as you go along, the harder you'll have to work to make up for lost time. Try to follow the schedule of readings for each course, but if you fall behind, don't panic. Here are some suggestions for getting back on track:

△ **A Marathon, Not a Sprint**

If you fall behind in your reading, you won't be alone—almost every student eventually does. Remember that your studies are more like a marathon than a sprint, so you should plan to make up lost ground slowly but steadily: Do your assigned readings, study with others, get help, and do not give up! Jerome Prevost/Getty Images

- **Plan to do the assigned readings as scheduled.** Add one or two hours a day to your study time so that you can go back and read what you missed. In particular, take advantage of every spare moment to read; for example, read during your lunch hour at work, or while you are waiting for public transportation or at the doctor's office.

- **Join a study group.** If each member of your study group reads a section of the assigned chapter and shares and discusses his or her notes, summary, or outline with the group, you can all cover the content more quickly.

- **Ask for help.** Visit your campus learning assistance center to work with a tutor who can help you with difficult concepts in the textbook.

- **Talk to your instructor.** If you have a valid reason for falling behind, such as sickness or a personal problem, ask for extra time to make up your assignments. Most instructors are willing to make an exception to help students catch up.

- **Do not give up.** You may have to work harder for a short period of time, but you will soon be back on track. ■

TRY IT!

FEELING CONNECTED ▷ Two (or More) Are Better Than One

One way to get immediate feedback on your reading comprehension is to work with a study partner or study group. The give-and-take that you will experience will improve your learning and your motivation. Another way that study group members can work together is to divide up a chapter for previewing and studying and then get together later to teach the material to one another.

Different Courses, Different Kinds of Textbooks

It's important to know how to get the most out of your textbook, whether it's printed or digital. Because of the variation in college textbooks, you will need to learn and use different reading strategies depending on the material in the text. Some books are better organized, written, or easier to understand than others, but you can depend on the four-step active reading plan you have reviewed in this chapter to help you navigate all of them.

Instructors use textbooks in different ways. Some instructors expect you to read the textbook carefully, while others are much more concerned that you understand broad concepts that come primarily from their lectures. Make time to read the first pages of the textbook, where you will likely find a preface, an introduction, and an "About the Author" section. This material will explain why the text was written, how it is organized, what material is covered, and how to use the chapter's features in the best way. Use the questions or activities in the chapter review material as a study guide or to quickly check your understanding of the chapter's main points.

If your textbook seems disorganized or hard to understand, let your instructor know your opinion; other students likely feel the same way. Your instructor might spend some class time explaining the text; he or she can also meet with you during office hours to help you with the material. You might visit the learning center for help as well.

Reading Math Textbooks

Textbooks in various major disciplines, or areas of academic study, tend to be quite different from one another. Let's start with math textbooks, which are filled with sample problems, graphs, and figures that you will need to understand in order to grasp the content as well as classroom presentations.

Math textbooks are also likely to have fewer lengthy blocks of text and more practice exercises than other textbooks. As you read, pay special attention to the definitions; learning the meaning of each term in a new topic is the first step toward complete understanding.

Math texts usually have symbols, derivations of formulas, and proofs of theorems. You must understand and be able to apply the formulas and theorems, but unless your course has an especially theoretical emphasis, you are less likely to be responsible for all the proofs. So if you get lost in the proof of a theorem, go on to the next item in the section.

When you come to a sample problem, work through it. Then look at the solution and think through the problem on your own. As you read the math text, you'll spend the most time completing the exercises that follow each section.

To be successful in any math or science course, you must keep up with all assignments. Always do your homework on time, whether or not your instructor collects it. After you complete an assignment, skim through the other exercises even if they weren't assigned. Just reading the unassigned problems will deepen your understanding of the topic and its scope. Finally, talk yourself through each assignment, focusing on understanding the problem and its solution, not just on memorization.

Reading Science Textbooks

Science textbooks have many similarities to math textbooks. Your approach to a particular science textbook will depend somewhat on whether you are studying a math-based science such as physics or a text-based science such as biology or zoology. First, you need to

△ **Getting the Most Out of Your Textbooks**
Math and science texts are filled with graphs and figures that you will need to understand in order to grasp the content as well as material presented in class. If you have trouble reading and understanding any of your textbooks, get help from your instructor or your learning center.

familiarize yourself with the overall format of the book. Review the table of contents, the glossary of terms, and the appendices. The appendices will include lists of physical constants, unit conversions, and various charts and tables.

As you begin an assigned section in a science text, skim the material quickly to get a general idea of the topic. Begin to absorb the new vocabulary and technical symbols. Then skim the end-of-chapter problems so that you'll know what to look for as you do a second and more detailed reading of the chapter. State a specific goal—for example, if you are taking a biology class: "I'm going to distinguish between mitosis and meiosis" or "Tonight I'll focus on the topics in this chapter that were stressed in class."

You may decide to underline or highlight words in a subject such as anatomy, which involves a lot of memorization of terms. Be restrained in your use of a highlighter; highlighting should pull your eye only to important terms and facts.

For most science textbooks, outlining the chapters is the best strategy. You can usually identify main topics, subtopics, and specific terms under each subtopic by the size of the type. Headings printed in larger type will introduce major sections; smaller type is used for subtopics within these sections. Refer to Figure 6.2 for an example of a chapter outline. To save time when you are outlining, don't write full sentences but include clear explanations of new technical terms and symbols. Pay special attention to topics that were covered in the lecture class or in the lab. If you aren't sure whether your outlines contain too much or too little detail, compare them with those of a classmate or the members of your study group.

Reading Social Science and Humanities Textbooks

Many of the suggestions that apply to reading science textbooks also apply to reading in the social sciences (sociology, psychology, anthropology, economics, political science, and history). Social science texts are filled with terms that are unique to a particular field of study. They also describe research and theory building and have references to many primary sources. In addition, your social science texts may describe differences in opinions or perspectives. Your reading can become more interesting if you seek out different opinions about a common issue by looking at a variety of resources in your campus library or on the Internet.

Textbooks in the humanities (philosophy, religion, literature, music, and art) provide facts, examples, opinions, and original material, such as stories and essays. You will often be asked to react to the reading by identifying central themes or characters.

Some professors believe that the way courses and majors are structured artificially divides human knowledge and experience. Those with this view may argue that subjects such as history, political science, and philosophy are closely linked and that studying each subject separately results in only partial understanding. These instructors will stress the connections between courses and encourage you to think in an interdisciplinary manner. You might be asked to consider how the book you're reading, the music you're studying, or a particular painting reflects the political atmosphere or prevailing culture of the period.

If English Is Not Your First Language

The English language is one of the most difficult languages to learn. You'll notice that words are often spelled differently from the

The Value of Primary Source Material

While textbooks cover a lot of material in a limited space, they can't tell you everything you might want to know about a topic, and they may omit things that would make your reading more interesting. If you find yourself fascinated by a particular topic, go to the primary sources—the original research or documents used in writing the text. You'll usually find these sources cited in footnotes or in endnotes at the end of each chapter or at the end of the book. If you are using an e-book or digital textbook, you might find more extensive primary source material or links that will take you directly to it.

Many primary sources were originally written for other instructors or researchers. Therefore, they often use language and refer to concepts you may have never heard before. If you are reading a journal article that describes a theory or research study, one technique for easier understanding is to read the article from the end to the beginning. Read the conclusion or "discussion" section, and then go back to see how the experiment was done. In almost all scholarly journals, each article is introduced by an abstract—a paragraph-length summary of the methods and major findings described in the article. Reading an abstract is sort of like reading a CliffsNotes study guide—you'll get the gist of the research article before you dive in. As you're reading research articles, always ask yourself: So what? Was the research important to what we know about the topic, or was it a waste of time and money, in your opinion?

way they sound and that the language is full of idioms—phrases that are peculiar and cannot be understood from the meaning of the individual words. If you are learning English and are having trouble reading your texts, don't give up. Reading the material slowly and more than once can help you improve your comprehension. Make sure that you have two good dictionaries—one in English and one that links English with your primary language—and look up every word that you don't know. Be sure to practice thinking, writing, and speaking in English, and take advantage of your campus's services, which may include ESL (English as a second language) tutoring and workshops. Ask your adviser or your college success instructor to help you locate these services. ■

TRY IT!

MANAGING TIME ▷ Plan Your Reading Assignments

Create a simple four-column table, with horizontal lines for all your reading assignments for this week. Following the example provided, use the first column to list each reading assignment. In the second column, rate each assignment on a scale of 1 to 5 according to how easy (1) or difficult (5) you think the reading will be. Estimate how many hours each assignment will take, and enter that estimate in the third column. (Remember that a difficult reading will take longer.) Use the fourth column to keep track of how much time you actually spend reading.

Estimated reading time this week:

Assignment	Difficulty (1–5)	Estimated time	Actual time
History (Ch. 1)	4	1.5 hr	2.0 hr
Psychology (Chs. 2 & 3)	4	1.5 hr	4.0 hr
Math (Ch. 3)	5	2.0 hr	2.5 hr
Speech (Ch. 2)	2	1.0 hr	1.25 hr
College Success (Ch. 5)	2	1.0 hr	1.0 hr

Total estimated reading time: 7 hrs

Total actual reading time: 10.75 hrs

Thoughts: *I used all four steps of active reading. My reading took me a bit longer, but I can tell that I learned much more. I also felt like I knew how to use my textbooks better after reading this chapter from my college success textbook.*

Estimated reading time this week:

Assignment	Difficulty (1–5)	Estimated time	Actual time

Total estimated reading time:

Total actual reading time:

Thoughts:

At the end of the week, record your total actual reading time, then go back and analyze the table. Did you spend more time or less time reading than you predicted? How accurate were your predictions about the difficulty of the different readings?

Use E-books

While textbook publishers continue to make traditional books available, the same content is increasingly available in digital formats. In most courses today, students are required to access some course material digitally. For students who are used to buying or renting printed books from the college bookstore, the transition to digital reading can be confusing. Maybe you aren't sure what device to buy to read e-books. Or maybe you are curious about the advantages and disadvantages that an e-book has when compared to a traditional book. Look at the "pros" and "cons" on this page to help you understand why you might or might not want to use e-books.

the GOAL

Embrace the e-book in your courses.

how TO DO it

Just like any technology, there are pros and cons to reading an e-book compared to a traditional book. Weigh the following factors, try it out, and decide for yourself.

Pros of E-books and E-readers:

- Digital reading devices are portable and can hold thousands of books.
- E-books save trees, can be bought without shipping costs, and have a low carbon footprint.
- E-readers let you buy books online from anywhere with Web access, and you can start reading within minutes.
- You can type notes in an e-book as well as highlight passages and copy and paste sections.
- You can print out pages simply by connecting the device to your printer.
- You can access many e-books for free from the public library.
- Some e-books come with bonus audio, video, or animation features.
- Many digital reading devices accept audio books and can read to you aloud.
- The backlit screen means that you can read in bed with the light off, without disturbing anyone.
- You can adjust the size of the text.
- Some e-readers have a built-in dictionary. Others can link to reference websites like Google or Wikipedia.
- E-books are searchable and even shareable.

Cons of E-books and E-readers:

- Digital reading devices are expensive and can break easily if you drop them.
- Looking at a screen can cause some eye fatigue.
- It's harder to flip through pages of an e-book than a printed book.
- If you have limited or temporary access to e-books for your courses, your access will expire after the academic term. But you can keep the print textbooks you buy and build your own library.

your TURN

Price your textbooks in both print and digital formats, including the cost of the e-reader (if you don't already have one). Which format is cheaper? Will you purchase an e-book of your textbook in the future?

Chapter Review

Reflect on Choices

In this chapter, you have learned that reading textbooks is an essential part of being a successful student. The choice of how to approach your reading is up to you. Reflect on the strategies that have been suggested, list those that you already use, and make a separate list of those you want to try in the future.

Apply What You've Learned

Now that you have read and discussed this chapter, consider how you can apply what you have learned to your academic and personal lives. The following prompts will help you reflect on the chapter material and its relevance to you, both now and in the future.

1. Choose a reading assignment for one of your upcoming classes. After previewing the material, begin reading until you reach a major heading or until you have read at least a page or two. Now stop and write down what you remember from the material, then go back and review what you just read. Were you able to remember all the main ideas?

2. It is easy to say that there is not enough time in the day to get everything done, especially when you are faced with a long reading assignment. However, your future depends on how well you do in college. Challenge yourself not to use that excuse. How can you modify your daily activities to make time for reading?

Use Your Resources

GO TO ▷ The learning center: If you need help with your reading. Most campuses have a learning center, and reading assistance is among its specialties. All types of students use the learning center, whether they are the best students, good students who want to be the best students, or students with academic difficulties. Learning center services are offered by both full-time professionals and highly skilled student tutors.

GO TO ▷ Fellow college students and peer leaders: If you need help understanding your reading assignments. Look for the best students—those who appear to be the most serious and conscientious. Hire a tutor if you can, or join a study group. You are much more likely to be successful if you do so.

GO ONLINE TO ▷ Resources maintained by your college or university: If you want to read helpful articles about reading and marking textbooks and other general study skills. Use a search engine to find Dartmouth College's "Active Reading: Comprehension and Rate"; Mount Saint Vincent University's "Reading Textbooks Effectively"; and Niagara University's "21 Tips for Better Textbook Reading," available through its Office for Academic Support.

LaunchPad Solo
macmillan learning

LaunchPad Solo for *Step by Step* is a great resource. Go online to master concepts using the LearningCurve study tool and much more. **launchpadworks.com**

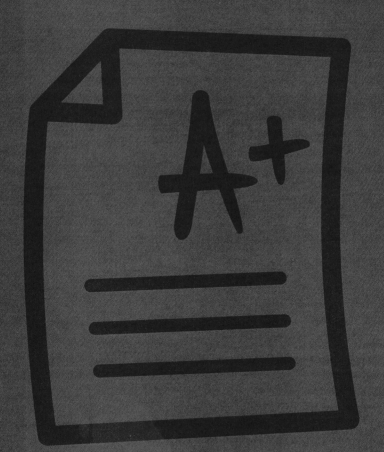

07

Taking Exams and Tests

In this chapter you will find advice for preparing academically, physically, and emotionally for tests and exams. This chapter also discusses what types of collaboration with other students are acceptable and reminds you why the guidelines for academic honesty and integrity are so important in college and beyond.

Does the thought of your first college test or exam make you anxious? Many students who have had particular problems with certain subjects, such as math or science, or with certain kinds of tests, will feel that they are doomed to repeat old problems in college. Nothing could be further from the truth. You were admitted to this college because of your potential to do well, but good grades on tests and exams don't happen by magic. It is your responsibility to attend all classes, take good notes, do all assigned readings, and seek help when you need it. Services available on most campuses include a learning center, tutoring, Supplemental Instruction, and special help from instructors with test-preparation sessions or one-on-one assistance. If you prepare and seek help when you have trouble, you should do well.

Most college instructors will expect you to be responsible for your own learning. They'll provide good information but won't always give you specific instructions about how to study and prepare for tests and major projects. Although some study strategies—such as not waiting until the last minute to prepare for an exam or start a project—will apply to all courses, the usefulness of other strategies will vary according to the subject matter. This chapter will help you determine the most effective study test-preparation strategies for different courses.

LaunchPad Solo
macmillan learning

To access ACES, the LearningCurve study tool, videos, and more, go to LaunchPad Solo for *Step by Step*. launchpadworks.com

Review Your ACES Score

Take a moment to reflect on your **Performing Well on Exams** and **Memory and Studying** ACES scores, and insert them in the boxes to the right. Now let's take action!

   Did you score in the high, moderate, or low ranges? Are you surprised by your scores? These scores will help you learn more about your strengths and weaknesses in understanding how to study, remembering information, and performing well on exams. Even if you already feel strong in these areas, be open to learning new strategies to help you improve your scores as you move through the chapter. This chapter will further your understanding of why these topics are essential to your success in college.

Score:

○ High
○ Moderate
○ Low

To find your ACES scores, log on to LaunchPad Solo for *Step by Step* at **launchpadworks.com**.

Preview the topic headings in this chapter. Then, in a journal or a readily accessible file, reflect on your current skills by answering the following questions:

▶ **What are your current strengths? Where do you feel challenged?**
▶ **What do you hope to learn from this chapter?**

Attitude Is Everything

Steve Debenport/Getty Images

I grew up all over the country, moving with my parents as part of a military family. I finished high school in Spokane, Washington, where I later met my husband. He died in Iraq soon after our son was born, and I had to find work to support the two of us. College was the furthest thing from my mind, but I realized that I wanted more for my son—and myself—and college was the best way to have a good future. Being a single mother motivates me, not only to provide a better life for both of us but also to set a good example for him.

   Part of going to college and raising a family involves finding a work–life balance in areas such as preparing for tests. I always thought I wasn't any good at taking tests or learning, so I usually finished in the middle of the pack on tests and exams. I quickly discovered that the first step in improving my test-taking abilities was changing my attitude about "Nicole's academic self." Once I improved my attitude, I began looking at test-preparation strategies that worked best for me, and I discovered that good note taking was essential. Now I make sure to take careful notes during class, underline key terms, and add margin notes. When I get home, I try to create associations between what I already know and the material I'm studying to help with my memory. I also know that my brain works best when I take care of my body, eat well, get daily exercise, and find time to relax. This isn't always easy with a toddler running around, but I know these methods are better for me in the long run than cramming. My advice to other first-year students? Remember that your attitude and your preparation are important if you are going to do well on tests and exams.

Nicole has made the most of her time in college by adjusting her attitude and finding a test-preparation strategy that works for her. Can you relate to Nicole's experience of not feeling like you are good at test taking? Why do you think her change in attitude allowed her to find ways to prepare more effectively? What ways can you adjust your own attitude and test preparation to succeed?

Preparing for Tests

In your first months of college, you will notice that students have different ways of preparing for tests. Some keep up with their assignments so that when the test day comes, they need only review what they have already studied. Others wait until the last minute and try to cram their test preparation into one night. Needless to say, cramming rarely results in good test grades.

Preparing for tests and examinations actually begins on the first day of the term. Note taking, assigned reading, and homework are all part of preparation; keeping up with all this work during each term will contribute to good test performance. Review assigned readings before class and again after class, and note any material covered in the reading assignments and in class. You will likely see this material again—on your test.

Work with Instructors, Peers, and Tutors

Preparing for tests does not have to be a lonely pursuit. In fact, it shouldn't be. Enlisting the help of others will help you succeed.

Start with your instructors. Pay close attention to what your instructors emphasize in class. Take good notes, and learn the material before each exam. Unless they tell you otherwise, instructors are likely to stress in-class material on exams. Before each exam, talk to your instructor to find out the types of questions you'll have to answer, the time you will have to complete them, and the content to be covered. Ask how the exam will be graded and whether all questions will have the same point value. Keep in mind, though, that most instructors dislike being asked, "Is this going to be on the test?" They believe that everything that goes on in class is important enough for you to learn, whether or not you'll actually be tested on it.

Use the information that you get from your instructor to design an exam plan. After checking exam dates on your syllabus (see Figure 7.1), create a schedule that will give you time to review effectively for the exam. Develop a to-do list of the major steps you need to take to be ready. Be sure you have read and learned all the

Figure 7.1 ▽ Exam Schedule from Sample Course Syllabus

History 111, US History to 1865
Fall 2018

Examinations

Note: In this course, most of your exams will be on Fridays, except for the Wednesday before Thanksgiving. This is to give you a full week to study for the exam and permit me to grade them over the weekend and return the exams to you on Monday. I believe in using a variety of types of measurements. In addition to those scheduled below, I reserve the right to give you unannounced quizzes on daily reading assignments. Also, current events are fair game on any exam! Midterm and final exams will be cumulative (on all material since the beginning of the course). Other exams cover all classroom material and all readings covered since the prior exam. The schedule is as follows:

Friday, 9/7: Objective type

Friday, 9/21: Essay type

Friday, 10/5: Midterm-essay and objective

Friday, 11/2: Objective

Wednesday, 11/21: Essay

Friday, 12/14: Final exam-essay and objective

material by one week before the exam. Try to attend all exam review sessions offered by your instructor. Whatever you do, don't wait until the night before the exam to begin your review.

Join a study group. Your instructor may allow class time for the formation of study groups. If not, ask your instructor, adviser, or campus tutoring or learning center to help you identify other interested students. Then, form a group, and decide on guidelines for your time together. For instance, group members should complete their assignments before the group meets and should prepare study questions or

points of discussion ahead of time. Study groups can meet throughout the term or just review for midterms or final exams.

Numerous research studies have shown that joining a study group is one of the most effective strategies you can use when preparing for exams. It allows you to hear other group members' views about your instructor's goals, objectives, and emphasis; have partners quiz you on facts and concepts; and gain the enthusiasm and friendship of others, which will help build and sustain your motivation.

Get a tutor. Tutoring is not just for students who are struggling. Often the best students seek tutorial assistance. Most campus tutoring centers offer their services for free. Ask your academic adviser or counselor about arranging for a tutor, or check in at the campus learning center. Learning centers frequently employ student tutors who have done well in the same courses you are taking. Many learning centers also have computer tutorials that can help you refresh basic skills. And think about eventually becoming a tutor yourself; tutoring other students will greatly deepen your own learning.

Prepare Properly for Math and Science Exams

More than in other academic areas, your grades in math and science courses will be determined by your scores on major exams. To pass a math or science course, you must perform well on timed tests. Here are some strategies you can use to prepare properly:

- **Ask about test rules and procedures.** Are calculators allowed? Are formula sheets permitted? If not, will any formulas be provided? Will you be required to give definitions? Derive formulas? State and/or prove theorems?

- **Work as many problems as you can before the test.** Practicing with sample problems is the best way to prepare for a problem-solving test (see Figure 7.2).

- **Practice understanding the precise meaning and requirements of problems.** Failure to read problems carefully and to interpret and answer what is being asked is the most common mistake made by students taking math and science exams.

- **Prepare in advance to avoid other common mistakes.** Errors with parentheses (failing to use them when they are needed, failing to distribute a multiplier) and mistakes with negative signs are common in math-based courses. Pay attention to these details in class so that you don't fall into the typical traps when you are taking an exam.

- **Study from your outline.** In a subject such as anatomy, which requires memorizing technical terms and understanding the relationships among systems, focus your preparation on your study outline.

Prepare Physically and Emotionally

Academic preparation—the studying you do to get ready for a test—is important, but physical and emotional preparation will also play a role

(c) What is the probability that a randomly chosen household will have a total income less than $50,000?

(d) What is the probability that a randomly chosen household will have a total income less than $100,000?

(e) Suppose two U.S. households were randomly selected. What is the probability that both households will have a total income less than $100,000?

28. Role-playing games like Dungeons & Dragons use many different types of dice. One type of die has a tetrahedral (pyramidal) shape with four triangular faces (see Figure 8.27). Each triangular face has a number (1, 2, 3, or 4) next to each of its edges. Because the top of this die is not a face but a point, the way to read it is by the number at the top of the face that is visible when the die comes to rest. Suppose that the intelligence of a character is determined by rolling this four-sided die twice and adding 1 to the sum of the results.

Brittny/Shutterstock

Figure 8.27 Rolling a pair of tetrahedral dice: red = 1 and green = 3; intelligence of character = 4 + 1 = 5, for Exercise 28.

(a) Give a probability model for the character's intelligence. (Start with a display in the style of Figure 8.7 on page 347, adapted for the outcomes of the two rolls of the four-sided die. These outcomes are equally likely.)

(b) What is the probability that the character has intelligence 7 or higher?

29. North Carolina State University posts the grade distributions for its courses online. Students in Statistics 101 in a recent semester earned 21% As, 43% Bs, 30% Cs, 5% Ds, and 1% Fs. Here is the probability model for the grade of a randomly chosen Statistics 101 student.

Grade	0 (= F)	1 (= D)	2 (= C)	3 (= B)	4 (= A)
Probability	0.01	0.05	0.30	0.43	0.21

(a) Make a probability histogram for this model. Does it have the shape of a normal distribution?

(b) What is the probability that the student got a grade of B or better?

30. How do rented housing units differ from units occupied by their owners? Here are probability models for the number of rooms for owner-occupied units and renter-occupied units, according to the Census Bureau:

# of Rooms	1	2	3	4	5
Owned	0.000	0.001	0.014	0.099	0.238
Rented	0.011	0.027	0.229	0.348	0.224
# of Rooms	6	7	8	9	10
Owned	0.266	0.178	0.107	0.050	0.047
Rented	0.105	0.035	0.012	0.004	0.005

Make probability histograms of these two models, using the same scale. What are the most important differences between the models for owner-occupied and rented housing units?

31. In each of the following situations, state whether or not the given assignment of probabilities to individual outcomes is legitimate—that is, satisfies the rules of probability. If not, give specific reasons for your answer.

(a) Choose a college student at random and record gender and enrollment status: P(full-time female) = 0.56, P(part-time female) = 0.24, P(full-time male) = 0.44, P(part-time male) = 0.17.

(b) Choose a college student at random and record the season of that student's birth: P(spring) = 0.39, P(summer) = 0.28, P(fall) = 0, P(winter) = 0.33.

32. What is the probability that a housing unit has five or more rooms? Use the models in Exercise 30 to answer this question for both owner-occupied and rented units.

33. Balanced six-sided dice with altered labels can produce interesting distributions of outcomes. Construct the probability model (sample space and assignment of probabilities for each sum) for rolling the dice that is featured in Joseph Gallian's article "Weird Dice" in the February 1995 issue of *Math Horizons*. Instead of using the regular values {1, 2, 3, 4, 5, 6}, one die has the labels 1, 2, 2, 3, 3, 4, and the other die has the labels 1, 3, 4, 5, 6, 8. How does this model compare with the model for regular dice?

8.5 Equally Likely Outcomes

34. If you play the lottery, there are two possibilities— you could either win or not win. Explain whether or not this means that you have a 1 out of 2 chance (i.e., a 50% probability) of winning.

in your success. Here are some tips for physical preparation:

- **Maintain a regular sleep routine.** To do well on exams, you need to be alert so that you can think clearly, and you are more likely to be alert when you are well rested. Last-minute, late-night cramming is not an effective study strategy.

- **Follow a regular exercise program.** Walking, running, swimming, and other aerobic activities are effective stress reducers. They provide positive and much-needed breaks from intense studying and may help you think more clearly.

- **Eat right.** Avoid drinking too many caffeinated drinks and eating too much junk food. Be sure to eat breakfast before a morning exam. Ask your instructor if you can bring a bottle of water with you to exams.

- **Know the material.** Study by testing yourself or by quizzing others in a study group so that you will be sure you really know the material. If you allow adequate time to review, you will enter the classroom confident that you are prepared on exam day.

- **Practice relaxing.** If you experience an upset stomach, sweaty palms, a racing heart, or other unpleasant physical symptoms of test anxiety before an exam, see your counseling center about learning relaxation techniques. Practice them regularly.

- **Use positive self-talk.** Instead of telling yourself, "I never do well on math tests," or "I'll never be able to learn all the information for my history essay exam," make positive statements, such as, "I have attended all the lectures, done my homework, and passed the quizzes. Now I'm ready to do well on the test." ■

TRY IT!

SETTING GOALS ▷ Be at Your Best for the Next Test

Doing your best on tests and exams takes more than hours of study. You must be physically and emotionally ready. Visualize the good grades you will earn, and imagine the pride you will feel in your accomplishments as a way to motivate yourself to prepare thoroughly. Set a goal to stay in good physical shape during the term and especially before midterms and final exams. That means not only paying attention to the suggestions in this chapter but also making sure that you get regular exercise and enough rest and that you maintain a nutritious diet. If you take care of yourself, you'll find that all the hard work you put into studying will really pay off.

Use the Cloud

Cloud computing allows you to use the Internet as a storage device. This comes in handy whether you are collaborating with your study group or need to access study materials and class notes wherever you are. Some sites even have pared-down versions of word processing, spreadsheet, and presentation software that you can use for free. Another great advantage of cloud computing is the ability to share your files or folders with others. You can create a personal digital library and decide who gets to check out what file. It also tracks the changes you and others have made to a file and keeps you from having multiple versions if you are sharing the file with a group.

Sign up for a free account from a cloud storage site. These sites allow you to save files to an online location, where you'll have your own private, password-protected storage space. Cloud storage is great for collaboration because you can choose to share all or some of your files with your classmates and friends. Here are four sites with free storage:

1. **Dropbox** is probably the best known cloud storage site. Users get 2 GB of free storage. You can upgrade to up to 500 GB for a monthly fee, or earn more storage space by referring others to the site.

2. **Google Drive** allows users to store and share documents up to 5 GB. A great feature of Google Drive is that you can edit documents in real time with others. If you're writing a group paper, your coauthors can view and edit the same document simultaneously.

3. **MediaFire** lets you work collaboratively and access your files using stand-alone apps on iPhone, iPad, and Android devices. Its key feature is 50 GB of free storage space.

4. **Microsoft OneDrive** uses the Microsoft Office suite and allows you to create, store, and share files. It comes with 15 GB of free space, but you can expand that space for a fee.

Studying to Make It Stick

In college, your memory will help you retain information and ace tests. After college, the ability to recall names, procedures, presentations, and appointments will save you energy and time and will prevent a lot of embarrassment. Learning how to exercise the "memory muscle" is just as important as using the tools and activities that can enhance memory.

Help Your Memory Help You

Psychologists and learning specialists have developed a number of strategies you can use to remember the information you study. Some of these strategies may be new to you, and others may be familiar. No matter what course you are taking, you need to remember concepts and ideas in order to complete the course successfully. To store concepts and ideas in your mind, ask yourself these questions as you review your notes and course material:

1. What is the basic idea here?

2. Why does the idea make sense? What is the logic behind it?

3. How does this idea connect to other ideas in the material or experiences in my life?

4. What are some possible arguments against the idea?

The human mind has discovered ingenious ways to remember information. Here are some tips that you may find useful as you're trying to sort out the causes of World War I or remember the steps in a chemistry problem:

- **Pay attention and avoid distractions.** This is perhaps the most basic and the most important suggestion. If you are sitting in class thinking about everything except what the instructor is saying, your memory doesn't have a chance. If you are reading and you find that your mind is wandering, you're wasting your study time. Force yourself to

focus, and pay attention to what you are hearing and reading.

- **Be confident that you can improve your memory.** Nearly everyone can improve his or her ability to remember and recall. Think of successes from the past when you learned things that you didn't think you could or would remember. Choose memory improvement strategies that best fit your preferred learning styles: aural, visual, read/write, or kinesthetic. Identify the courses in which you can make the best use of each memory strategy.

- **Overlearn the material.** Once you think you understand the material you're studying, go over it again to make sure that you'll retain it for a long time. Test yourself or ask someone else to test you. Recite what you're trying to remember aloud and in your own words.

- **Explain the material to another person.** Researchers who study learning know that the best way to learn something is to teach it to someone else.

- **Make studying a part of your daily routine.** As Figure 7.3 shows, after nine hours, we remember less than 40 percent of the information we just encountered. To counter this forgetting curve, be sure to review course material and reread notes within twenty-four hours of learning new information. Also, don't allow days to go by when you don't open a book or work on course assignments. Make studying a daily habit.

- **Check the Internet.** If you're having trouble remembering what you've learned, Google a keyword and try to find interesting details that will engage you in learning more about the subject. Many first-year courses cover such a large amount of material that you'll overlook the more interesting information unless you seek it out and explore it for yourself. As your interest increases, so will your memory.

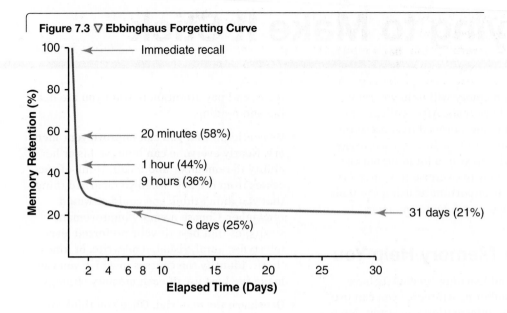

Figure 7.3 ▽ Ebbinghaus Forgetting Curve

- **Use online quizzing.** Many textbooks have related websites that offer a number of study tools, such as flash cards, videos, or online quizzing. Ask your instructors about these resources, and also check the preface of your textbooks for information on accessing these sites.

- **Go beyond memorizing, and focus on understanding.** Keep asking yourself questions: What is the main point here? Is there a big idea? Whenever you begin a course, review the syllabus, talk with someone who has already taken the course, and look briefly at all the reading assignments. Having the big picture in mind will help you understand and remember the details of what you're learning. For example, the big picture of a first-year college success class is to give students the knowledge and strategies to be successful in college.

- **Look for connections between your life and the content of your courses.** Finding connections between course material and your daily life can help you remember what you're learning. For example, if you're taking a sociology class and studying marriage and the family, think about how your own family experiences relate to those described in your readings or in the lectures.

- **Look for repeated ideas, themes, and facts as you reread your notes.** These are likely to appear on tests.

- **Think through and say aloud the key concepts and terminology of the course.** The more your brain uses these ideas and words, the more likely you are to remember them.

- **Get organized.** If your desk and computer are organized, you won't waste time trying to remember where you put a particular document or what name you gave a file. And as you rewrite your notes, ordering them in a way that makes sense to you (for example, by topic or by date) will help you learn and remember them.

- **Manage stress.** We don't know how much worry or stress causes us to forget, but most people agree that stress can be a distraction. Healthful, stress-reducing activities such as eating well, meditating, exercising, and getting enough sleep are especially important. Remember, too, that your college probably has a counseling center or health center where you can seek help in dealing with whatever might be causing stress in your daily life.

Use Review Sheets, Mind Maps, and Flash Cards

To prepare for an exam covering large amounts of material, you need to condense the volume of notes and text pages into manageable study units. Review your materials with these questions in mind: Is this one of the key ideas in the chapter or unit? Will it be on the test? You may prefer to highlight, underline, or annotate the most important ideas, or you may create outlines, lists, or visual maps containing the key ideas.

Use your notes to develop review sheets. Make lists of key terms and ideas that you need to remember. Also, do not underestimate the value of using a recall column from your lecture notes to test yourself or others on information presented in class. A recall column is a narrow space on the left side of your paper that you can use to rewrite the ideas from the lecture that you most want to remember. A mind map is essentially a review sheet with a visual element that shows the relationships between ideas and these patterns provide you with clues

to jog your memory. The words and visual patterns provide you with graphic clues to jog your memory. If you have already used a wheel or branching map to organize your reading, you'll find that the mind map offers you even more opportunity to be creative—to use art, color, and graphics to map your learning. You can also use these maps when you're studying several chapters for a test. The maps can help you make connections between the concepts in each chapter. Because the mind map approach is visual, it helps many students recall information easily. You can find many apps for creating mind maps on your computer or mobile device. Figure 7.4 shows a mind map of this chapter created by using an app called Coggle. Other apps include Total Recall and MindMeister.

In addition to using review sheets and mind maps, you may want to create flash cards. An advantage of flash cards is that you can keep them in a pocket or backpack and pull them out anywhere to study. Apps such as Chegg Flashcards and StudyBlue enable you to create flash cards on your electronic devices. Flash cards can help you make good use of time

Figure 7.4 ▽ Sample Mind Map

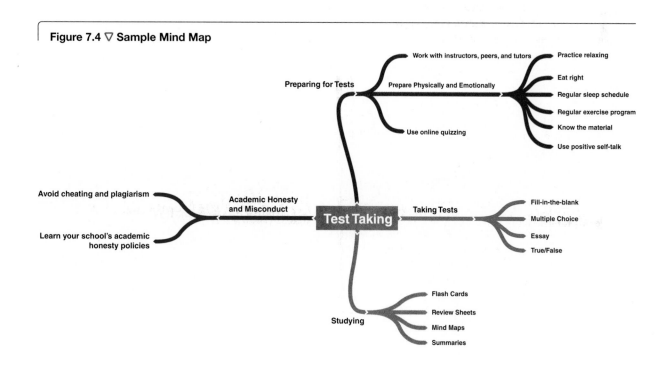

that might otherwise be wasted, such as time spent riding the bus or waiting for a friend. Flash cards are excellent tools for improving your vocabulary, especially if you are learning English as a second language.

Create Summaries

Writing summaries of course topics can help you prepare for tests, especially essay and short-answer exams. By condensing the main ideas into a concise summary, you store information in your long-term memory so that you can retrieve it when it's time to answer an essay question. Here's how to create a good summary in preparation for taking a test:

1. **Read the assigned material, your class notes, and your instructor's PowerPoint slides.** Underline or mark main ideas as you go, make explanatory notes or comments about the material, or make an outline on a separate sheet of paper. Predict test questions based on your active reading.

2. **Make connections between main points and key supporting details.** Reread to identify each main point and the supporting evidence. Create an outline in the process.

3. **Review underlined material.** Put those ideas into your own words and in a logical order.

4. **Write your ideas in a draft.** In the first sentence, state the purpose of your summary. Follow this statement with each main point and its supporting ideas. See how much of the draft you can develop from memory without relying on your notes.

5. **Review your draft.** Read it over, adding missing details or other information.

6. **Test your memory.** Put your draft away, and try to repeat the contents of the summary out loud to yourself or to a study partner, who can let you know whether you have forgotten anything.

7. **Schedule time to review your summary and double-check your memory shortly before the test.** You might want to do this with a partner, but some students prefer to review alone. Some instructors might be willing to help you in this process and give you feedback on your summaries. ■

Taking Tests and Exams

Throughout your college career, you will take tests in many different formats, in many subject areas, and with many different types of questions. Some test-taking tips, however, apply to nearly all test situations:

- **Write your name on the test.** Unless you're directed not to, write your name on the test and on the answer sheet.

- **Analyze, ask, and stay calm.** Read all the directions so that you understand what to do. Ask the instructor or exam monitor for clarification if anything confuses you. Be confident. Don't panic.

- **Use your time wisely.** Quickly survey the entire test, and decide how much time you will spend on each section. Be aware of the point values of different sections of the test.

- **Answer the easy questions first.** Expect that you'll be puzzled by some questions. Make a note to come back to them later. If different sections consist of different types of questions (such as multiple-choice, short-answer, and essay), complete the types you are most comfortable with first. Be sure to leave enough time for essays.

- **If you feel yourself starting to panic or go blank, stop whatever you are doing.** Take a long, deep breath and slowly exhale. Remind yourself that you know the material and can do well on this test. Then take another deep breath. If necessary, go to another section of the test and come back later to the item that triggered your anxiety.

- **If you finish early, don't leave.** Stay and check your work for errors. Reread the directions one last time. If you are using a Scantron answer sheet, make sure that the question number on the answer sheet corresponds to the number of the question on the test and that all your answer bubbles are filled in accurately and completely.

Be Ready for Every Kind of Pitch

Just like a batter in baseball has to be ready for any pitch—fastball, curve, slider, change-up—on test day, you have to be ready for whatever may be coming your way. Some test-taking tips depend on the type of exam you are taking or the type of test questions that you have to answer within the exam. Different types of exam questions call for different strategies.

Essay questions. Essay exams include questions that require students to write a few paragraphs in response. Some college instructors have a strong preference for essay exams for one simple reason: They promote critical thinking, whereas other types of exams tend to be exercises in memorization. To succeed on essay exams, follow these guidelines:

1. **Budget your exam time.** Quickly survey the entire exam, and note the questions that are easiest for you to answer, along with their point values. Take a moment to weigh their values, estimate the approximate time you should allot to each question, and write the time beside each item number. Be sure you understand whether you must answer every question or choose among the questions provided.

2. **Actively read the whole question.** Many well-prepared students write a good answer to a question that was *not* asked; when that happens, they may lose points or even fail the exam. Many other students write a good answer to only part of the question; they also may lose points or even fail the exam.

3. **Develop a brief outline of your answer before you begin to write.** First make sure that your outline responds to all parts of the question. Then use your first paragraph to introduce the main points, and use subsequent paragraphs to describe each point in more depth.

If you begin to lose your concentration, you will be glad to have the outline to help you regain your focus. If you find that you are running out of time and cannot complete an essay question, at least provide an outline of key ideas. Instructors usually assign points based on your coverage of the main topics from the material. Thus, you will usually earn more points by responding to all parts of the question briefly than by addressing just one aspect of the question in detail.

4. **Write concise, organized answers.** Some students answer essay questions by quickly writing down everything they know about the topic. Long answers are not necessarily good answers. Answers that are too general, unfocused, or disorganized may not earn high scores.

5. **Know the key task words in essay questions.** The following key task words appear frequently on essay tests: *analyze, compare, contrast, criticize/critique, define, describe, discuss, evaluate, explain, interpret, justify, narrate, outline, prove, review, summarize,* and *trace.* Take time to learn them so that you can answer essay questions accurately and precisely.

Multiple-choice questions.

Multiple-choice questions provide any number of possible answers, often between three and five; the answer choices are usually numbered (1, 2, 3, 4) or lettered (a, b, c, d), and the test taker is supposed to select the correct or best answer for each question. Preparing for multiple-choice tests requires you to actively review all the course material. Reciting from flash cards, summary sheets, mind maps, or the recall column in your lecture notes is a good way to review.

Take advantage of the many cues that multiple-choice questions include. Note terms in the question such as *not, except,* and *but* so that the answer you choose fits the question. Also, read each answer choice carefully; be suspicious of choices that use words such as *always, never,* and *only.* These choices are often (but not always) incorrect. Often the correct answer is the option that is the most comprehensive.

To avoid becoming confused by answer choices that sound alike, predict the answer to each question before reading the options. Then choose the answer that best matches your prediction. If a question totally confuses you, place a check mark in the margin and come back to it later. Sometimes a question that appears later in the exam will provide a clue for the one you are unsure about. If you have absolutely no idea, look for an answer that has at least some familiar pieces of information. If there is no penalty for guessing, fill in an answer for every question, even if it is just a guess. If there is a penalty for guessing, don't just choose an answer at random; leaving an answer blank might be a wiser choice. Finally, if you have time at the end, always go back and double-check that you chose the right answer for the right question, especially if you are using a Scantron form.

Fill-in-the-blank questions.

Fill-in-the-blank questions consist of a phrase, sentence, or paragraph with a blank space indicating where the student should provide the missing word or words. In many ways, preparing for fill-in-the-blank questions is similar to getting ready for multiple-choice questions, but fill-in-the-blank questions can be harder because you do not have a choice of possible answers right in front of you. Not all fill-in-the-blank questions are constructed the same way. Sometimes the answer consists of a single word, while at other times the instructor is looking for a phrase. In the latter case, there may be a series of blanks to give you a clue about the number of words in the answer, or there may be just one long blank. If you are unsure, ask the instructor whether the answer is supposed to be one word or more than one word.

True/false questions.

True/false questions ask students to determine whether a statement is accurate or not. For the statement to be true, every detail in the statement must be true. As in multiple-choice tests, statements containing words such as *always, never,* and *only* tend to be false, whereas statements with less definite terms—such as *often* or *frequently*—suggest that the statement may be true. Read through the entire exam to see if information in one question will help you answer another. Do not second-guess what you know or doubt your answers just because a sequence of questions appears to be all true or all false.

Matching questions. Matching questions are set up with terms in one column and descriptions in the other, and you must make the proper pairings. Before matching any items, review all the terms and descriptions. Match those terms you are sure of first. As you do so, cross out both the term and its description, and then use the process of elimination to assist you in matching the remaining items. ∎

TRY IT!

MANAGING TIME ▷ **Time Flies—Especially during an Essay Test**

Have you ever taken an essay test or exam and the instructor called "time" before you had finished all your answers? Don't let this happen to you. Remember that writing long responses to the first few questions can be a costly error, because doing so takes up precious time that you may need to answer the questions at the end of the exam. Divide the total time available by the number of questions, wear a watch to monitor your time as you move through the exam, and remember to give yourself enough time at the end for a quick review.

You Bombed a Test—Now What?

Has your college experience already included bombing a test—maybe even a test that you studied hard for? You're not alone. Almost all first-year students are occasionally surprised by a bad test grade that they didn't expect. What can you do now? First and foremost, be sure to review the test to understand what questions you missed and why. If you throw the test in the trash without figuring out what went wrong, you lose a golden opportunity to learn from your mistakes (and it's always possible that your instructor made an error in grading or that there was a glitch if the test was machine scored). Be sure to make an appointment with your instructor to discuss the test and get his or her advice on how you can do better next time. You might be embarrassed and tempted to avoid your instructor, but that's not a smart move. When you take the initiative to talk over your test,

find out what you misunderstood, and get the clarification you need, your instructor will know that you're a serious student.

Did the test you bombed cover more in-class lecture or discussion material than what you read in your text, or vice versa? Think about how you are studying now. Are you spending too much time studying the wrong material? And did you honestly put in enough study time, or did you think you could do well by just skimming the material? Did you study alone with no distractions, or did you study with other students? Both techniques have value, and over time you'll figure out what works best for you.

Finally, once you have analyzed why you earned a poor test grade, be resilient—don't let a bad grade get you down! Make some changes in what and how you study, and find the motivation to succeed on your next test.

Ace Your Online Tests

Many students will take online tests in traditional, hybrid, and online courses in college. Online tests might include any of the question types described in this section. You can prepare for online tests in much the same way you prepare for traditional tests, but be aware that online testing environments present their own particular challenges.

▶ how TO DO it

Which of these is NOT a strategy for overcoming procrastination?

○ promising yourself a reward for finishing the task
● completing the most interesting tasks first
○ breaking down big jobs into smaller steps
○ creating a to-do list

Submit answer

1. **Don't rely just on your notes.** Many instructors will allow you to reference your notes when taking an online test. For this reason, online tests are often harder than traditional tests. So don't get complacent. Prepare for an online test as if you won't have access to your notes, and during the test, get in the habit of referencing your notes only if you really need to.

2. **Resist the temptation to look online for answers.** The answer you discover might not be what your instructor is looking for. It's much better to check your notes to see what you were taught in class.

3. **Collaborate if it is allowed.** If your instructor doesn't forbid collaboration on tests, open up an instant message window with a fellow student. Take the test together, and take it early.

4. **Don't get distracted.** When you're taking an online exam, it's easy to fall prey to real-life diversions, like Twitter, Netflix, or a sudden urge to rearrange your closet. Whatever you do, take the test seriously. Go somewhere quiet where you can concentrate—not Starbucks. A quiet, remote spot in the library is ideal. You might also try wearing noise-canceling headphones.

5. **Be aware that you might lose your Internet connection in the middle of the test, and plan accordingly.** To be on the safe side, type all your answers and essays into a Word document. Then leave time at the end to cut and paste them into the test itself.

6. **Use any extra time wisely.** Take a few minutes to obsessively check your answers and spelling. Your online test platform may not have spell-check. (Of course, double-checking your answers is good advice for traditional tests, too.)

7. **Be aware of the testing environment.** For example, some online tests won't let you change your answer once you hit "submit," and others might have time limits for how long you can spend on each question. Some online tests will let you skip around, provided you finish the test in a certain amount of time. Be sure to ask your instructor what you can expect. If possible, ask your instructor if you can practice in the online platform before taking the test.

▶ your TURN

Have you taken an online test before? In a small group, discuss your experience with your peers. What were some common pitfalls you and your group members faced? How might you approach your online test in the future? Use the strategies above, or brainstorm your own.

Academic Honesty and Misconduct

Imagine what our world would be like if researchers reported fraudulent results that were then used to develop new machines or medical treatments or to build bridges, airplanes, or subway systems. Integrity is a cornerstone of higher education, and activities that compromise that integrity damage everyone: your country, your community, your college or university, your classmates, and yourself.

Cheating

Institutions vary widely in how they define broad terms such as *lying* or *cheating*. One university defines cheating as "intentionally using or attempting to use unauthorized materials, information, notes, study aids, or other devices . . . [or engaging in] unauthorized communication of information during an academic exercise." This would apply to looking over a classmate's shoulder for an answer, using a calculator when it is not authorized, obtaining or discussing an exam (or individual questions from an exam) without permission, copying someone else's lab notes, purchasing a term paper over the Internet, watching the movie version of a book instead of reading it, and duplicating computer files.

▽ **Exam Day—Give It Your Best**
Whether or not your exams are monitored by the instructor, be sure to do your own work and protect it from the wandering eyes of others. Put away all materials, including your mobile devices, so that you will not arouse the suspicion of the instructor. Chris Ryan/Getty Images.

Plagiarism

Plagiarism, or taking another person's ideas or work and presenting it as your own, is especially intolerable in an academic culture. Just as taking someone else's property constitutes physical theft, taking credit for someone else's ideas constitutes intellectual theft. On most tests, you don't have to credit specific sources. In written reports and papers, however, you must give credit any time you use (1) another person's actual words; (2) another person's ideas or theories, even if you don't quote the person directly; or (3) information that is not considered common knowledge.

Many schools prohibit certain activities in addition to lying, cheating, getting unauthorized assistance, and plagiarizing. Some examples of prohibited behaviors are intentionally inventing information or results, earning credit more than once for the same piece of academic work without permission, giving your work or exam answers to another student to copy during the actual exam or before that exam is given to another section, giving or selling a paper you have written to another student, and bribing someone in exchange for some kind of academic advantage. Most schools also prohibit helping or attempting to help another student commit a dishonest act.

Consequences of Cheating and Plagiarism

Although some students may seem to be getting away with cheating or plagiarizing, such behaviors can have severe and life-changing consequences. In recent years, college students have been suspended or expelled for cheating on examinations or plagiarizing major papers, and some college graduates have even had their degrees revoked. Writers and journalists such as Jayson Blair, formerly of *The New York Times*, and Stephen Glass, formerly of the *New Republic*, have lost their jobs and their journalistic careers after their plagiarism was discovered. Even college

presidents have occasionally been guilty of using the words of others in writing and speaking. Such discoveries can result not only in embarrassment and shame but also in lawsuits and criminal actions.

Because plagiarism can be a problem on college campuses, faculty members are now using electronic systems, such as www.turnitin.com, to identify passages in student papers that have been plagiarized. Many instructors routinely check their students' papers to make sure that the writing is original. So even though the temptation to cheat or plagiarize might be strong, the chance of possibly getting a better grade isn't worth misrepresenting yourself or your knowledge and suffering the consequences.

Reducing the Likelihood of Academic Dishonesty

To avoid becoming intentionally or unintentionally involved in academic misconduct, consider the reasons why it could happen:

- **Ignorance.** Some students are unaware of the rules for academic honesty in each class. In a survey at the University of South Carolina, 20 percent of students incorrectly thought that buying a term paper wasn't cheating. Forty percent thought that using a test file (a collection of actual tests from previous terms) was fair behavior. Sixty percent thought that it was acceptable to get answers from someone who had taken the exam earlier in the same or a prior term.

- **Cultural and campus differences.** In other countries and on some U.S. campuses, students are encouraged to review past exams as practice exercises. Some student government associations maintain test files for student use. Make sure you know the policy on your campus.

- **A belief that grades are all that matter.** This misconception might reflect our society's competitive atmosphere. It also might be the result of pressure from parents, peers, or teachers. In truth, grades mean nothing if you have cheated to earn them. Even if your grades help you get a job, what you have actually learned is what will help you keep the job and be promoted. If you haven't learned what you need to know, you won't be ready to work in your chosen field.

- **Unclear boundaries and concern that you'll seem rude.** If another student asks you to help him or her cheat, clearly state your boundaries. Tell the student that you both would risk failing the assignment, failing the course, or worse. Protect your paper during an exam. During class or outside class, resist showing another student your homework or a major paper you have written unless your judgment says that doing so presents a good opportunity for student collaboration and you can ensure that your work doesn't leave your sight. Turning someone down can be hard because so many of us are instinctively polite and helpful, but assure yourself that saying no is the right thing to do.

- **Lack of preparation or inability to manage your time and activities.** If your lack of preparation is a time-management problem, be honest with yourself and unlearn old habits of procrastination. If you've done your best and still need extra time, ask an instructor to extend a deadline so that a project can be done well.

- **Feeling overwhelmed and alone.** Find out where you can obtain assistance with study skills, time management, and test taking. If your methods are in good shape but the content of the course is too difficult, consult your instructor, join a study group, or visit your campus learning center or tutorial service. As a last resort, consider withdrawing from the course. Your college will have a deadline for dropping a course without penalty. But before withdrawing, be sure to talk with your academic adviser or instructor.

- **Impossibly high standards of family and friends.** Rather than giving in to unfair pressure from others to achieve impossibly high standards, stick to your own goals. If you are being pressured to enter a career that does not interest you, sit down with a counselor or career services professional to explore alternatives. ∎

TRY IT!

MAKING GOOD CHOICES ▷ Ignorance Is No Excuse

Make a decision to learn about the rules of academic honesty for each of your classes by asking questions in class or by setting up appointments with your instructors during their office hours. Some rules will be the same for all classes; others will depend on how the course is taught or how students are expected to study. Pleading ignorance of the rules is not a good strategy. Having all the information at hand each term will allow you to make good decisions with regard to maintaining your academic integrity.

Chapter Review

Reflect on Choices

Test taking is an inevitable part of college life. But you can choose how you are going to prepare for tests, deal with any test anxiety you might feel, and pay attention to your grades and instructor feedback. Reflect on your biggest problem in taking tests. Is it with certain types of tests or with all of them? Is it related to certain subjects or to any subject? Write a brief summary of strategies you have learned in this chapter to deal with this problem.

Apply What You've Learned

Now that you have read and discussed this chapter, consider how you can apply what you have learned to your academic and personal lives. The following prompts will help you reflect on the chapter material and its relevance to you, both now and in the future.

1. Identify your next test or exam. What class is it for? When is it scheduled (morning, afternoon, or evening)? What type of test will it be (problem-solving, multiple-choice, open-book, etc.)? List the specific strategies described in this chapter that will help you prepare for and take this test.

2. Do you know how your institution or your different instructors define cheating or plagiarism? Look up the definitions of these terms in your institution's student handbook, and read about the penalties for students who are dishonest. Then check your syllabi for class-specific guidelines. If you still have questions about what behaviors are or are not acceptable in a particular class, check with your instructor.

Use Your Resources

GO TO ▷ **The learning center:** If you need help solving your academic problems. All types of students use the learning center, whether they are the best students, good students who want to be the best students, or students with academic difficulties. Learning center services are offered by both full-time professionals and highly skilled student tutors.

GO TO ▷ **Your college's counseling services center:** If you need help dealing with test anxiety. College and university counseling centers offer a wide array of services, often including workshops and individual or group counseling.

GO TO ▷ **Fellow college students and peer leaders:** If you need help staying on track academically. Seek the help of classmates who are serious, purposeful, and directed. Or you can secure a tutor or join a study group.

GO ONLINE TO ▷ **College and university exam preparation resources:** If you need help studying and preparing for exams. Helpful online exam preparation resources are available from many institutions. For example, use your search engine to find Florida Atlantic University's (FAU) list of tips to help you prepare for exams, available through the Center for Learning and Student Success (CLASS). Or check out Shaniese Alston's "Scientifically, the Best Ways to Prepare for Final Exams" on the State University of New York's blog for strategies on exam preparation. Do your own search using terms like "test preparation and academic support" to locate other online resources.

LaunchPad Solo
macmillan learning

LaunchPad Solo for *Step by Step* is a great resource. Go online to master concepts using the LearningCurve study tool and much more. launchpadworks.com

118

08

Developing Information Literacy and Communication Skills

Domofon/Shutterstock

 LaunchPad Solo
macmillan learning

To access ACES, the LearningCurve study tool, videos, and more, go to LaunchPad Solo for *Step by Step*. **launchpadworks.com**

To participate fully in the information age, you will need to develop your information literacy skills: finding, evaluating, and using information that others have communicated through writing and speaking. Your communication skills—especially the ability to write and speak clearly, persuasively, and confidently—will make a tremendous difference in how the rest of the world perceives you and how well you communicate throughout your life. Furthermore, in almost every occupation, you will be expected to think, create, manage, lead, and communicate.

At its most basic, information literacy is the ability to manage the overwhelming amount of information available today. In addition to learning how to retrieve and select the best resources to meet your needs, you will learn how to synthesize and write or speak about the sources you have found. In assigned research projects, you will process information, pulling ideas and concepts together to create new information and ideas that other people can use.

Some students look at writing, speaking, and information literacy as tasks to be mastered and then forgotten. Nothing could be further from the truth. These are processes (step-by-step methods for reaching your final goal) that can help you create products (such as a final research paper, answers to an essay exam, or a presentation) throughout your education and career.

119

Review Your ACES Score

Take a moment to reflect on your **Information Literacy and Communication** ACES score, and insert it in the box to the right. Now let's take action!

Did you score in the high, moderate, or low range? Are you surprised by your score? This score will help you learn more about your strengths and weaknesses in understanding how to find and use information as well as write and speak effectively. Even if you already feel strong in this area, be open to learning new strategies to help you improve your score as you move through the chapter. This chapter will further your understanding of why this topic is essential to your success in college.

Score:

⬚

○ High
○ Moderate
○ Low

To find your ACES score, log on to LaunchPad Solo for *Step by Step* at **launchpadworks.com**.

Preview the topic headings in this chapter. Then, in a journal or a readily accessible file, reflect on your current skills by answering the following questions:

▶ **What are your current strengths? Where do you feel challenged?**
▶ **What do you hope to learn from this chapter?**

The Early Bird Gets the A

When I was looking into going to college, Montclair University in New Jersey had everything I wanted—a wide range of majors and lots of student activities. Plus, it had a good library system, which would allow me to conduct research both on and off campus.

Writing research papers in high school is much different from writing college research papers. In high school I usually got As on my papers, so the D that I received on my first graded paper at Montclair was a huge shock. I had waited until the day before it was due to begin working on it, but I still thought it was good. My instructor had a different opinion. "Your paper reads like something that was written in a few hours at the last minute," she said. "And your bibliography cites Wikipedia more than the actual source material."

The instructor also pointed out a couple of places where I had copied material from a source without referencing it. "Analee, you're going to need to get your writing up to a college level. The best source of help for you will be the writing center, so make an appointment right away."

Now I start working on my papers early—as soon as I receive the assignment. I give myself plenty of time to do research in the library and online. Because I don't procrastinate, I can get help from the writing center without any last-minute stress. The strong grades I am now earning prove that working this way pays off.

Not everyone arrives at college with the same expectations or the same high school preparation. As Analee's story illustrates, developing good habits for writing college research papers provides many benefits that can last throughout one's entire college experience, including less stress and better grades. What did Analee learn about the amount of time she should have spent on that first paper? What did Analee do next to build on what she learned through this first assignment? What can you learn from Analee's story?

Information Literacy

Information literacy, a skill demanded by most twenty-first century employers, is the ability to find, interpret, and use information to meet your needs. Information literacy requires that you also develop computer literacy, media literacy, and cultural literacy.

- **Computer literacy** is the ability to use electronic tools for conducting searches and for communicating and presenting to others what you have found and analyzed.

- **Media literacy** is the ability to think deeply about what you see and read via television, film, advertising, radio, magazines, and the Internet.

- **Cultural literacy** is having deep knowledge about the world around you—both past and present.

Learning to Be Information Literate

People are amazed at the amount of information available to them everywhere, especially online. What can you do about information overload? To become an informed and successful user of information, keep three basic goals in mind:

1. **Know how to find the information you need.** Once you have figured out where to look for information, you'll need to ask good questions and learn how to search information systems, such as the Internet, libraries, and databases.

2. **Learn how to interpret the information you find.** It is important to find information, but

△ **Stay Connected**
In today's world, information literacy is one of the most important skills a person can have. This means developing computer, media, and cultural literacy, along with learning how to find, interpret, and use the information you need. Hero Images/Getty Images

> " There are several ways to search for information, but before you start searching, you need to have a clear idea of what you're looking for. "

it is even more important to make sense of that information. What does the information mean? Is the information correct? Can the source be trusted?

3. **Have a purpose for collecting information, and then put it to use.** Even the best information won't do you much good if you don't know what to do with it. Decide how to put your findings into an appropriate format, such as a research paper for a class or a presentation for a meeting.

In this chapter, you'll explore ways to work toward each of these goals—doing so is really what college is all about.

Choosing, Narrowing, and Researching a Topic

Assignments that require the use of library materials will be a part of most of your classes. There are several ways to search for information, but before you start searching, you need to have a clear idea of what you're looking for.

Choosing a topic is often the hardest part of a research project. Your instructor may assign a general topic, but you'll probably want to narrow it down to a particular area that interests you. Imagine, for example, that your assignment is to write a research paper on the topic of global warming. First, you will want to get an overview of this topic through a search engine, like Google. Once you've found basic information, you have a decision to make: What aspects of global warming will you research? You may realize that global warming includes many related subtopics, and you can use this new information to create keywords—words or phrases that tell an online search engine what you're looking for. For example, for the topic "global warming," keywords may include "climate change," "greenhouse effect," "ozone layer," "smog," or "carbon emissions." Even these terms will generate a large number of hits, and you will probably need to narrow your search even more. Aim to identify twelve or so focused and highly relevant hits on an aspect of global warming that you can use to write a well-organized research paper.

If you are having trouble coming up with keywords, one place to begin your research is an encyclopedia—a book or an electronic database with general knowledge on a range of topics. You have probably used an encyclopedia recently without thinking about it: *Wikipedia*. A *wiki* is a type of website that allows many different people to edit its content. Many instructors feel that the information on *Wikipedia* is not reliable because anyone can change it; instead, they want students to use sources that have gone through a formal review process. Your instructors might even forbid *Wikipedia*; if so, avoid it altogether. Even if an instructor permits the use of *Wikipedia*, it's best to use it only as a *starting point* for your research. Do not plan to cite *Wikipedia* in your final paper.

Even with an understanding of various types of sources, it can be difficult to determine what exactly you need for your assignment. Figure 8.1 provides an overview of when to use common research sources, and gives examples of what you'll find in each source. ■

Figure 8.1 ▽ Using Common Research Sources
This chart differentiates the most common research sources. You will access these types of sources in your classwork, for your job, and in your personal life. Source: "Best Practices for Online Communication," adapted from Steven McCornack, *Reflect & Relate: An Introduction to Interpersonal Communication*, 4th ed. Copyright © 2016 by Bedford/St. Martin's. All rights reserved. Used by permission of the publisher, Macmillan Learning.

INFORMATION TIME LINE		
Source	**When to access information**	**What it offers**
Newspapers (print and online)	Daily/hourly after an event	Primary-source, firsthand discussions of a current event, and of what happened at the time of the event; short articles
Magazines	Weekly/monthly after an event	Analysis by a journalist or reporter of an event days or weeks after it occurred; longer articles than in newspapers; informally credits sources; might include more interviews or research as well as historical context
Scholarly articles	Months after an event	In-depth analyses of issues; research-based scientific studies with formally credited sources, written and reviewed by experts; contains graphs, tables, and charts
Books	Months/years after an event	A comprehensive overview of a topic with broad and in-depth analyses

Research: Information Literacy in Action

In the past, you might have completed assignments that asked you to find a book, journal article, or website related to a particular topic. While finding information is an essential part of research, it's just the first step. Research is not just copying a paragraph from a book or putting together bits and pieces of information without adding any of your own comments. In fact, such behavior could easily be considered plagiarism, which could result in a failing grade—or worse. We address plagiarism later in this chapter.

Research is a process that includes asking questions, collecting and analyzing data related to those questions, and presenting one or more answers. Good research is information literacy in action. If your instructor asks you to select and write about a topic, you might search for information about it, find multiple sources, select and organize a few of those sources, write a paper or prepare a presentation that cites your sources, draw conclusions of your own, and submit the final product. The conclusions that you make based on your research represent new information.

It takes time to go through all the steps of conducting good research. Some steps will be difficult, and you might be tempted to take shortcuts. However, learning to persist at these kinds of tasks in college will pay off in your career. You will find that the research and writing process becomes easier, and you will be more successful.

Using the Library

Libraries are no longer the cold, silent places that some of us remember. Today, they are inviting and friendly, and so are the people who work in them. You can use libraries to read books and articles and to find online information and quiet spaces for study. Most libraries also have computers and printers that you can use to complete your assignments. Many libraries now also house tutoring and learning centers and have areas where you can grab a cup of coffee or a snack, socialize, relax, and work in groups.

Whenever you have research to do for a class, for your job, or for your personal life, visit a library in person or access it online. Although we might think that all valuable information can be found online, many resources are still stored in traditional print formats or in your college library database. A key component of being information literate is determining the kinds of sources you need to satisfy your research questions. Librarians at your college or university work with instructors to determine the kinds of materials that support their teaching. Most libraries house not only books but also government documents, microfilm, photographs, historical documents, maps, music, and films.

Of course, no one library can possibly own everything you might need or enough copies of each item, so groups of libraries share their materials with one another. If your college library does not have a journal or book that you need, or the item you need is checked out, you can use interlibrary loan—a service that allows you to request an item at no charge from another college or university library.

△ **Does This Library Look Familiar?**
College libraries are changing as information goes digital and space for group work becomes a priority. This facility contains both quiet spaces for individuals or groups and a digital classroom. Have you explored your college library? Are you making the most of this important academic resource? Learning Commons, 2012, Atlanta University Center, Robert W. Woodruff Library Photographs, Atlanta University Center, Robert W. Woodruff Library

> ❝ Whenever you have research to do for a class, for your job, or for your personal life, visit a library in person or access it online. ❞

If it is difficult for you to get to your college library, you will still have off-campus online access to library materials through a college-provided ID and password. You can also have online chats with librarians. To learn more, check out your library's website, or e-mail or phone the reference desk. Be sure to use the handouts and guides that are available at the reference desk or online, as well as tutorials and virtual tours that will help you become familiar with the collections, services, and spaces available at your library.

Library Resources

Many college-level research projects will require you to use a variety of sources to find information and do research. The most commonly used resources that college libraries offer are scholarly journals and periodicals.

Scholarly journals are collections of original, peer-reviewed research articles written by experts or researchers in a particular academic discipline. Examples are the *Journal of Educational Research* and the *Social Psychology Quarterly*. The term *peer-reviewed* means that other experts in the field read and evaluate the articles in the journal before it is published. You can find scholarly articles by using an online database that is organized by certain subject areas or by your library's catalog and is accessible on or off campus. You may also be able to find some scholarly articles by using Google Scholar—a web search engine that searches for information only within scholarly journals.

A periodical is a journal, magazine, or newspaper that is published multiple times a year. Scholarly journals fit into this category, but most periodicals are popular rather than scholarly. The articles in *Rolling Stone*, for instance, do not go through a peer-review process like the articles in scholarly journals. Magazines can be legitimate sources for your research, unless your assignment specifically requires all sources to be scholarly articles or books. Look back at Figure 8.1 for a breakdown of different types of sources.

Books are especially useful for research projects. Often students in introductory classes must write research papers on broad topics like the Civil War. While many scholarly articles have been written about the Civil War, they will not provide the kind of general overview of the topic that is available in books. Many books are also available electronically, and some of these e-books can be easily accessed online. ∎

Evaluating Sources

The Internet makes research easier in some ways and more difficult in others. Through Internet search engines such as Google or Bing, you have immediate access to a great deal of free information, but many of the links will not take you to valid sources for serious research. For one thing, the order of the search results can be misleading; order is determined not by a website's importance but by search formulas that depend both on popularity and on whether someone pays for a source to be at the top of the list. Anyone can put up a website—a famous professor, a professional society, or a fifth grader.

Some students might at first be excited about receiving 243,000,000 hits from a search on global warming, but they may be shocked when they realize that the information they find is not sorted or organized. Think carefully about the usefulness of the information based on three important factors: relevance, authority, and bias.

Relevance

The first thing to consider in looking at a possible source is whether it is relevant: Does it relate to your subject in an appropriate way?

How well does it fit your needs? The answers to these questions depend on your research project and the kind of information you are seeking.

- **Is it introductory?** Introductory information is basic and elementary. It does not require background knowledge about the topic. Introductory sources can be useful when you're first learning about a subject.

- **Is it comprehensive?** Look for sources that consider the topic in depth and offer plenty of evidence to support the conclusions.

- **Is it current?** Give preference to recent sources, although older, primary sources can sometimes be useful.

- **Is it meaningful?** Use the "So what?" test: So what does this information mean? Why does it matter to my project?

Authority

Once you have determined that a source is relevant to your research project, make sure that it was created by someone qualified to write or speak on the subject. For example, a fifth grader would generally not be considered an authority, but if your topic is bullying

> ◁ **The Ten-Minute Rule**
> If you have been working hard for ten minutes to locate information for a research project and haven't found what you need, ask a librarian for help. Let the librarian know what searches you've tried, and he or she will be able to help you figure out new strategies to find the sources you need. In addition, the librarian can help you develop strategies to improve your research skills. Doing research without a librarian is like driving cross-country without using a map or GPS— technically, you can do it, but you might get lost along the way. Get to know at least one librarian as your go-to expert. Blend Images/Hill Street Studios/ Getty Images

in elementary schools, a fifth grader's opinion might be exactly what you're looking for.

Determine whether your project calls for scholarly publications, magazines and newspapers, or both. Many journalists and columnists are extremely well qualified, and their work might be appropriate for your needs. But as a general rule, scholarly sources have more credibility in a college research project than do newspapers and magazines (see Figure 8.1).

Bias

Research consists of considering and analyzing multiple perspectives on a topic and creating something new from your analysis. Signs of bias—overly positive or overly harsh language, hints of a personal agenda, or a stubborn refusal to consider other points of view—indicate that you should question the credibility and accuracy of a source. Although nothing is wrong with citing someone's particular point of view, as a researcher you will want to be aware that bias exists, and you may need to exclude strongly biased sources from your research. For example, if you are writing about climate change, you'll want to examine sources for evidence of political or personal agendas. The following questions can help you evaluate your sources:

- Who is the author?

- What is the author's goal in writing about this topic?

- Does the author present facts, personal opinions, or both?

- Does the author provide evidence that is based on other sources?

- What is the basis for the author's conclusions—sound evidence or personal opinion? ■

Using Your Research in Writing and Presentations

You have probably heard the saying "Knowledge is power." But knowledge gives you power only if you use it to create a product—a piece of writing or a presentation. Consider your audience and how you will present the information. What do you hope to accomplish by sharing your conclusions? Make it a point to do something with the results of your research; otherwise, why bother? You researched information to find the answer to a question; now is the time to share that answer with others.

Many students construct a straightforward report that summarizes what they found, and sometimes that's enough. A more powerful report will include an analysis of the information. To do an analysis, first consider how the facts, opinions, and details you found from your different sources relate to one another. What do they have in common, and how do they differ? What conclusions can you draw from these similarities and differences? Essentially, what you're doing at this stage of any research project is synthesis, a process in which you put together parts of ideas to come up with a whole result. By accepting some ideas, rejecting others, combining related concepts, and pulling it all together, you'll create new information and ideas that other people can use. Your final paper or presentation will include analysis and synthesis of the sources you found through your research. Remember: You must clearly state which thoughts and ideas came from the sources you found, and which are yours.

Conduct Effective Searches

Most of us frequently do casual research. But while Google, Wikipedia, and IMDb.com can provide some helpful answers, you will have to ramp it up a notch for a college-level research project. When academic research is done properly, the question being researched is clear and the answers that are found become part of the body of research that other professionals in that field would recognize and respect. When doing academic research, you need to be picky and filter out what is not helpful by using your critical-thinking skills. You also need to be smart about how you search.

the GOAL

Use your search engine and your library's database to find relevant, scholarly sources.

how TO DO it

"It's a new syndrome we're seeing more of... "Google-itis"."

www.CartoonStock.com

Your college library offers free online access to a wealth of academic databases, e-journals, and so on. If you have any questions about how to use them or about what kinds of materials qualify as academic research in general, make an appointment with a reference librarian. Here are some quick tips:

- **Hone your online research skills.** Make sure that you understand common Boolean operators, such as the words AND, OR, and NOT. How you use them affects your search results.

- **If you are looking for an exact phrase, use quotation marks or asterisks.** For instance, searching for "rock and roll 1957" or *rock and roll 1957* will bring up results that include that exact phrase. If you get too few hits, omit a search term.

- **Become familiar with your library's databases.** Many colleges subscribe to over one hundred databases. In advance of assignments, make yourself aware of the kinds of information you are likely to find in the various databases. Come up with your own list of questions, and see which database yields the best results in answering them. Databases often offer tools to help you save, store, and cite that information for your research.

your TURN

Explore what's out there. Look over your upcoming assignments, whether research papers or projects. Pick one assignment, and talk to a reference librarian about a database that might be helpful for you in completing it. Commit to exploring that database as you develop your approach to the assignment.

The Writing and Speaking Process

In college, you will be required to write often. In addition to writing original essays presenting your ideas, reflection papers on assigned readings, and lab reports in your science courses, you'll be required to articulate your ideas and research through formal presentations. Like research, good writing and speaking take practice, and it is always a good idea to ask for help. First, we will look at the writing process and consider step-by-step guidelines for effective writing.

Steps to Good Writing

The writing process typically includes the following three steps:

1. Prewriting
2. Drafting
3. Revising

Let's look more closely at each of these steps.

Step 1: Using prewriting to discover what you want to say. Prewriting is a powerful process for discovering ideas you didn't know you had. It simply means writing things down as they come to mind without trying to organize your thoughts, find exactly the right words, or think about structure. Sometimes called freewriting, prewriting can involve filling a page, whiteboard, or screen with words, phrases, or sentences. Prewriting also helps you avoid the temptation to try to write and edit at the same time.

When you prewrite, you might discover that you have more ideas than you can fit into one paper; this is very common. Prewriting helps you figure out what you really want to say as you make connections among different ideas.

Step 2: Drafting. When you have completed your research with the help of your librarian, gathered a lot of information sources and ideas, and done some prewriting, it's time to move to the drafting stage. Before you start writing your draft, you need to organize all the ideas you generated in the prewriting step and form a thesis statement, a short statement that clearly defines the purpose of the paper (see Figure 8.2).

Thesis: Napoleon's dual personality can be explained by examining incidents throughout his life.

1. Explain why I am using the term "dual personality" to describe Napoleon.
2. Briefly comment on his early life and his relationship with his mother.
3. Describe Napoleon's rise to fame from soldier to emperor. Stress the contradictions in his personality and attitudes.
4. Describe the contradictions in his relationship with Josephine.
5. Summarize my thoughts about Napoleon's personality.
6. Possibly conclude by referring to opening question: "Did Napoleon actually have a dual personality?"

Figure 8.2 ◁ Example of a Thesis Statement
A thesis statement will clearly and succinctly express the purpose of your paper.

Most students find that creating an outline helps them organize their thoughts, resulting in a clear structure from the thesis to the conclusion (see Figure 8.3 for an example). Once you've set the structure for your paper and have added analysis and synthesis of your research findings, you'll be well on your way. If you have chosen the thesis carefully, you will want to check to make sure that each sentence relates to your main idea. When you have completed this stage, you will have the first draft of your paper in hand.

Step 3: Revising. The key to good writing is revising, which is taking a good piece of writing and making it great. Revising is usually the most time-consuming step in the writing process. After you draft your paper, read it through once, twice, or even more times. You may need to reorganize your ideas, cut unnecessary words, rewrite some sentences or paragraphs, or use stronger words.

After you revise your paper, put it aside for at least a day, then reread it. Distancing yourself from your writing for a while allows you to see it differently. You may find more grammatical and spelling errors that need to be corrected or problems with organization that need revising. Taking a second look at your writing will almost always make it stronger.

It also might help to ask a classmate or someone in the writing center to review your paper. Once you have talked with your reviewers about their suggested changes, it will be your decision to either accept or reject them. At this point, you are ready to finalize your writing and turn in your paper. Reread the paper one more time, and double-check your spelling and grammar.

Figure 8.3 ▽ Example of an Outline
An outline is a working document; you do not need a complete outline to begin writing. Note how this author has included a placeholder for another example; she has not yet decided which example from her research to use.

Outline for Napoleon Paper

    I. Thesis—Napoleon's dual personality can be explained by examining incidents in his life

    II. Dual Personality

        a. What is it?

        b. How does it apply to Napoleon?

    III. Napoleon's Rise to Fame

        a. Contradictions in his personality and attitudes

            i. Relationship with Josephine

            ii. Example #2 (to come)

    IV. Summary of my thoughts about Napoleon's personality

    V. Conclusion

        a. Restate and answer thesis

            i. Yes, he had a dual personality because:

                1. Josephine

                2. Example #2

Time and the Writing Process

Many students turn in poorly written papers because they skip the first step (prewriting) and the last step (revising) and make do with the middle step (drafting). The best writing is usually done over an extended period of time, not as a last-minute task.

When planning the amount of time you'll need to write your paper, make sure to add enough time for the following:

• Doing more than a single round of revising as part of the writing process

• Asking your instructor for clarification on the assignment and for examples of papers that have received good grades; some instructors will even be willing to review a draft of your paper before you turn in the final version

• Seeking help from a librarian or from staff and trained peers in the writing center or learning center

• Narrowing or expanding your topic, which might require finding some new sources

• Balancing other assignments and commitments

• Dealing with technology problems

△ **Write. Review. Revise.**
Good writers spend more time revising and editing their written work than they spend writing the original version. Never turn in your first draft; spend the necessary time to reread and improve your work. © Radius Images/Alamy

Knowing Your Audience

Before you came to college, you probably spent much more time writing informally than writing formally. Think about all the time you've spent writing e-mails, texts, and tweets. Now think about the time you've spent writing papers for school. The informal style that you use to write an e-mail, a text, or a post is not the style you'll use to write a formal research paper. When writing research papers or essays in college, assume that your audience includes instructors and other serious students who will make judgments about your knowledge and abilities based on what and how you write. You should not be casual or sloppy when writing a formal paper.

TRY IT!

MANAGING TIME ▷ **Is It Worth Some Extra Time to Improve Your Writing?**

Think for a minute about your writing process—the steps you go through when you write a major paper. Do you rush through or skip the prewriting or revising stage to save time? Would you produce a better product by spending more time on it, especially on revising and polishing your writing? For your next research paper, devote an appropriate amount of time and attention to each step of the writing process, and based on the quality of the paper and the grade you earn, decide whether it was worth it.

Citing Your Sources and Avoiding Plagiarism

At some point you'll present your findings, whether you are writing an essay, a formal research paper, a script for a presentation, or a page for a website. Remember that you must include complete citations, which are references that enable a reader to locate a source based on its identifying information, such as the author's name, the title of the work, and its publication date.

Citing your source serves many purposes. For one thing, acknowledging the information and ideas you've borrowed from other writers distinguishes between other writers' ideas and your own and shows respect for their work. Source citations show your audience that you have based your conclusions on good, reliable evidence. They also provide a starting place for anyone who is curious about how you reached your conclusions or would like more information about the topic. Most important, citing your sources is the simplest way to avoid plagiarism—taking another person's ideas or work and presenting them as your own. Plagiarism is unacceptable in a college setting and in the workforce, and it can have severe consequences beyond just the shame and embarrassment of being caught. Writers and journalists who have been found guilty or even suspected of plagiarism have jeopardized their careers, as in the case of Fareed Zakaria in 2012, who was suspended from his job at *Time* and CNN after being accused of plagiarizing material from the *New Yorker*.

Some students consider plagiarizing because they think that doing so will help them get a better grade, but you can avoid the temptation if you keep in mind the high likelihood of getting caught, as well as the serious consequences that will follow if you do get caught. In order to reduce plagiarism on college campuses, instructors are now using electronic systems such as Turnitin (www.turnitin.com) to identify passages in student papers that have been plagiarized. Because plagiarism is a form of cheating, students who are caught plagiarizing are likely to face severe penalties, such as a failing grade on the assignment, a failing grade in the course, or even expulsion from the college or university.

Source citation includes many details and can get complicated, but it all comes down to three basic rules:

- If you use somebody else's exact words, you must give that person credit.

- If you use somebody else's ideas or theories, *even if you use your own words to express those ideas*, you must give that person credit.

- If you use any information that is not considered common knowledge, you must cite your sources.

Your instructors will tell you about their preferred method for citation: footnotes, references in parentheses included in the text of your paper, or endnotes. If you're not given specific guidelines or if you simply want to make sure you do it right, use a handbook or style manual. One standard manual is the *MLA Handbook for Writers of Research Papers*, published by the Modern Language Association. Another is the *Publication Manual of the American Psychological Association*. Both of these resources are available online. You can also download MLA and APA apps on your mobile devices from Google Play or iTunes.

Speaking Effectively

What you have learned in this chapter about writing also applies to public speaking—both are processes that you can learn and master, and each results in a product. Since the fear of public speaking is very common—more common, studies show, than the fear of death—you might be thinking along these lines: What if I plan, organize, prepare, and practice my

TRY IT!

SETTING GOALS ▷ Seek Out Speaking Opportunities

Are you occasionally asked to speak before a group—maybe a club, your coworkers, or your class? Don't avoid those chances to hone your speaking skills. The only way you will develop more self-confidence in speaking before a group is to do it. So gather your courage and step up to the next speaking opportunity that comes your way.

speech, but my mind goes completely blank, I drop my note cards, or I say something totally embarrassing? Remember that people in your audience have been in your position and will understand your anxiety. Your audience wants you to succeed. Just be positive, rely on your wit, and keep speaking. Just as there is a process for writing a paper, there is a process for developing a good speech. The guidelines in Table 8.1 can help you improve your speaking skills and lose your fear of speaking publicly. ∎

Table 8.1 ▽ Steps to Successful Speaking

1: Clarify your objective.	Begin by identifying the goals of your presentation. What do you want your listeners to know, believe, or do when you are finished?
2: Understand your audience.	To understand the people you'll be talking to, ask yourself the following questions: • Who is my audience? • What do they already know about my topic? • What do they want or need to know? • What are their attitudes toward me, my ideas, and my topic?
3: Organize your presentation.	Build your presentation so that your listeners can connect the ideas they already have to the new information you are presenting. You may want to write an outline for your speech.
4: Choose appropriate visual aids.	Use software programs, such as Prezi or PowerPoint, to prepare your presentation. By using Prezi templates or PowerPoint slides, you are creating images and videos to support your ideas while making your presentation animated, engaging, and interactive. You might also choose to prepare a chart, write on the board, or distribute handouts. When using visual aids, follow these guidelines: • Make visuals easy to follow. • Proofread carefully. • Use font colors to make your slides attractive. • Explain each visual clearly. • Give your listeners enough time to process visuals. • Maintain eye contact with your listeners while you discuss the visuals. • Don't turn your back to the audience. Remember that a fancy slide show can't make up for lack of careful research or sound ideas.
5: Practice your delivery.	Practice your delivery before an audience: a friend, your dog, or even the mirror. If you practice in front of others, ask for feedback so that you can make changes. Practice your presentation aloud several times. Consider recording yourself to hear or see your mistakes. Use eye contact and smile.
6: Pay attention to word choice and pronunciation.	As you reread your presentation, make sure that you have used the correct words to express your ideas. If you aren't sure how to pronounce some words, get help ahead of time. Try your best to avoid *like, um, uh, you know,* and other fillers.
7: Dress appropriately.	Leave the baseball cap, T-shirt, and sneakers at home. Don't overdress, but do look professional.
8: Request feedback from someone in your audience.	After you have completed your speech, ask a friend or your instructor to give you some honest feedback.

Communicating with Others in a Digital Age

While learning how to write formal research papers and speak in public are important parts of succeeding in college and your career, it is also important to be aware of how you are communicating with others in your day-to-day life. So much of our communication with others occurs through e-mail, text and picture messaging, mobile apps, and posting on social networking sites. Online communication enables us to connect with others, whether we're forming new friendships or romantic relationships or maintaining established ones. Online communication also gives us a broad sense of community.

Social networking sites and apps such as Facebook, Twitter, Instagram, Viber, Telegram, WhatsApp, and Snapchat are popular with college students; it's likely that you use sites and apps such as these throughout the day to keep up with your friends. While social media outlets have both positives and negatives, one thing is certain: As students enter college, most do not carefully examine what they share through social media. Online statements, posts, and messages can have a strong impact, so you should be careful about everything you put into public view. Today it is common for employers to check job applicants' online images before making a job offer. Given how often we use technology to communicate with others, it is critically important to use it properly. When you do, you are strengthening, and not weakening, your relationships. Here are some helpful suggestions for improving online communication.[1]

1. **Match the seriousness of your message to your communication medium.** Know when to communicate online versus offline. *Online* is best for transmitting quick reminders or messages that require time and thought to craft. Texting a friend to remind her of a coffee date you've already set up likely makes good sense—calling or reminding her in person could be disruptive. E-mail may be best when dealing with problematic people or trying to resolve certain types of conflicts. When you use e-mail, you can take the time to think about what you want to say, then carefully draft and revise your response before sending it—something that isn't possible in a brief text message or during face-to-face interactions.

   Offline, and ideally face to face, is better for sharing personal information, such as news of health issues, or for in-depth, lengthy, and detailed explanations of professional or personal problems or important relationship decisions. Even though online communication is being used more and more for big announcements, many people still expect important news to be

△ **Devices, Devices, Everywhere**
These days, wherever you look you see people on their various devices. Although digital devices offer ways to connect with others, consider how these devices are limiting our ability to communicate effectively. © iStock/Getty Images

---

[1] Adapted from Steven McCornack, *Reflect & Relate: An Introduction to Interpersonal Communication*, 3rd ed., pp. 24–27. © 2013 Bedford/St. Martin's. Boston, MA.

shared in person. For example, most of us would be startled if our spouse revealed a long-awaited pregnancy through e-mail, or if a friend disclosed a serious illness through a text message.

2. **Don't assume that online communication is always more efficient.** If your message needs a quick decision or answer—like deciding when to meet for lunch—a phone call or a face-to-face conversation may be better. Often a one-minute phone call or a quick face-to-face exchange can save several minutes of texting and can avoid having to wait for a response to an e-mail. Issues that may cause an emotional reaction are more effectively and ethically handled in person or over the phone, but opt for online communication if you want to give someone time to respond.

3. **Presume that your posts are public.** You may be thinking of the laugh you'll get from friends when you post the funny picture of yourself drunkenly hugging a houseplant on Instagram. But would you want family members, future in-laws, or potential employers to see that picture? Even if you have privacy settings on your personal page, what's to stop friends from downloading your photos and posts and distributing them to others? Keep in mind that anything you've sent or posted online can potentially be seen by anyone. Follow this rule: If you wouldn't want a message to be seen by the general public, don't send it or post it online.

4. **Remember that your posts are permanent.** Assume that what goes online or is shared through a mobile app lives forever, despite claims to the contrary of some sites and apps. Old e-mails, photos, videos, tweets, blogs, you name it—all of these may still be accessible years later. As just one example, everything you have ever posted on Facebook is stored on the Facebook server, even if you delete it. And Facebook legally reserves the right to sell your content, as long as the company first deletes personally identifying information (such as your name). Think before you post.

> ❝ **If you wouldn't want a message to be seen by the general public, don't send it or post it online.** ❞

5. **Practice the art of creating drafts.** Get into the habit of saving text and e-mail messages as drafts, then revisiting them later and editing them as needed for appropriateness, effectiveness, and ethics. Don't feel pressured to answer an e-mail immediately. Taking time to respond will result in a more competently crafted message. Online communication makes it easy to fire off a message that you will later regret, so be sure of what you want to say before hitting send.

6. **Protect your online identity.** Choose secure passwords for websites of financial institutions, such as banks and credit card companies; your social networking sites; and course sites where your grades might be listed. Limit the amount of personal information available on your social media profiles, ratchet up your security settings, and accept friend requests only from people you know.

7. **Exercise caution and common sense when online correspondence turns into a face-to-face meeting.** Keep in mind that some people tell lies on their profiles and posts. Select a public meeting place, and be sure a friend, family member, or roommate knows about your plans. ∎

TRY IT!

MAKING GOOD CHOICES ▷ Your Online Image through an Employer's Eyes

Look at either your or a friend's postings on social media. Do you see anything on Twitter, Snapchat, Instagram, or Facebook that puts you or your friend in a negative light? Think about how you would alter them.

Chapter Review

Reflect on Choices

Your campus library is a valuable resource for finding information and a great place to study. Although your instructors will sometimes require you to use the library, at other times, it will be your choice. Reflect on your use of the library so far in your college experience. Make a list of the pros and cons of going to the library to study or do research, and share that list with other students in your class.

Apply What You've Learned

Now that you have read and discussed this chapter, consider how you can apply what you have learned to your academic and personal lives. The following prompts will help you reflect on the chapter material and its relevance to you, both now and in the future.

1. It is important to familiarize yourself with all the resources in your campus library. Think about a book that you love that was turned into a movie (for example, *The Lord of the Rings* or the Harry Potter series). Search your library catalog to find the print copy and an e-book version. See if the library has it as an audiobook or in a language other than English. Find the DVD or soundtrack in your library's media collection, or see if you can download the music. Write a short paragraph describing your process for finding these resources and your experience. How easy was it to find these resources? Would you modify your search technique in any way?

2. Before reading this chapter, had you considered the differences between writing an exam response and writing a blog post or a response to someone on Facebook? Think about your online communications in the past week. Can you say for certain that you knew exactly who your audience was each time? Did you send or post anything that could be misinterpreted or read by someone outside your intended audience? What advice about online communications would you give to other students?

Use Your Resources

GO TO ▷ Your instructor: If you need help understanding his or her expectations for writing, speaking, or research assignments.

GO TO ▷ The library: If you need help working on an assignment. Head over to the reference desk and talk with a librarian about the assignment you are working on.

GO TO ▷ The writing center: If you need help finding effective writing and research tools. Most campuses have one; it is frequently part of the English department.

GO TO ▷ The departments of speech, theater, and communications: If you need help finding resources and specific courses to help you develop your speaking skills.

GO ONLINE TO ▷ Purdue University's Online Writing Lab: If you need help with documenting print or electronic sources or with understanding different forms of citation.

GO ONLINE TO ▷ Toastmasters International's public speaking tips: If you need help developing your public speaking skills. Search for "Toastmasters Public Speaking Tips" to access the website.

LaunchPad Solo
macmillan learning

LaunchPad Solo for *Step by Step* is a great resource. Go online to master concepts using the LearningCurve study tool and much more. launchpadworks.com

09

Considering Majors and Careers

To access ACES, the LearningCurve study tool, videos, and more, go to LaunchPad Solo for *Step by Step*. **launchpadworks.com**

College is a time for gaining academic knowledge and exploring career opportunities with the goal of developing into a productive member of the global economy. Have you already been thinking about a specific career after college, or are you still exploring different possibilities? For many students, the road to a career begins with a strong interest in an academic major. For others, selecting a major is harder than deciding on a career path. Some students may enter with one major in mind and change to another. Regardless, your selection of a major and a career should ultimately fit with your overall life goals, purpose, values, and beliefs.

The National Center for Educational Statistics released findings from a recent

study reporting that nearly 80 percent of college students who declare academic majors aren't sure if they've made the right choice. The same study revealed that many college students change majors about three times on average before settling into a major that leads to a career. Whether you do or don't change majors, be sure to make connections with academic and career advisers who will work with you to ensure you are on the right path to thrive in today's fast-paced economy. As this chapter emphasizes, how you connect your classes with extracurricular pursuits and work experiences will prepare you for a first career—or, if you have been in the labor force for some time, for career advancement.

Review Your ACES Score

Take a moment to reflect on your **Academic and Career Planning** ACES score, and insert it in the box to the right. Now let's take action!

Did you score in the high, moderate, or low range? Are you surprised by your score? This score will help you learn more about your strengths and weaknesses in understanding how to develop a strong academic and career plan. Even if you already feel strong in this area, be open to learning new strategies to help you improve your score as you move through the chapter. This chapter will further your understanding of why this topic is essential to your success in college.

Score:

○ High
○ Moderate
○ Low

To find your ACES score, log on to LaunchPad Solo for *Step by Step* at **launchpadworks.com**.

Preview the topic headings in this chapter. Then, in a journal or a readily accessible file, reflect on your current skills by answering the following questions:

▶ **What are your current strengths and challenges?**
▶ **What do you hope to learn from this chapter?**

When the Best-Laid Plans Need to Change

michaeljung/Shutterstock

I had always wanted to be a nurse. When I was in high school, I was an after-school volunteer in our local hospital, and I loved seeing people smile when I would visit them in their rooms. My choice of major seemed clear, and I started my first year of college in a pre-nursing curriculum. But it didn't take long for reality to set in. I learned that I still had to be admitted into the nursing program, and only about 20 percent of students who want to be nurses actually make it. There were so many other students who wanted to enter the program, but I still believed that I could be part of that 20 percent. I was a good student in science and math, and I thought I had a strong chance of achieving my dream.

But then I had an opportunity to see what being a nurse would be like on a day-to-day basis. My college offered a special first-year seminar for pre-nursing students, and we were able to shadow a nurse in order to experience what nursing is all about. Let me tell you: Being a nurse is very different from being a hospital volunteer. I quickly discovered that nursing involves a lot more than seeing people smile. In fact, after a week of following a real nurse around the hospital and watching her deal with patients who were really sick, I realized that even if I got into the program, nursing wouldn't be the right career for me.

A visit to my college's career counselor, Mr. Holt, was the next step. "Well, Beth, since you have always been interested in a health-related career," said Mr. Holt, "why don't we explore other possibilities?" I considered many different options and, with Mr. Holt's help, finally decided on physical therapy. Most of the courses I was taking in pre-nursing were the same ones I would need for physical therapy, so I didn't have to start over. I know that physical therapy programs are also competitive, and there are no guarantees that I'll be admitted to one, but I believe I have a good chance. I'm going to give it my best shot!

As Beth's story shows, college students should be realistic about their degree plans and try to experience what their work life would be like before committing to it. Beth was also wise to talk to a career counselor to help her explore another option. What steps can you take to make sure your chosen major is a good fit? If you are having doubts, what resources are available to help you?

Careers and the New Economy

During your lifetime, economies in the United States and throughout the world have undergone significant changes as powerful forces—including technology, free markets, and workforce realignment—collided. Although in some of those years there has been an economic recession, today there is hope for a bright economic future for college graduates—a hope that comes with more expectations for higher-level competencies; professional experiences before graduation; and attention to the importance of resiliency, curiosity, and hard work.

Since 2010, the labor market for college graduates has steadily improved, far outpacing the general labor market. In fact, according to the annual recruiting projects made by Michigan State University, graduating seniors enjoyed more employment opportunities from 2013 to 2016 than at any time since 2000.[1] This trend is welcome, and the availability of jobs is expected to remain strong for the next several years.

Although there is more good news than bad news, economic uncertainty remains a reality. Therefore, it is important to make decisions about your major and career path based on information about yourself and the underlying factors that drive today's economy.

Characteristics of Today's Economy

The characteristics of today's economy are quite different from those of twenty years ago. Our economy today is global, fast, disruptive, innovative, boundaryless, customized, ever-changing, and networked. Think about

the potential impact of these characteristics on your program of study and possible career path.

It's global. Many organizations operate in multiple countries, and they look for opportunities to expand markets, identify sources of cheap talent to keep their prices low, and secure access to capital and resources. Competition on a global level presents challenges and opportunities for American workers, as all workers are potentially threatened by cheaper labor somewhere else.

The introduction of so many college-educated individuals worldwide into the economy will continue to shape how U.S. college students need to prepare for, and make the transition into, the labor market. As a U.S. student, you cannot be complacent about the impact of highly educated global talent on your chances of finding employment both here and around the world.

It's fast. Companies need to seek ways to produce goods faster, revamp services to stay ahead of competitors, or take advantage of new opportunities. Getting a new product to market just a few weeks ahead of a competitor can mean capturing that market niche and returning a profit. This means that new employees have to complete assignments and projects on time; there is no such thing as an extension or a redo.

It's disruptive. A pervasive and threatening disruption to the economy is the rapid infusion of smart technologies based on artificial intelligence. Smart technologies are replacing many human workers and taking over the running of some basic operations. While smart machines and software will not replace workers completely, every occupation will be affected. As technology changes, we also have to change and adapt by learning new skills, identifying

[1] "Recruiting Trends Report Briefs 2016–17," CERI (College Employment Research Institute), Michigan State University, accessed December 5, 2016, http://www.ceri.msu.edu/recruiting-trends/recruiting-trends-report-briefs-2016-17/.

opportunities to use new technologies, and understanding our current systems.

It's innovative. At no time before has the economy depended more on individual creativity. Organizations are seeking talented individuals who can employ new work methods, test new technologies, service delivery systems or processes, and identify new paths to reach team and organizational goals.

It's boundaryless. Organizations have learned that the lines separating functional, company, national, and cultural divisions have simply disappeared. No one works or lives in isolation anymore. Organizations are responding by seeking talent that can navigate boundaries. You may be a financial adviser, a product designer, or an event planner and find that, in order to complete your assignment, you have to interact with different units within and beyond your organization. Being able to cross boundaries means developing strong skills in communication, empathy, team management, cultural awareness, and possibly a foreign language.

It's customized. As consumers, you face many choices every day. Purchasers of goods and services want those purchases tailored to their specific needs. For instance, the popular frozen yogurt franchise Orange Leaf allows customers to "become the master" of their dessert by building their own yogurt treats. We customize our cell phone ringtones, our coffee, and our music playlists. Some colleges and universities even allow students to customize their majors.

It's always changing. No one likes a lot of change, particularly in the workplace. Yet organizations are constantly changing their missions and their expectations of employees. Although change may make you uncomfortable, the simple fact is that you will not be able to avoid it. So turn change into a positive while you're in college by being open to new ideas, continuing to learn, taking advantage of new challenges, and even seeking out change.

It's networked. Like many of your peers, you are likely to have a Facebook account with hundreds of friends. In addition, you may have Instagram, Twitter, Snapchat, YouTube, Pinterest, Tumblr, Reddit, and Meetup accounts, as well as accounts with a number of other social media outlets. We are a highly networked society and have many relationships, both personal and professional, which constitute our "social capital." *Social capital*, defined as the value of social networks (who people know) and the tendency that arises from these networks to do things for each other, has a long and important economic and social role in the development of our country. For a company or an organization, the social capital derived from all of its employees can be used to advance its ability to produce goods and deliver services. Your personal and professional network, or your social capital, is a potentially critical resource for both you and your employers.

Building a Professional Mindset for Life after College

Career development is a lifelong process. Even after you have landed a job, you will be expected to continue learning and developing yourself. You will also need a professional mindset—a point of view about how to be successful in the workplace. While developing this mindset, here are some important things to keep in mind:

- **There are no guarantees.** With a college degree, more opportunities—financial and otherwise—will be available to you than if you did not have a degree. However, just because you want to work for a certain organization or in a certain field doesn't mean that the job will be available when you graduate.

- **You will need to take some risks.** This advice may seem unwise, as most of us try to avoid risks. However, employers expect some level of risk-taking among their employees, even their new ones. Being a risk-taker requires

courage, because others—particularly family members—may depend on you to provide income. Nevertheless, you will have to extend yourself in order to maintain and even advance your career.

- **Your first job is seldom your dream job.** Few people get a perfect job right after graduation. Think of your first job as an audition for your next job. Employers want to see how quickly you learn, how well you adapt to and maneuver through the workplace, and how well you perform before providing more demanding and challenging positions.

Now for the good news: Hundreds of thousands of graduates find jobs every year, even in recessionary times. Some graduates might have to work longer to get where they want to be, but persistence pays off. If you start preparing now and continue to do so over your college years, you'll build a portfolio of academic, co-curricular, and pre-professional experiences that will add substance to your career profile. ■

TRY IT!

MAKING GOOD CHOICES ▷ **Ponder Your Choice of Academic Major**

This week, find another student who has the same major as you. Ask that person why he or she chose this major. Does the person seem passionate about the major? Why or why not? Why did *you* choose this major? Are you excited, or do you have a ho-hum attitude about it?

Working with an Academic Adviser

Academic planning is a vital step in your college career, and it should be an ongoing process that starts early in your first term. An *academic plan* lists the courses you need to complete in your major to graduate with a degree. Before you register for classes next term, sit down with your academic adviser. On most campuses, you will be assigned an adviser who is typically either an instructor or staff person in your field or a professional adviser. A good adviser can help you choose courses, decide on a major, weigh career possibilities, and map out your degree requirements. He or she can also recommend instructors and help you simplify the different aspects of your

> **Before you register for classes next term, sit down with your academic adviser.**

academic life. In this section, we will review a few ways to make sure that your first meeting with your adviser is a valuable experience.

Prepare for Your First Meeting with Your Academic Adviser

Take these steps before meeting with your academic adviser:

- **Review your college course catalog, think about the available majors, and familiarize yourself with campus resources.** If you haven't decided on a major, ask your adviser about opportunities for taking an aptitude test or a self-assessment to help you narrow down your options.

- **Prepare materials to bring to the meeting.** Even if you submitted your high school academic transcript with your application, bring a copy of it to the meeting. The transcript is an important tool; it shows your academic adviser what courses you have taken and your academic strengths.

- **Make a list of majors that appeal to you.** Academic advisers love it when students are passionate and take their futures seriously.

- **Map out your time frame and goals.** Be prepared to answer the following questions: Are you enrolling as a full-time or part-time student? When do you plan to graduate, and with what degree? Are you planning to transfer? Are you a student returning after a break? Do you want to go to graduate school?

◁ **Sit Down with Your Adviser**
The relationship you form with your academic adviser can become one of the most valuable relationships of your life. iStock.com/bowdenimages

Know the Right Questions to Ask

Once you've chosen a major, you'll need to understand how to meet the necessary requirements. You will have *prerequisites*—the basic core courses you need to take before you can enroll in upper-level classes in your major. Your major may also have *corequisites*—courses you have to take in conjunction with other courses during the same term, such as a chemistry lab along with your chemistry class. To acquire this knowledge, you will need to ask the following:

- How many credits must I take each term to graduate on time?

- What are the prerequisites and corequisites for my major?

- If I have any AP credits or dual-enrollment credits, can I use them to fulfill some of my major's requirements?

- Will I be able to finish a degree that prepares me for my desired career, or will I need to transfer?

Leave the meeting with a printout of your current course schedule and a plan for taking classes in the next term and beyond. Check in with your adviser at least once a term to make sure you're on a positive track, especially if you plan to transfer or apply to graduate school.

Learn How to Select Your Classes

Your academic adviser can not only inform you about your major's requirements, but also help you decide how many and which specific courses to take each term.

- Most full-time students take four to six courses a term. Decide which courses you want to take, find out which days and times they meet, and make sure they don't overlap.

- To get the courses you want, make sure to register as early as possible—in person or online.

- Resist the temptation to cram all your courses into one or two days. It's better to aim for a manageable workload by spreading your classes throughout the week.

- Go for a mix of hard and easy classes. Especially at the beginning, you might not realize how challenging college courses can be or how much outside work they entail. If you load up on organic chemistry, Russian 101, and advanced thermodynamics, your grades and general well-being could suffer.

- If you are currently at a two-year college and are planning to transfer to a four-year college or university, be sure to research transfer requirements at each institution where you intend to apply. Requirements can vary from campus to campus. You don't want to come up short, and you don't want to waste time and money taking courses that won't count later on!

Explore Course Options, and Pay Attention to Your Grades

College gives you the opportunity to explore a variety of courses, but trying to pad your grades or avoid hard work by taking easy classes is not viewed positively by employers or graduate school application committees. Grades are important, especially when you're seeking a position that is directly linked to an academic discipline, such as accounting, engineering, or finance. Grades also become an easy way to eliminate candidates in a competitive field. Remember that good grades show that you have a solid knowledge base and a strong work ethic—two characteristics that all employers value.

Deal with a Mismatch

What if there are problems with your adviser? Your college success instructor will know where you can go if you feel that you need a different adviser. You have a right to make a change; academic planning is so critical to your success in college that it's worth persevering until you find an adviser with whom you feel comfortable. ∎

Find and Use Campus Resources

Your college or university will likely have a number of resources available to help you investigate and decide on a career. Your campus career center most likely employs career advisers, who can be partners in your college success. In addition to understanding how academic majors link to careers, these resource persons can provide one-to-one guidance and can help you take these important first steps:

- **Explore the career center website.** Your college's career center website will likely have resources for planning your career and, later, your job search strategy. You will be able to link to campus-wide listings for full- and part-time positions, internships, cooperative (co-op) programs, and seasonal employment, as well as take self-assessments to provide insights on yourself and your career choice. The website will provide details on employer visits; special events, such as career fairs and workshops; and on-campus interviewing opportunities.

- **Engage in at least one career center-sponsored event per term.** Even as a first-year student, you may find programs and events that are geared toward helping you discover possible occupations, introducing you to recent graduates, and allowing you to interact with alumni from different career areas. A common misconception is that the career center's services are just for graduating students who have an immediate need for assistance in finding a job. Career experts agree that students can benefit from a variety of career services *throughout the course of their educational experience*.

- **Build your professional network daily.** Work to develop a mentor–mentee relationship with faculty, guest speakers, alumni, other students, or professional staff members on your campus. You can also build a mentor–mentee relationship through off-campus opportunities, such as internships, employment, or volunteer activities. If you haven't already done so, create and develop an account on LinkedIn, a professionally focused social media platform.

Getting to Know Yourself

Getting to know yourself while you're in college can help you make decisions about your future. Don't wait until graduation to think back on what your experiences have taught you about yourself. Here are some questions that you should think about periodically:

- Do I understand my strengths, aptitudes, and needs for improvement?

- Are my academic experiences preparing me for what I aspire to do?

- Am I gaining confidence to pursue my purpose through developing competencies and strengthening my abilities?

- Do I know what employers or graduate school faculty expect of me in terms of abilities, attitudes, and behaviors?

- Am I aware of the next steps I need to take in order to move further toward my goals?

Clarify Your Personal and Workplace Values

Your values, formed through your life experiences, are the things you feel most strongly about. During your college experience, your values will become clearer; sometimes your values will be challenged, and at other times new values will become important to you. Because you will bring your values into the workplace, it is important that you recognize the values held by the organization where you are seeking employment.

Your *personal values* may reflect your need for family, security, integrity, wealth, compassion, fairness, creativity, ambition, adaptability, and personal fulfillment. People vary widely on the values they hold. Your ability to talk about the values that are important to you is critical—especially in a job interview. This is something you may wish to practice and role-play.

Workplace values are the values held by a company or an organization. These are usually written in a mission or values statement available on the organization's website. We do not always get the workplace that we want, but knowing that your values are compatible with workplace values before taking a job can help you avoid early career problems.

Employers also hold expectations about the values new hires should possess when they arrive for the first day of work. Some employers are even shifting to value-based recruiting to ensure that important organizational values are reflected in their candidate pool. Here are some values that employers believe their potential new hires must possess:

- **Accountability:** takes responsibility for work and behavior

- **Strong work ethic:** demonstrates a strong willingness to work

- **Maturity:** displays sound judgment and controls feelings or emotions in work situations

- **Willingness to cooperate:** cooperates with coworkers in a respectful, sincere manner

- **Passion:** conveys passion for work and career

- **Adaptability:** functions effectively in an ever-changing environment

- **Punctuality:** completes assignments and commitments on time

- **Integrity:** acts and performs with integrity

- **Initiative:** shows the ability to work without immediate supervision

In general, being aware of what you value, as well as what potential employers may value, is important, because a career choice that is closely related to your core values is likely to be the best choice.

Understand Your Skills, Aptitudes, Personality, and Interests

Each job or career is different, and each job you explore will be a good or poor fit, depending on your personal characteristics. These characteristics include your skills, your natural abilities or aptitudes, your personality, and your interests.

Personal, workplace, and transferable skills.

You are continuously building your skills and competencies through practice in activities both in and out of the classroom. New abilities emerge as your skill set grows and combines in new ways. To identify your particular skill set, look for skills assessments at your campus career center.

Skills typically fall into three categories:

1. **Personal.** Some skills come naturally or are learned through experience. Examples of these skills are teamwork, self-motivation, and conflict management.

2. **Workplace.** Some skills can be learned on the job; others are gained through training designed to increase your knowledge or expertise in a certain area. Examples include designing websites, bookkeeping, and providing customer service.

3. **Transferable.** Some skills gained through previous jobs or hobbies or through everyday life can be transferred to a career. Examples include planning events, motivating others, paying attention to detail, solving problems, and thinking critically.

Employers begin their search for talent by focusing on personal and workplace skills in addition to anticipated educational credentials. Once they have identified potential candidates, their focus shifts to transferable skills. Transferable skills help you because they allow you to quickly adapt to changing situations, extend your career options beyond your academic major, and gain promotions. Table 9.1 provides a list of transferable skills and how they link to specific abilities.

Table 9.1 ▽ Transferable Skills

Transferable Skills	Abilities
Communication	Being a clear and persuasive speaker Listening attentively Writing well
Presentation	Justifying Persuading Responding to questions and serious critiques of presentation material
Leadership	Taking charge Providing direction
Teamwork	Working with different people while maintaining control over some assignments
Interpersonal	Relating to others Motivating others to participate Easing conflict between coworkers
Personal traits	Being motivated Recognizing the need to take action Being adaptable to change Having a strong work ethic Being reliable and honest Acting in an ethical manner Knowing how to plan and organize multiple tasks Being able to respond positively to customer concerns
Critical thinking and problem solving	Identifying problems and their solutions by combining information from different sources and considering options

Job Candidate Skills and Qualities Ranked as *Very Important* by Employers

Employers seek job candidates who can do the following:

- Work in a team structure
- Make decisions and solve problems
- Plan, organize, and prioritize work
- Communicate (verbally or in writing) with persons inside and outside the organization
- Obtain and process information
- Analyze quantitative data
- Demonstrate that they have technical knowledge related to the job

Therefore, the ideal job candidate is a team player and a good communicator who can make decisions, solve problems, and prioritize. Does this describe you? If not, don't panic. This chapter is intended as a guide for you to *develop into* the ideal candidate.

Source: National Association of Colleges and Employers, *Job Outlook 2018* (Bethlehem, PA: National Association of Colleges and Employers, 2017).

Aptitudes. Your acquired or natural ability for learning and proficiency in a particular area is referred to as aptitude. Manual dexterity, musical ability, spatial visualization, and memory for numbers are examples of aptitudes that have a lot to do with the way you learn. Each of us has aptitudes that we can build on. The trick is to discover a path in which your aptitudes become your best intellectual assets. Remember: Navigating the future depends on your aptitude for learning, so uncover the ways you learn best.

Personality. One of the things that make college such a fun place is that all of us are different. On a daily basis, you will meet a variety of characters among your fellow students, professors, and school staff. But could you work with any of them? Could you do a team project with a randomly selected group of students? How do you feel in new situations? Your personality makes you who you are, and it can't be ignored when you make career decisions.

Interests. From birth, we develop particular interests that will help shape our career paths and might even define them. Good career exploration begins with considering what you like to do and relating that to your career choices. For example, if you enjoyed writing for your high school newspaper, you might be interested in writing for your college newspaper, with an eye toward a career in journalism. Don't get trapped trying to live someone else's interests; take time to explore your interests through assessments or job shadowing.

△ **Matching Passions with a Profession**
Are you interested in American history? Do you enjoy talking with the public? Do you value education? Do you value the preservation of our natural landmarks? People who answer yes to these questions might find that a career as a park ranger suits them. How does the career that you plan to pursue align with your values, interests, and personality? If you're coming up empty, you might want to reconsider your plans. Matt McClain for The Washington Post/Getty Images

Using the Holland Model

John Holland, a psychologist at Johns Hopkins University, developed tools and concepts that can help you organize the various dimensions of yourself so that you can identify potential career choices (see Table 9.2).

Table 9.2 ▽ Holland Personality and Career Types

Category	Personality Characteristics	Career Fields
Realistic (R)	These people describe themselves as concrete, down-to-earth, and practical doers. They exhibit competitive/assertive behavior and show interest in activities that require motor coordination, skill, and physical strength. They prefer situations involving action solutions rather than tasks involving verbal or interpersonal skills, and they like taking a concrete approach to problem solving rather than relying on abstract theory. They tend to be interested in scientific or mechanical areas rather than the arts.	Environmental engineer, electrical contractor, industrial arts teacher, navy officer, fitness director, package engineer, electronics technician, Web designer
Investigative (I)	These people describe themselves as analytical, rational, and logical problem solvers. They value intellectual stimulation and intellectual achievement, and they prefer to think rather than to act and to organize and understand rather than to persuade. They usually have a strong interest in physical, biological, or social sciences. They are less apt to be people oriented.	Urban planner, chemical engineer, bacteriologist, flight engineer, genealogist, laboratory technician, marine scientist, nuclear medical technologist, obstetrician, quality-control technician, computer programmer, environmentalist, physician, college professor
Artistic (A)	These people describe themselves as creative, innovative, and independent. They value self-expression and relating with others through artistic expression and are also emotionally expressive. They dislike structure, preferring tasks involving personal or physical skills. They resemble investigative people but are more interested in the cultural or the aesthetic than the scientific.	Architect, film editor/director, actor, cartoonist, interior decorator, fashion model, graphic communications specialist, journalist, editor, orchestra leader, public relations specialist, sculptor, media specialist, librarian
Social (S)	These people describe themselves as kind, caring, helpful, and understanding of others. They value helping and making a contribution. They satisfy their needs in one-on-one or small-group interaction using strong speaking skills to teach, counsel, or advise. They are drawn to close interpersonal relationships and are less apt to engage in intellectual or extensive physical activity.	Nurse, teacher, social worker, genetic counselor, marriage counselor, rehabilitation counselor, school superintendent, geriatric specialist, insurance claims specialist, minister, travel agent, guidance counselor, convention planner
Enterprising (E)	These people describe themselves as assertive, risk taking, and persuasive. They value prestige, power, and status and are more inclined than other types to pursue it. They use verbal skills to supervise, lead, direct, and persuade rather than to support or guide. They are interested in people and in achieving organizational goals.	Banker, city manager, FBI agent, health administrator, judge, labor arbitrator, salary and wage administrator, insurance salesperson, sales engineer, lawyer, sales representative, marketing manager
Conventional (C)	These people describe themselves as neat, orderly, detail oriented, and persistent. They value order, structure, prestige, and status, and possess a high degree of self-control. They are not opposed to rules and regulations. They are skilled in organizing, planning, and scheduling, and are interested in data and people.	Accountant, statistician, census enumerator, data processor, hospital administrator, insurance administrator, office manager, underwriter, auditor, personnel specialist, database manager, abstractor/indexer

Source: Table 9.2 and Figure 9.1: Holland Personality and Career Types Table and Holland's Hexagonal Model of Career Fields. Reproduced by special permission of the Publisher, Psychological Assessment Resources, Inc. (PAR), 16204 North Florida Avenue, Lutz, Florida 33549. From *The Self-Directed Search Professional's User's Guide* by John L. Holland, PhD. Copyright © 1985, 1987, 1994, 1997 by PAR. Further reproduction is prohibited without permission from PAR.

Figure 9.1 ▽ **Holland's Hexagonal Model of Career Fields.**
Holland's model can help you address the questions surrounding career choice. Start by identifying career fields that are consistent with what you know about yourself. Once you've come up with your list of fields, you can begin to identify the harmony or conflicts of each by using the career center or online resources to get more information about specific jobs in those fields, such as daily activities, interests and abilities required, preparation required for entry, working conditions, salary and benefits, and employment outlook.

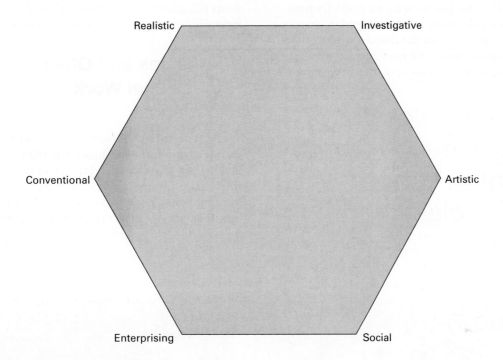

Holland suggests that people are separated into six general categories based on their interests, skills, values, and personality characteristics, or their preferred approaches to life. Holland's system organizes career fields into the same six categories. Career fields are grouped according to both the skills and personality characteristics most commonly associated with success in those fields and the interests and values most commonly associated with satisfaction. As you view Table 9.2, highlight or note the characteristics that you believe you share, as well as those that are the least closely matched.

Your career choices will involve a complex assessment of the factors that are most important to you. To display the relationship between career fields and the potential conflicts people face as they consider them, Holland's model is commonly presented in a hexagonal shape (see Figure 9.1). The closer the types are, the closer the relationships are among those career fields; the farther apart the types are, the more conflict there is among those career fields. ∎

Gaining Professional Experience

Once you have determined your interests and career goals, you can start to gain experience that will move you toward your goals. Gaining professional experience means working in relevant settings outside the classroom. Students in health professions gain experience through their clinical rotations, student teachers through their student teaching experience, and social workers and counselors through practicums. Most students will gain their experience through an internship or a cooperative education experience.

> " Gaining professional experience means working in relevant settings outside the classroom. "

Internships and Other Professional Work Experiences

You will need to plan early if you want to fit an internship into your academic plan. Should you choose not to pursue an internship, other options are available. For instance, some employers offer paid summer positions but not internships. Start thinking

△ **Linking Classroom and Career**
This student studies computer science and works part time in the college's computer lab, helping other students with their technology problems. His work experience links to what he is learning in his courses.
Goodluz/Shutterstock.com

now about the experiential learning opportunities available to you, such as service learning, volunteer activities, study abroad programs, internships, co-op programs (in which you alternate studies and work), and student competitions and projects.

Part-Time Work in College

Paid opportunities for getting experience are particularly beneficial because they can support the attainment of your college goals, provide you with the financial means to complete college, and help you structure your time so that you are a much better time manager. Remember, however, that overextending yourself—working more than twenty hours per week—can potentially interfere with your college success.

Your first decision will be whether to work on campus or off. If you choose to work on campus, look for opportunities early in the term. One benefit of on-campus employment is that the work schedules are often flexible. Another benefit is that you might be able to connect with instructors and administrators whom you can later consult as mentors or professional references. Finally, students who work on campus are more likely to graduate from college than are students who work off campus; keep this

MAKING GOOD CHOICES ▷

Let Previous Work Experience Guide Future Career Choices

What kinds of jobs have you had, either for pay or as a volunteer? Why did you choose those jobs? Which of them was your favorite, and which did you dislike? How could your prior job experience help you make good choices in the future? Be prepared to discuss your ideas in class and offer thoughts about what your work experience has taught you about yourself and which careers you should choose—or avoid—in the future.

fact in mind as you consider mixing college and work.

You may, however, decide that you would rather work off campus. An off-campus job might pay better than an on-campus one, be closer to your home, or be in an organization where you want to continue working after you finish college. The best place to start looking for off-campus jobs is your campus career center, which might have listings or websites featuring off-campus employment opportunities. ▪

Network Online

Members of different professions have their own ways of doing things, their own terminology, particular leaders, and important events. As a college student, you need to learn how to join your intended professional community and network with others in your chosen profession. You can and should start now.

▶ the GOAL

Learn about the industries, companies, and professional groups you would like to work with.

▶ how TO DO it

1. **Conduct industry and career research.** A great place to start is O*NET OnLine, a site with an interactive application for exploring occupations. Identify specific companies or organizations that interest you, as well as roles in which you could see yourself. Research individual employers of interest, too.

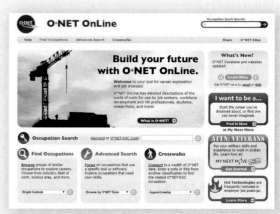
△ U.S. Department of Labor

2. **Do some research on yourself.** Even if you already have an idea about what you want to pursue, several online resources—such as the O*NET OnLine Interest Profiler or CAREERwise Education—will give you important feedback about what professions match your interests, personality, values, and skills.

3. **Get familiar with professional organizations.** Every profession has one or more groups whose members exchange ideas, hold events, or conduct trainings. Explore these organizations' websites to find local chapters or local events you can attend to learn more. In addition, many professional groups have a presence on LinkedIn, where you can see who is in a group and join an online conversation about a topic of interest.

4. **Find ways to gain real experience.** Check with your college's career center to find out what kinds of internship opportunities are available. You can look online, too:
   - Internships.com
   - Indeed
   - Idealist
   - LinkedIn

▶ your TURN

Visit work environments you want to explore. Find a person, through either LinkedIn or your college's alumni or career center, who will grant you an informational interview. You can also seek an opportunity for job shadowing. Here are a few questions to get your interview off to a strong start:

- Describe the moment when you knew this was the job for you.
- What is the most interesting thing that has happened to you in this profession?
- What changes would you make in your career preparation if you were entering this field today?
- Describe the most satisfying professional accomplishment you have had.

Marketing Yourself and Putting It All Together

You may never have thought you were responsible for your own start-up company, but in a sense, you are. This company—which we'll call "You, Inc."—is all about understanding your brand (what you bring to the table in terms of knowledge, skills, attitudes, behaviors, and values) and how to market yourself. You have been building your brand for years, whether you realized it or not, but now you have to take your brand much more seriously.

Branding You, Inc.

Building your brand begins the first day on campus. How you interact with new people, how you approach your academics, how you engage in campus life—each is an important ingredient in who you are and how you are seen by others. Through your experiences and your growing understanding of yourself, you establish your presence on campus, create name recognition among faculty and peers, and shape your reputation. This is a personal responsibility that you accept for a lifetime. It is more than getting a job; it is the navigation system—a sort of GPS—that will guide your professional and personal aspirations.

Here are a few points to consider:

- **You must take control of your own image.** No one is better equipped to portray *you* as accurately as *you* are. Remember to share your career goals with instructors, academic and career advisers, friends, and family;

△ **Standing Out from the Crowd**
A big part of developing You, Inc. is figuring out how to set yourself apart from others. Will you do it through commitment to getting good grades, community service, engagement in campus activities, or a unique niche in your industry? At the beginning of college, start thinking about the endgame and continually revisit where you're headed, making adjustments along the way. JeremyRichards/Shutterstock

they can help market you if they get to know you! The more others know about your professional goals, the more they can help you make professional connections.

- **Got ideas? Share them.** You may be hesitant about sharing your ideas or providing direction to others, but guess what? If you don't, you may be left with a good idea that no one else knows about.

- **Realize that it isn't all about you.** A perfect candidate who employers compete to hire can not only bring out the best in themselves but also bring out the best in others. For team dynamics and success, your ability to assist others to succeed is powerful.

- **Actions speak louder than words.** When you were in high school, you may have realized that good grades and extracurricular activities were ways to feel positive about your college applications. Or you may have discovered how poor grades or lack of involvement in school activities made it more difficult to feel confident in those applications. Professional résumés are similar; you want to be mindful of what makes a strong résumé and act accordingly. It is never too early to develop your résumé and a well-written cover letter. These two items are critical marketing collateral, so to speak, for You, Inc.

Building a Résumé

A good résumé is an excellent and necessary way to market yourself. Before you finish college, you'll need a résumé, whether it's for a part-time job, for an internship or co-op position, or to show to an instructor who agrees to write you a letter of recommendation. Typically, there are two types of résumés. One is written in a chronological format, and the other is organized by skill. If you have related job experience, choose the chronological résumé; if you can group skills from a number of jobs or projects under several meaningful categories, choose the skill-based résumé. Your career center can help you choose the format that is right for you given your experience and future goals.

On average, employers spend seven to ten seconds screening each résumé to glean their first-round picks when it's time to fill a job. Many employers also use résumé-scanning software to identify key terms and experiences that are most important to them. If you are a new professional, a one-page résumé is usually appropriate. Add a second page only if you have truly outstanding skills or work experience that won't fit on the first page, but consult with your career center for guidance on this point. If you are in college to be retrained and change your career, make sure to update the information on your résumé.

Writing a Cover Letter

A cover letter is *more important* than a résumé and much harder to write well. Even if an employer says a cover letter is optional, take the time to write one! When sending a cover letter, think about who will receive it—typically the hiring manager for the position or a human resources professional. Your career center can help you address your letter to the right person; so can the Internet. Use proper grammar, spelling, and complete sentences. These are details that employers pay attention to, and a mistake in your letter may cost you an interview.

TRY IT!

FEELING CONNECTED ▷
Marketing Yourself to Employers

Working with a small group of classmates, help one another develop a marketing strategy that each person could use to sell him- or herself to a potential employer. Which characteristics and aptitudes should each group member emphasize? Do other group members agree or disagree? Be honest and respectful in your comments to one another.

> " A good résumé is an excellent and necessary way to market yourself. "

Use the cover letter to highlight your relevant skills for every requirement of the position, and explain how hiring you will benefit the organization. It is important to review the organization's website to find out what skills and experience its employees have. Make sure to use resources at your college—such as the career center, a peer, or an instructor—to help you write and proofread your cover letter. Spending time on writing an excellent cover letter also prepares you for the interview by allowing you to think about how your background matches the needs of the position and the organization. ■

Creating an Online Portfolio

Developing an online portfolio is one of the best ways to display your accomplishments and to give employers access to examples of your work. For example, if you are a writer, you can post pieces of writing that demonstrate your ability to effectively communicate an idea and persuade an audience. Or if you are an aspiring software engineer, you can showcase your finished products as well as the code behind it. There are free platforms that will allow you to create a website quickly without any web development experience, such as Weebly, about.me, or Wix. Here are a few tips to keep in mind when creating your online portfolio:

1. **Include your résumé and a professional bio.** Be sure to add information about your professional and educational experience, interests, and skills.

2. **Identify your best work.** You should be proud of the work you post online. It should demonstrate what you can bring to an employer and ultimately make a strong argument for why that employer should hire you.

3. **Provide a brief explanation for everything you post.** Describe the project, explain your process for completing it, and connect it to a skill set.

4. **Make your portfolio visually interesting with photos and videos.** For example, if you are explaining the steps you took in your engineering project, post pictures and screenshots of your process. This will help prospective employers better understand your problem-solving abilities.

As with your résumé and cover letter, make sure to proofread your portfolio for any errors in spelling or grammar.

Chapter Review

Reflect on Choices

Most students are in college to prepare for a career. This chapter provides essential information on how you can structure your college experience—both in and outside class—to gain knowledge and skills that will help you, no matter what your employment future holds. Think about careers you are considering, and jot down some steps you can take in your very first term of college to help you prepare for your first job after graduation.

Apply What You've Learned

Now that you have read and discussed this chapter, consider how you can apply what you have learned to your academic and personal lives. The following prompts will help you reflect on the chapter material and its relevance to you, both now and in the future.

1. Sometimes it's hard to know if you're headed in the right career direction. Describe two steps you can take to make sure your career plans are realistic.

2. The best way to learn about a career is to talk to someone who is working or teaching in that field. Set up an appointment to talk with a professor who teaches in the field in which you are interested. Find out as much as possible about the education required for a specific career in that field.

Use Your Resources

GO TO ▷ Your college website and career center: If you need help learning about specific jobs and careers, preparing an effective résumé and cover letter, or getting ready for an interview. Continue to use these and other institutional services and resources, such as the learning center, throughout college.

GO TO ▷ Academic advisers and first-year counselors: If you need help finding supportive networks to connect academic learning to co-curricular and extracurricular learning.

GO TO ▷ A career adviser: If you need specialized help pertaining to your career. Career advisers can be found in either your career center or your campus counseling center.

GO TO ▷ Faculty: If you need help connecting your academic interests to careers. A faculty member can recommend specific courses that relate to a particular career. If you are a racial or ethnic minority student on your campus, seek out faculty or staff members who share your racial or ethnic profile and experiences.

GO TO ▷ The library: If you need help finding information about careers.

GO TO ▷ Knowledgeable students and your peer leaders: If you need help navigating courses and finding important resources.

GO TO ▷ Student organizations: If you need help finding leadership development opportunities. If you are a veteran or an active-duty military student, your campus may have a special organization designed to help you take advantage of special veterans or military benefits.

GO ONLINE TO ▷ The Occupational Outlook Handbook of the U.S. Bureau of Labor Statistics: If you need career information. This website, maintained by the U.S. Department of Labor, serves as a guide to hundreds of occupations.

GO ONLINE TO ▷ Mapping Your Future: If you want to start exploring potential careers.

 **LaunchPad Solo** macmillan learning — LaunchPad Solo for *Step by Step* is a great resource. Go online to master concepts using the LearningCurve study tool and much more. **launchpadworks.com**

10

Connecting with Others in a Diverse World

WunderfulPixel/Shutterstock

LaunchPad Solo
macmillan learning

To access ACES, the LearningCurve study tool, videos, and more, go to LaunchPad Solo for *Step by Step*. launchpadworks.com

What does success in college have to do with connecting with others? Very simply, the quality of the relationships you develop and maintain in college will have an important effect on your success. Not only will you develop relationships with students who look, act, and think like you, but you will also have the opportunity to get to know students whose life experiences and worldviews are different from yours. A college or university serves as a microcosm of the real world—a world that requires us all to live, work, and socialize with people from diverse ethnic, cultural, and economic groups. In fact, few real-world settings create opportunities for members of these different groups to interact in such close proximity as they do on a college campus.

You will also maintain relationships with members of your family and friends from your community, although those relationships may change in some ways. It will be especially important for you to keep the lines of communication open with family members in order to increase their understanding of your college experience.

Review Your ACES Score

Take a moment to reflect on your **Connecting with Others** ACES score, and insert it in the box to the right. Now let's take action!

Did you score in the high, moderate, or low range? Are you surprised by your score? This score will help you learn more about your strengths and weaknesses in understanding how to create strong relationships and embrace diversity during college. Even if you already feel strong in this area, be open to learning new strategies to help you improve your score as you move through the chapter. This chapter will further your understanding of why this topic is essential to your success in college.

Score:

○ High
○ Moderate
○ Low

To find your ACES score, log on to LaunchPad Solo for *Step by Step* at **launchpadworks.com**.

Preview the topic headings in this chapter. Then, in a journal or a readily accessible file, reflect on your current skills by answering the following questions:

▶ **What are your current strengths and challenges?**
▶ **What do you hope to learn from this chapter?**

Finding Help When You Least Expect It

© bo1982/iStock

Last week during Professor Velez's office hours, I went to see her with some questions about a lecture she had given a couple of days before. I noticed a photo of two people who I thought might be her mother and father, and we ended up having a really interesting talk about our families. Professor Velez told me that she was the first person in her family to go to college. It was a surprise for me to learn that, at first, her parents were suspicious of a psychology major and the whole idea of college and were afraid for her to leave home. I told her that I have been having a lot of trouble dealing with my family since I came to college—especially my mother. She has been calling me every day and trying to tell me what courses I should take, how much I should study, what my major should be, and even what time I should go to bed.

Professor Velez said she understood why I was frustrated. "I know you wish your parents would let you make your own decisions, Frank, but remember that they really care about you and want you to have a great experience. Perhaps if you call your mom every few days and tell her what's going on in your life, she will call you less often." I decided to follow her suggestion. My mom was really surprised when I called her yesterday. I spent about thirty minutes telling her everything that was happening to me, and I promised to call again over the weekend. I'm keeping my fingers crossed that she'll call less often and let me make my own decisions from now on.

What challenges do college students face when they move away from their family? What are some strategies for maintaining communication with your family while still making your own decisions? What did Frank learn from Professor Velez that will help him in the future?

Personal Relationships

One of the best things about going to college is meeting new people. In fact, scholars who study college students have found that students learn as much—or more—from other students as they learn from instructors. Although not everyone you meet in college will become a close friend, you will likely find a few special relationships that may even last a lifetime. Some relationships will be with people who have a background that is different from yours.

Roommates

For students whose college experience involves living in a residence hall or other off-campus housing, adjusting to a roommate can be a significant transition. Although it's tempting to room with your best friend from high school, that friend might not make a good roommate for you. In fact, many students lose friends by rooming with them. A roommate doesn't have to be a close friend, just someone with whom you can share your living space comfortably. Often, a roommate is someone you might not have selected if you had been given a choice, but you find that sharing a living space works well. Many students end up developing a lasting relationship with someone who, at first, was a total stranger. Some students, however, end up with an exasperating acquaintance they wish they'd never met.

It's important for roommates to establish in writing their mutual rights and responsibilities. Many colleges provide contract forms that you and your roommate might find useful if things go wrong. If you have problems with your roommate, talk them out promptly. Speak directly—politely, but plainly. Conflicts with roommates provide good opportunities to practice communication skills and can help build emotional intelligence. If the problems persist, or if you don't know how to talk them out, ask your residence hall adviser for help. Working through issues such as roommate challenges helps build resilience. Throughout your life, you will inevitably have conflicts with others that you will have to navigate.

◁ **Group Selfie**
The memories you create with your college friends will stay with you forever. © William Perugini/ Shutterstock

> ❝ College allows you to meet people from different backgrounds who share common interests. ❞

Romantic Relationships

You may already be in a long-term committed relationship, or your first serious romance might be with someone you meet on campus. Given that college allows you to meet people from different backgrounds who share common interests, you might find it easier to meet romantic partners during college than it ever was before. Whether you commit to one relationship or keep yourself open to meeting others, you'll grow and learn about yourself and those with whom you become involved.

If you are thinking about getting married or entering a long-term relationship, consider this: Studies show that the younger you are when you marry, the lower your odds are of enjoying a successful marriage. It is important not to get married until both you and your partner are certain of who you are and what you want.

Breakups

Breaking up is hard, but if it's time to end a relationship, do it calmly and respectfully. Explain your feelings, and talk them out. If you don't get a mature reaction, take the high road; don't join someone else in the mud.

Almost everyone has been rejected or dumped at one time or another. Let some time pass, be open to emotional support from your friends and family, and, if necessary, visit your college

MAKING GOOD CHOICES ▷ **What about Online Relationships?**

Have you met someone interesting online? Do you plan to meet him or her in person? While some online relationships can blossom into long-term friendships or romantic relationships when the parties meet face to face, others can be disappointing or even dangerous. If you want to get together in person with someone you've met online, it's a good idea to meet in a public place and to bring a friend along for that first meeting. At that point, based on your interaction, you can choose whether you want to see this person again or whether one "date" was enough.

counselor or school chaplain. These professionals have assisted many students through similar experiences, and they can be there for you as well.

Relationship No-Nos

One type of involvement you should definitely avoid is a romantic relationship with an instructor or someone who supervises you at your job. When a romantic partner has power over your grades or your employment status, you are setting yourself up for trouble down the road. If you find yourself becoming attracted to an instructor or someone else who has the power to affect your grades or your job, remember this: It is never wise to get involved with someone who is in a power relationship with you—unbalanced relationships create opportunities for abuses of power and/or sexual harassment. Plus, it is difficult to heal from a breakup if you must continue to work with (or even report to) your ex. You won't be sorry if you choose to maintain strictly professional relationships in the classroom and in the workplace. ■

Family Connections

Almost all first-year students, no matter their age, are connected to family members. Your family might be a spouse and children, a partner, or parents and siblings. The relationships that you have with family members can be a source of support throughout your college years, and it's important to do your part to maintain these relationships.

If you come from a cultural background that values family relationships and responsibilities above everything else, you will also have to work to balance your home life and college. In some cultures, if your grandmother or aunt needs help, that might be considered just as important—or more important—than going to class or taking an exam.

If you are living at home with one or more family members, you may have to bargain for time and space to study. This can be especially tough if you have children who demand your attention or if you live in a small space; in such situations, you might be forced to study after others have gone to sleep. Unless you have to study at home so that you can provide care for family members, you might want to find a study space on campus or at a nearby public library, especially before an upcoming test or exam.

Negotiating the demands of college and family can be difficult. However, most college instructors will be flexible with requirements if you have a problem meeting a deadline because of family obligations. It's important that you explain your situation to your instructors; don't expect them to be able to guess what you need. As the demands on your time increase, it's also important that you talk with family members to help them understand your role and responsibilities as a student.

Marriage and Parenting during College

While marriage and parenting can coexist positively with being a college student, meeting everyone's needs—your own, your spouse's,

◁ **Sweet Success**
Whether you are single or have a spouse or partner, being a parent while being a college student is one of the most challenging situations you can face. Find other students who have children so that you have a support system—it can make all the difference. You may not believe it now, but you are functioning as an important role model for your children. They will learn from you that education is worth striving for, even in the face of many obstacles.
© Paul Barton/Getty Images

your children's—is not easy. If you are living with a partner in a long-term (or committed) relationship, you need to become an expert at negotiating—whether or not you have children. If you do have children, find out what resources your college or university offers to help with childcare.

Sometimes going to college can create conflict between you and your partner as you take on a new identity and new responsibilities. Financial problems are likely to put extra pressure on your relationship, so both you and your partner have to work hard at paying attention to each other's needs. Be sure to involve your partner and children in your decisions. Bring them to campus at every opportunity, and let your partner (and your children, if they are old enough) read your papers and other assignments. Finally, set aside time for your partner and your children just as carefully as you schedule your work and your classes.

Relationship with Parents

Your relationship with your parents will never be quite the same as it was before you began college. On the one hand, you might find it uncomfortable when your parents try to make decisions on your behalf, such as choosing your major, determining where and how much you work, and setting rules for what you do on weekends. On the other hand, you might find that it's hard to make decisions on your own without talking to your parents first. While communicating with your parents is important, don't let them make all your decisions. Your college can help you draw the line between the decisions that should be yours alone and the decisions your parents should help you make. Many college students are living in blended families, meaning that more than one set of parents is involved in their college experience. If your father or mother has remarried, you might have to negotiate with both family units.

During this period of transition, a first step in establishing a good relationship with your parents is to make sure the lines of communication are open. Your parents may have concerns about your safety and well-being— you will understand these concerns better when you become a parent yourself. Your parents may be worried that you'll get hurt in some way. They might still see you as young and innocent, and they don't want you to make the same mistakes they might have made or experience the dangerous situations that have been publicized in the media. They might be concerned that your family values or cultural values will change or that you'll never really come home again, and for some students, that is exactly what happens.

Remember, though, that parents generally mean well even if their good intentions aren't always expressed in productive ways. Most of them love their children and want to protect them, even if their children are grown. To help your parents feel more comfortable with your life in college, try setting aside regular times to update them on how things are going for you. Ask for and consider their advice. You don't have to take it, but your parents will likely appreciate the chance to weigh in on your decisions. Thinking about your parents' suggestions can be useful as you consider the many factors that will help you make decisions.

Even if you're successful in establishing appropriate boundaries between your life and your parents' lives, it's hard not to worry about what's happening at home, especially when your family is in a crisis. If you find yourself in the midst of a difficult family situation, seek help from your campus's counseling center or from a chaplain. And whether or not your family is in crisis, if they are not supportive, reach out to others who can offer the emotional support you need. With your emotional needs satisfied, your reactions to your real family will be much less painful. ■

Thriving in Diverse Environments

So far in this chapter, you have learned about various ways to connect with others while in college and also about how being in college changes many of the relationships in your life. A logical next step is to increase your awareness of differences and similarities among people, which is an important component of your ability to connect with others and to build and maintain healthy relationships. Colleges and universities attract students with different backgrounds; as a result, the ethnicity, cultural background, economic status, and religion of college students may vary widely on your campus. Because almost all colleges and universities value rationality and fairness, they offer an ideal environment for exploring, understanding, and appreciating human differences.

Diversity can be defined as the difference in social and cultural identities among people. A diverse community has many advantages, including exposure to various cultures, historical perspectives, and ways of thinking. Diversity, however, can also be a source of misunderstanding and suspicion of the beliefs and behaviors of others. Through self-assessment, discovery, and open-mindedness, you can begin to understand your perspectives on diversity and become aware of situations in which conflicts and misunderstandings might arise. This work, although difficult at times, will add to your educational experiences, personal growth, and development. Thinking critically about your personal values and beliefs will allow you to understand others, to have a greater sense of belonging and to make a positive contribution to our multicultural society.

◁ Expand Your Worldview
How has going to college changed your experience with diversity? Are you getting to know people of different races or ethnic groups? Do your classes have both traditional-aged and older students? Are you seeking out people who are different from you and sharing personal stories and worldviews? © Digital Vision./Getty Images

Other Differences You Will Encounter in College

When we hear the word *diversity*, most of us immediately think of differences in race or ethnic group. But you will experience many other kinds of human difference during your years in college.

Age. Although some students enter college around age eighteen, others choose to enter or return to college in their thirties and beyond. Age diversity in the classroom gives everyone the opportunity to learn from others who have different life experiences. Many factors determine when students enter higher education for the first time and whether they leave college and then reenter.

Sex and gender. The words *sex* and *gender* are often used interchangeably, but as you become part of an academic community, you might start to think differently about these related terms. While a person's sex is often thought of as being either male or female, some students identify as nonbinary, transgender, or intersex (individuals born with both male and female sex characteristics). Beyond sexual anatomy, multiple *gender* definitions and experiences are generally understood as existing on a continuum or on a spectrum. To offer support to students across the gender spectrum, many colleges and universities are now asking students to identify gender affiliation and gender expression voluntarily on admission applications.

You are probably familiar with the terms *gay*, *straight*, *homosexual*, *heterosexual*, *bisexual*, and *transgender*. You might be less familiar with the categories *queer*, *questioning*, *intersex*, *asexual*, and *ally*. These two sets of terms describe people whose sexual orientation or gender expression is represented by the acronym LGBTQIA (lesbian, gay, bisexual, transgender, queer, intersex, and asexual). The LGBTQIA community advocates for human rights and fights against laws that do not include consideration and just treatment for LGBTQIA individuals.

In college, you will meet students, staff members, and instructors whose sexual orientation or gender expression is similar to or different from yours. Some people are lucky enough to come from welcoming environments; for many students, however, college is the first time they have been able to openly express their sexual or gender identity. These topics can be difficult to talk about, and it is important that you respect all individuals. Avoid making judgments about what you believe is appropriate or inappropriate for one group or another, and give others a chance to become educated without fear of judgment. Consider attending educational events about sexual or gender identity on your campus to increase awareness and expand your and others' worldviews.

Economic status. The United States is a country of vast differences in wealth. This considerable economic diversity can be either a positive or a negative aspect of college life. On the positive side, you will be exposed to, and can learn from, students with a wide range of economic differences. Meeting others who have grown up with either more or fewer opportunities than you did is part of learning how to live in a democracy.

Try to avoid developing exaggerated feelings of superiority or inferiority based on wealth. What matters now is not what you had or didn't have before you came to college; what matters is what you *do* in college. You have more in common with other students than you think. Now that you're in college, your individual efforts, dreams, courage, determination, and ability to stay focused can be your success factors.

Religion. Many students come to college with deeply held religious views, and some of them will create faith communities while on campus. Their religions will be not only those with a common Judeo-Christian heritage but also Islam, Hinduism, and Buddhism. Learning about different faith perspectives is another way you can explore human difference.

Some students and instructors may consider themselves atheists or agnostics, either denying or doubting the existence of a divine creator. Whatever *your* religious views may be, it is important that you respect the views of others. Learning more about world religions can help you better understand your own faith perspective.

Physical and learning challenges.

The majority of college students have average physical and learning abilities; however, the number of students with physical or learning challenges is rising on most college campuses, as is the availability of services for these students.

> " A person with a physical or learning challenge wants to be treated just like anyone else—with respect. "

Physical challenges include hearing impairment, visual impairment, paralysis, and specific disorders, such as cerebral palsy or multiple sclerosis. As discussed earlier in this book, many students have some form of learning disability that makes college work a challenge.

A person with a physical or learning challenge wants to be treated just like anyone else— with respect. If a student with such a challenge is in your class, treat him or her as you

△ **Can You Find Yourself?**
Are you a student who has recently come to the United States from another country? Perhaps you have immigrated to the United States with family members, or perhaps you came on your own. Whatever your particular situation, learning the unique language, culture, and expectations of a U.S. college or university can be a challenge. Do instructors' expectations and students' behaviors seem different from what you experienced in your home country? Seek out ESL (English as a second language) courses or programs if you need help with your English skills. You can also talk with international student counselors at your college to find out how you can continue to increase your understanding of life in the United States, both on and off campus. © Elaine Thompson/AP Images

would any student; too much eagerness to help might be seen as an expression of pity.

If you have, or think you might have, a learning disability, visit your campus learning center for testing, diagnosis, and advice on getting extra help as needed. Be sure to inform someone in the appropriate office if you require accommodations.

Stereotyping and Microaggressions

Many of our beliefs are the result of our personal experiences, whereas others are the result of stereotypes. A stereotype is a generalization—usually exaggerated or oversimplified and often offensive—that is used to describe or distinguish a group. Things we may have heard throughout our lives from family members, friends, or neighbors about members of a particular group may have resulted in our stereotyping of people in that group. We may acquire stereotypes about people we have never met before, or we may accept a stereotype without even thinking about it. Children who grow up in an environment in which dislike and distrust of certain groups of people are openly expressed might adopt those judgments, even if they have had no direct interaction with those being judged.

Sometimes interacting in the diverse environment that college represents can result in microaggressions, which are subtle but offensive comments that reinforce stereotypes of minority populations.[1] For instance, suppose a white person interviewed a person of color for a position with an advertising agency or another corporate setting and said, "Wow, you are very well spoken!" This statement suggests that most of the people in the interviewee's racial or ethnic group are not expected to be well spoken, which is an offensive generalization.

Or what if, in an effort to build rapport or make small talk, a white woman asks an Asian American woman, "So, where are you from, and what language do you speak?" Assuming a person is not originally from the United States based purely on that person's appearance can be offensive. Consider also what this kind of assumption says about the person who makes it.

In a college classroom, if the discussion topic is race relations, should one minority student be expected to speak on the topic as if he or she were speaking for the entire race? Of course not, but sometimes this happens. Although most of us would not intentionally insult someone of a different race or ethnic group, we do so when we aren't careful about the language we use or the assumptions we are inclined to make. While you are in college, learn to approach topics with an open mind and an appreciation for different cultures, behaviors, and beliefs. Enjoy the diverse perspectives around you, and learn from them. When meeting people for the first time, keep the following suggestions in mind:

1. **Focus on the person:** Put aside any of your previous ethnic, racial, or other stereotypes. Get to know the person as a blank slate. You may be fascinated by what you have in common.

2. **Avoid guesswork:** Do not attempt to guess a person's race, language, diet, expected behavior, age, or knowledge based only on their appearance.

3. **Practice the Golden Rule:** Treat others as you want to be treated. If you are curious about someone's ethnicity or background, use conversation starters like "Tell me about yourself" or "Where did you attend high school?" Avoid questions that reflect assumptions or come off as insensitive such as, "So, what are you?"

TRY IT!

FEELING CONNECTED ▷ Prejudice Affects Everyone

Often, when we think about prejudice or stereotyping, we immediately consider race or ethnicity. But there are many kinds of prejudice evident in our society. Have you ever experienced prejudice from others because of the way you talk, your gender, your weight, your religion, your socioeconomic status, or your political views? Think about an incident you would be willing to share with others in which you were affected by prejudice not related to your race or ethnic group.

[1] John McWhorter, "Microaggression' Is the New Racism on Campus," *Time*, March 21, 2014, http://time.com/32618/microaggression-is-the-new-racism-on-campus/.

Creating a Welcoming Environment on Your Campus

Your college experience will be enriched if you are open to the possibility of learning from all members of the campus community. In college, you might encounter personal values and belief systems that run counter to yours. Talking about diversity with someone whose beliefs seem to conflict with your own can be very rewarding. Learn not to make assumptions, rely on stereotypes, or rush to judgment. Give yourself time to get to know different people before forming opinions about them.

Colleges are working to provide a welcoming and inclusive campus environment for all students. In response to acts of violence, intimidation, and ignorance occurring on campuses, college administrators have established policies against any and all forms of discriminatory actions, racism, and insensitivity. Many campuses have adopted zero-tolerance policies that prohibit verbal and nonverbal harassment as well as hate crimes, such as physical assault, vandalism, and intimidation. If you have been the victim of a discriminatory, racist, or insensitive act, report it to the proper authorities.

Whatever form these crimes might take on your campus, it is important to examine your thoughts and feelings about their occurrence. Ask yourself: Will you do something about it, or do you think it's someone else's problem? Commit to becoming involved in making your campus a safe place for all students. ■

Sexual Harassment: A New Spotlight on an Old Problem

Sexual assault is easy to define; it involves unwanted physical contact of a sexual nature—groping, rape, or attempted rape. Sexual harassment, however, covers a much wider list of unwanted behaviors, ranging from inappropriate touching to comments that make someone feel uncomfortable or threatened sexually. While sexual harassment is nothing new, recent allegations of sexual harassment by movie producers, TV and film stars, politicians, and other public figures have put this societal problem under a spotlight.

No matter your gender or sexual orientation, you may have had an encounter that made you feel uncomfortable or even violated. You may have responded forcefully, or you may have tried to laugh it off. Some victims of sexual harassment are confused; they wonder if they were at fault or if they behaved in a way that unintentionally invited the action.

Fortunately, universities and colleges are becoming more aware of the negative effects of these behaviors. Students who are harassed sexually often find themselves less able to concentrate, study, or participate in class. Harassment may negatively affect how they feel about themselves or even their willingness to attend classes or social events. The bottom line is that sexual harassment can affect any student's overall feeling of safety.

Writing for the *Huffington Post*, Emily May, Debjani Roy, and Jae Cameron describe sexual harassment on campus as a "gateway crime . . . that creates a culture where words can escalate to physical contact and other forms of violence, including stalking, assault or rape."[2] If you or someone you know experiences harassment of a sexual nature, whether on or off campus, do not be silent. Confront the harasser firmly, but also talk to a trusted instructor or counselor about the situation and what steps you can take to prevent it in the future, including filing a formal complaint with officials on your campus.

[2] Emily May, Debjani Roy, and Jae Cameron, "What about Sexual Harassment on Campus?," *Huffington* Post, January 27, 2014, https://www.huffingtonpost.com/hollaback/about-sexual-harassment-college_b_4662080.html.

Look Beyond the Filter

College will give you the opportunity to expand your horizons, but you have to be willing to motivate yourself to branch out, try new things, and embrace new perspectives. The Internet, however, can thwart these efforts. Computer algorithms learn about your preferences and interests based on your online behavior and feed you more and more of that content. Author Eli Pariser defines this effect as the "filter bubble," which he describes as an unintended consequence of web companies tailoring their services—including news and search results—to our personal tastes.[3] This effect causes us to miss a large amount of information that we might like or learn from—we never see it because it is being filtered away from us.

[3] Eli Pariser, *The Filter Bubble: What the Internet Is Hiding from You* (New York: Penguin Books, 2011).

the GOAL

Expose yourself to new perspectives.

how TO DO it

It may not surprise you that one of the best ways to escape the filter bubble is to get offline and experience things in real life. Take advantage of the following suggestions to expand your worldview:

- **Join clubs or student groups to expand your interests.** College can be a time for you to meet new people and learn new things, and not all of this will happen in the classroom. You can develop new interests by talking to new people about new things.

- **Find ways to be of use.** Volunteering or interning can help you meet new people, explore new interests, understand others, and learn new skills. Additionally, the interests you explore and the skills you learn can be important to your future career and long-term goals.

- **When you are online, search in places other than Google, Facebook, or YouTube for new things to see, hear, or experience.** As you saw in chapter 8, "Developing Information Literacy and Communication Skills," your college maintains access to a number of databases containing all kinds of cool information. These databases are not searchable by external search engines such as Google or Bing, and your preferences and interests are not automatically tracked and mirrored back to you. If you take time to explore these databases, many of which contain unusual videos and music as well as text, you will become a better researcher and find new things to guide your professional interests.

your TURN

Set a goal to expose yourself to new things by using one or more of these suggestions. In small groups, reflect on this experience. Why is exposing yourself to new ideas important but challenging? How will you combat the filter bubble in your lives?

Connecting through Involvement

A college or university can seem to be a huge and unfriendly place, especially if you went to a small high school or grew up in a small town. Getting involved in campus life will help you feel comfortable in your new environment, enrich your college experience, and help you make friends, so make sure to take advantage of student activities on your campus. Getting involved is not difficult, but it will take some initiative on your part. Consider your interests, and choose some activities to explore. You might be interested in joining an intramural team, performing community service, running for student government, or getting involved in a structured campus-wide club or organization. Some clubs are related to professions, while others are related to general interests.

While involvement is the key, it's important to strike a balance between finding a niche where you are immediately comfortable and challenging yourself to have new and different interactions with others. Keeping an open mind and experiencing diversity will prepare you for changes in the workforce that you'll experience in the years ahead. Also, challenge yourself to learn about various cultural groups in and around your college and home community, and participate in campus ethnic and cultural celebrations to learn about unique traditions, ideas, and viewpoints.

Almost every college has numerous organizations you can join; check them out through printed brochures, open houses, activity fairs, websites, Facebook pages, and so on. If a particular organization interests you, consider attending one of the organization's meetings before you decide to join. Find out what the organization is like, what the expected commitment is in terms of time and money, and whether you feel comfortable with its members. Students who become involved in at least one organization are more likely to complete their first year and remain in college.

Be careful not to overextend yourself when it comes to campus activities. Although it is important to get involved, joining too many clubs or organizations will make it difficult to focus on any one activity and will interfere with your studies. Future employers will see a balance in academics and campus involvement as a desirable quality in prospective employees. Don't fall into the trap of thinking that more is better. As with many things, when it comes to campus involvement, quality is much more important than quantity.

> " Getting involved in campus life will help you feel comfortable in your new environment, enrich your college experience, and help you make friends. "

TRY IT!

FEELING CONNECTED ▷ Explore Involvement Opportunities

Get together with four or five students in your class, and share what you have learned about how to get involved and participate in clubs or organizations. Share both the positives and the negatives of your involvement experiences so far, as well as your beliefs about how many extracurricular clubs or organizations a first-year student should join.

Connecting by Working

One of the best ways to develop meaningful relationships on your campus is to get an on-campus job, either through the federal work-study program or directly through the college. Generally, on-campus supervisors will be much more flexible than off-campus employers in helping you balance your study demands and your work schedule. You might not make as much money working on campus as you would in an off-campus job, but the relationships you'll develop with influential people who care about your success in college and who will write those all-important reference letters make on-campus employment well worth it. Consider finding a job related to your intended major. For instance, if you are a pre-med major, you might be able to find on-campus work in a biology or chemistry lab. Such work will help you gain knowledge and experience as well as make connections with faculty experts in your field.

If an on-campus job is not available or you can't find one that appeals to you, an off-campus job will allow you to meet new people in the community. If you already had a job before starting college, talk to your employer about the new demands on your time. Also keep in mind that some employers offer tuition assistance in certain circumstances; ask whether any such opportunities are available to you.

Wherever you decide to find a job, it's important that you limit work to a reasonable number of hours per week. Although some students have to work to pay their tuition or living expenses, many college students work too many hours just to support a certain lifestyle. Be careful to maintain a reasonable balance between work and study. Don't fall into the trap of thinking that you can do it all. Too many college students have found that trying to do it all means not doing anything well.

Connecting through Community Service

As a first-year student, one way to support causes important to you and expand your experience with diversity is to consider volunteering for a community service project, such as serving the homeless at a soup kitchen or helping build or renovate homes for needy families. Your campus's division of student affairs might have a volunteer or community service office that offers other service opportunities, such as working with elementary school students who are learning to read, tutoring in an after-school program, participating in a campus cleanup, or working in a local animal shelter. You can also check online at VolunteerMatch for opportunities in your area. Simply enter your zip code and, if you wish, keywords to help you find volunteer work in your field of interest.

◁ The Power of Social Media

Online communities can also be powerful catalysts for social commentary, awareness, and change. For example, the "Me Too" movement, created by Tarana Burke in 2007, was popularized by Alyssa Milano with a post on Twitter. Now "#MeToo" has been posted on social media by millions of women and men who have been affected by sexual assault and harassment, increasing awareness of the pervasiveness of this problem in our society.

Chelsea Guglielmino/Getty Images

Connecting through Online Communities

If you're taking an online course, you are part of one kind of online community. Hopefully your online course gives you opportunities to get to know other classmates in chat rooms or through one-on-one interactions. If you're like many college students, however, social media groups—such as Facebook, Instagram, Twitter, and Snapchat—may be the online communities in which you spend the most time and energy. These communities are valuable ways to stay in touch with old friends and meet new ones, engage in professional networking, and uncover new passions and interests. However, this kind of unfiltered online communication can pose many challenges. Have you been drawn into a nasty Facebook argument you never intended, or tempted to post "too much information" that might hurt you as well as others? Remember that many forms of social media can be viewed not merely by one person but by multitudes. Take advantage of social media to connect with others, but exercise caution. ■

Seek Diversity in the Workplace and in Life

Diversity enriches us all, and understanding the value of working with others and the importance of keeping an open mind enhances your educational and career goals. Your college campus is diverse, and so is the workforce you will enter.

Expanding your worldview during your time in college prepares you to work successfully with others in any field. Has your instructor already given you an assignment to join a group of classmates to complete a graded project? The rationale behind group work is not only to help you develop the ability to function in a group setting but also to help you understand each person as an individual in spite of his or her differences. Learning the characteristics and strengths of each person and using them collectively to complete the goal and do well on the project can propel your productivity in a team environment.

In the workplace, a director or supervisor might ask you to lead a team charged with resolving a particular issue your employer is facing. Your first step would be to get to know and establish rapport with every member of your team, no matter their age, gender, race, or ethnic group; then you can successfully communicate the goals of the project. In a workplace situation, prejudice against another coworker reduces your ability to be productive and achieve workplace goals. Therefore, it will not be tolerated. To prepare for your future in this diverse world, consider the following:

- **Learn about various groups in your community, at your college, and in any job you hold.** These settings might differ ethnically and culturally, giving you an opportunity to develop your relationship skills.
- **Attend events and celebrations sponsored by other groups.** These events can take place on campus or in the general community. Taking advantage of special cultural events is a good way to experience traditions that are specific to the groups being represented.
- **Incorporate people from different cultures into your inner circle of friends.** As you begin your college experience, you will meet people who are not like you but who share common goals and aspirations. Some of these people have the potential to be future business partners, coworkers, managers, or employers.
- **Practice communicating clearly and respectfully, especially when you disagree.** When you encounter people with different backgrounds, opinions, or experiences from you, misunderstandings are inevitable. When you're in college, some of those misunderstandings may result in conflict with an instructor, a friend or roommate, or a family member. As you pursue your career, similar situations may arise with supervisors, coworkers, a spouse or partner, or even your children. Basic rules apply: Discuss your perspective respectfully and thoughtfully rather than exchanging angry e-mails or engaging in a shouting match. Try to see the situation from the other person's point of view and negotiate your differences.
- **Make time to travel.** Seeing the world and its people can be an uplifting experience. Travel will expose you to diverse ways of thinking that will challenge your ideas about who you are and what you have been taught.

Finally, if you want to learn more about a culture or group, ask a member of that group for information, but do so tactfully. Most people will be happy to share information about their viewpoints, traditions, and history.

Chapter Review

Reflect on Choices

College is a great time to build and nurture relationships with others from diverse backgrounds. The choice of whether to find new relationships and get to know others who are different is up to you. College offers many ways to get involved. Consider finding a part-time job, participating in community service, and engaging with diversity in order to enrich and energize your learning. Write a one-page essay about someone you have already met who helped you understand a different way of thinking.

Apply What You've Learned

Now that you have read and discussed this chapter, consider how you can apply what you have learned to your academic and personal lives. The following prompts will help you reflect on the chapter material and its relevance to you, both now and in the future.

1. If you are not already involved in on-campus activities and clubs, visit your college's website or activities office to learn more about the kinds of clubs, organizations, service-learning opportunities, sports teams, and volunteer work that are offered. Find at least one activity that seems interesting to you, and learn more about it. When does the group meet and how often, and how many students are involved?

2. Reflecting on your personal identity and values is a step toward increasing self-awareness. Read and answer the following questions to the best of your ability: How do you identify and express yourself ethnically and culturally? Are there practices or beliefs with which you do not agree? If so, what are they? Why do you have difficulty accepting these beliefs? What aspects of your identity do you truly enjoy?

Use Your Resources

GO TO ▷ The counseling center: If you need help thinking and talking about your relationships and making appropriate decisions. It is normal to seek such assistance. This kind of counseling is strictly confidential (unless you are a threat to yourself or others) and is usually provided at no charge, which is a great benefit.

GO TO ▷ A campus chaplain: If you need help from a member of the clergy in dealing with a relationship problem. Many public and private colleges have religiously affiliated chaplains, most of whom have specialized training in pastoral counseling. They also organize and host group activities in campus religious centers, which you might want to take advantage of.

GO TO ▷ Student organizations: If you need help finding a small group of other students who share the same interests with you.

GO ONLINE TO ▷ The University of Chicago's Student Counseling Virtual Pamphlet Collection: If you need help finding websites devoted to relationship problems. Browse among the many links to see whether any information applies to you.

GO ONLINE TO ▷ The Community Toolbox's chapter, "Cultural Competence in a Multicultural World": If you need help finding a good resource for becoming culturally competent. The Community Toolbox, a public service of the University of Kansas, is a free online resource for those working to build healthier communities and bring about social change. Its mission is to promote community health and development by connecting people, ideas, and resources.

GO ONLINE TO ▷ AACU's Diversity and Democracy project: If you need help finding resources related to civic learning and democratic engagement, global learning, engagement with diversity, and social responsibility.

GO ONLINE TO ▷ Teaching Tolerance: If you need help accessing resources for dealing with discrimination and prejudice both on and off campus.

 **LaunchPad Solo**
macmillan learning

LaunchPad Solo for *Step by Step* is a great resource. Go online to master concepts using the LearningCurve study tool and much more. launchpadworks.com

11

Managing Money

Whether we like it or not, we can't ignore the importance of money. Money is often symbolically and realistically the key ingredient to independence and even, some people have concluded, to a sense of freedom. You probably know of instances in which money divided a family or a relationship or seemed to drive someone's life in a direction he or she would not have taken otherwise. Money can also affect people's specific academic goals, causing them to select or reject certain academic majors or degree plans.

Sometimes parents will insist that students major in a field that is more likely to yield a good job and a good salary. Given the cost of college today, these attitudes are understandable.

Although your primary goal in college should be to achieve a strong academic record, the need for money can be a significant distraction, making it more difficult to complete your degree. Sometimes, in their attempt to survive financially, students will overuse credit cards and get themselves in serious financial trouble. Educators recognize that not understanding personal finances can hinder a student's progress, and mandatory personal finance classes are now being added in high schools and are available as options at some colleges. The purpose of this chapter is to provide basic information and suggestions so that money issues will not be a barrier to your success in college. There are sources of financial assistance through loans, grants, and work-study programs, and this chapter will help you develop a strategy for investigating your options. Think of this chapter as a summary of needed financial skills; if you want more information, consider taking a personal finance class at your college or in your community.

Review Your ACES Score

Take a moment to reflect on your **Personal and Financial Health** ACES score and insert it in the box to the right. Now let's take action!

Did you score in the high, moderate, or low range? Are you surprised by your score? This score will help you learn more about your strengths and weaknesses in understanding how to manage your financial health. In this chapter, we will focus on money management and financial literacy. Even if you already feel strong in this area, be open to learning new strategies to help you improve your score as you move through the chapter. This chapter will further your understanding of why this topic is essential to your success in college.

Score:

○ High
○ Moderate
○ Low

To find your ACES score, log on to LaunchPad Solo for *Step by Step* at **launchpadworks.com**.

Preview the topic headings in this chapter. Then, in a journal or a readily accessible file, reflect on your current skills by answering the following questions:

▶ **What are your current strengths and challenges?**

▶ **What do you hope to learn from this chapter?**

Eating Your Words

Monkey Business Images/Shutterstock

My first year at college was a financial struggle. I lived on campus and ate in the dining hall. But I was always hungry late at night after the dining hall closed, and I made frequent trips to the pizza joint just across the street from my residence hall. My parents were sending me a fixed monthly allowance, and it seemed that there was always "too much month at the end of the money." Before my sophomore year, my dad bought me a used car, so I decided to move off campus and buy and cook my own food. I was convinced that cooking my own food would save money and give me the extra I needed for late-night pizza.

"This is a bad idea, Jeff," said my mother when I told her of my plan. "When are you and your roommates going to have time to cook, and what are you going to eat besides a lot of junk food?"

"Oh, we can do it," I said. "It'll be cheaper in the long run. My roommates and I are going to take turns shopping and cooking."

We did take turns, for the first week or so. Sam made pizza. Nick made burritos. I made my famous spaghetti. Occasionally, we made enough for leftovers. But all of a sudden, around the first of October, no one had time to go to the grocery store, much less cook. In fact, it was hard to even eat a bowl of cereal in the morning because we were always out of milk. It got to the point where I ate out all the time, and in two months my food budget for the entire semester was totally gone and I was dipping into my rent money. I had to call and tell my parents that I'd maxed out my credit card, drained my bank account, and run up over $200 in credit card penalties—all on food.

"I know I should have kept track of what I was spending," I admitted. "It just added up so fast."

"See, I warned you," my mother said. "You learned a painful lesson." An ominous pause followed. "So . . . how will you make it to the end of the term? What kind of job will you get?"

Why is it so important to track your spending in college? What steps could Jeff take to manage his money more carefully? While some students track their expenses precisely, others seem unaware of how much money they're spending. If they run out, they risk having to rely on credit cards. Spending more than you have can sabotage your college experience as well as your life after college.

Living on a Budget

Face it: College is expensive, and most students have limited financial resources. Not only is tuition a major cost, but day-to-day expenses can add up quickly. No matter what your financial situation, a budget for college is a must. Although a budget might not completely eliminate debt after graduation, it can help you become realistic about your finances so that you will have a basis for future life planning.

A budget is a spending plan that tracks all sources of income (such as student loan disbursements and money from parents) and expenses (like rent and tuition) during a set period of time (such as a week or a month). Creating and following a budget will allow you to pay your bills on time, cut costs, put some money away for emergencies, and finish college with as little debt as possible.

Creating a Budget

A budget will condition you to live within your means, put money into savings, and possibly invest down the road. Here are a few tips to help you get started.

Gather income information. To create an effective budget, you need to learn more about your income and where you spend money. First, determine how much money is coming in and when. Sources of income might include a job, your savings, gifts from relatives, student loans, scholarship dollars, or grants. List all your income sources, making note of how often you receive each type of income (weekly or monthly paychecks, quarterly loan disbursements, one-time gifts etc.), and how much money you can expect each time. Knowing when your money is coming in will help you decide how to design a budget. For example, if most of your income comes in on a monthly basis, you'll want to

> ❝ No matter what your financial situation, a budget for college is a must. ❞

create a monthly budget. If you are paid every other week, a biweekly budget might work better.

Gather expense information for your college or university. Your expenses will include tuition; residence hall fees if you live on campus; and textbooks, course materials, lab fees, and membership dues for any organizations you might join. Some institutions offer a separate January or May term. Although your tuition for these one-month terms is generally covered in your overall tuition payment, you would have extra expenses if you wanted to travel to another location in the United States or abroad.

Gather information about living expenses. First, do a reality check. How do you think you're spending your money? To find out for sure where your money is going and when, track your spending for a few weeks—ideally, for at least a full month—in a notebook or in a table or spreadsheet. The kinds of expense categories you should consider will vary depending on your situation. If you are a full-time student and you live with your parents or other family members, your living expenses won't be the same as those of a student living in a campus residence hall or in an off-campus apartment. If you are a returning student holding down a job and have a family of your own to support, you will calculate your expenses differently.

Whatever your situation, keeping track of your expenses and learning about your spending behaviors are important habits. Consider which of the following expense categories are relevant to you:

- Rent/utilities (electricity, gas, water)
- Cell phone/cable/Internet
- Transportation (car payment, car insurance, car repairs, gas, public transportation)
- Child care
- Groceries
- Medical expenses (prescriptions, doctor visits, hospital bills)
- Clothing/laundry
- Entertainment (dining out, hobbies, movies)
- Personal grooming (haircuts, toiletries)
- Miscellaneous (travel, organization dues)

Be sure to recognize which expenses are fixed and which are variable. A fixed expense is one that will cost you the same amount every time you pay it. For example, your rent is a fixed expense because you owe your landlord the same amount each month. A variable expense is one that may change. Your textbooks are a variable expense because the number and cost of them will be different each term.

Find out how you are doing. Once you have a sense of how your total income compares to your total weekly or monthly expenses, you can get a clearer picture of your current financial situation.

Make adjustments. Although your budget might never be perfect, you can strive to improve it. In what areas did you spend much more or much less than expected? Do you need to reallocate funds to better meet your immediate needs? Be realistic and careful about how you spend your money, and use your budget to help meet your goals, such as planning for a trip or buying a new pair of jeans.

Whatever you do, don't give up if your bottom line doesn't turn out to be what you expected. Be resilient and get back on track. Budgeting is a lot like dieting; you might slip up and eat a pizza (or spend too much buying one), but all is not lost. If you stay focused and flexible, your budget can help you achieve financial stability and independence.

Cutting Costs

Once you have put together a working budget and have tried it out and adjusted it, you're likely to discover that your expenses still exceed your income. Don't panic. Simply begin to look for ways to reduce those expenses. Here are some tips for saving money in college.

Recognize the difference between your needs and your wants. A need is something you must have. For example, tuition and textbooks are considered needs. Your wants are goods, services, or experiences that you wish to purchase but could reasonably live without. For example, concert tickets and mochas are wants. Your budget should always provide for your needs first.

△ **Go Vintage**
Saving money doesn't mean you have to deprive yourself. Shopping at thrift stores for your clothes or apartment furnishings is a fun, affordable way to get one-of-a-kind items and not break the bank. Raphye Alexius/Getty Images

Use low-cost transportation. If you live close to campus, consider whether you need a car. Take advantage of lower-cost options, such as public transportation or biking to class, to save money on gasoline and parking. If you live farther away, check to see whether your institution hosts a ride-sharing program for commuter students, or carpool with someone in your area.

Seek out inexpensive entertainment options. Take advantage of discount or free entertainment offered through your college. Most institutions use a portion of their student fees to provide affordable entertainment options, such as discount or free tickets to concerts, movie theaters, sports events, or other special activities.

Embrace secondhand goods. Use Craigslist, Freecycle.org, and thrift stores such as Goodwill to expand your wardrobe; purchase games and sports equipment; or furnish and decorate your room, apartment, or house.

Avoid unnecessary fees. Making late payments on credit cards and other bills can lead to expensive fees and can lower your credit score (which in turn will raise your interest rates). Note payment due dates carefully on your calendar to avoid this type of costly mistake. ■

Benefits of Being a Good Money Manager

You may be wondering how money management is related to academic success. Well, we have worked with college students for decades. We have watched many of them experience major money problems and, as a result, get in serious financial trouble with a bank or credit card company, develop a poor credit rating that will follow them for many years, lose their motivation for academic work, and ultimately struggle to achieve their life and career goals. Occasionally, money problems are out of a student's control; but more often, they result from poor money management.

How you manage money while you're in college will affect the rest of your life. This is true whether you have a generous allowance from your family or no financial help at all. You might know students who often hit others up for money. These students are probably wasting money and will still be wasting money when they are in their thirties, forties, and fifties. You might also know students who are frugal, tracking virtually every penny they spend. These students may actually save money while they're in college, and this habit of saving will be with them throughout their lives. Are you in either of these groups? And how important is it, really?

As it turns out, your ability to manage money is likely to affect your job prospects. Some employers run credit checks on all or some potential new hires. Especially when there is competition for a job, employers may want to consider not only your academic qualifications or experience but also your ability to manage money. This is especially true if you are applying for a job in a bank, a brokerage house, the government, or other financial institutions where the potential exists for fraud and embezzlement.

Here is the bottom line: If you develop the habit of budgeting and money management while you're a college student, it will pay off for the rest of your life, no matter how much or how little money you ultimately have. But if you are in the habit of wasting money now, you might always waste it, and this may be a sign to a potential employer that you lack a sense of personal responsibility. Practice now by developing good budgeting strategies; don't let money management be a lifelong struggle for you.

Manage Your Personal Budget

Technology can really help you when it comes to keeping track of your money—knowing how much you have, how much you need, and whether there are any problems with transactions moving through your accounts.

▶ the GOAL

You've created a budget. Now what? Use one of the many electronic tools available to track and manage your budget for this term.

▶ how TO DO it

- **Check with your banking institution.** See what apps and online services it offers. Many banks offer free online access to your accounts so that you can deposit funds, make purchases, transfer funds, and receive deposit or withdrawal notifications via your cell phone or e-mail. These services allow you to review your account information and help you make better decisions about how you use your money.

- **Use your bank's app and online tools to help you with your budget.** Check out some of these useful apps:

  - **Mint (mint.com).** This website and phone app allow you to combine information from all your financial accounts in one place. You can see your entire financial picture at once—your investments, income, loans, and payments.

  - **PayPal Mobile (paypal.com).** This app allows you to spend money and allows other people to give you money.

  - **Pocket Budget (mapeapps.com).** This app installs on your phone and is a simple way to keep track of your budget.

- **Beware of scams.** As you improve how you track your finances, remember to exercise caution in dealing with banks, credit card companies, and all financial institutions.

  - Do not transmit personal information (social security number, bank details, credit or debit card numbers, passwords, etc.) through e-mail.

  - Do not answer questions about vital personal information over the phone if you didn't make the call.

  - Do not reply to e-mails, pop-ups, or text messages that ask you to reveal personal information.

▶ your TURN

Do you have an electronic method for keeping track of your expenses? If not, give one of these apps a try.

Understanding Financial Aid

Few students can manage the costs of college tuition, academic fees, textbooks, room and board, bills, and random expenses without some kind of help. Luckily, financial aid options—student loans, grants, scholarships, work-study programs, and other sources of money to support a college education—are available to help cover your costs.

> **"** Few students can manage the costs of college tuition, academic fees, textbooks, room and board, bills, and random expenses without some kind of help. **"**

Types of Aid

While grants and scholarships are unquestionably the best forms of aid because they do not have to be repaid, the federal government, states, and colleges offer many other forms of assistance, such as loans, work-study opportunities, and cooperative education. A student loan is a form of financial aid that must be paid back with interest.

Grants are funds provided by the federal government, state governments, and the educational institutions themselves to help students pay for college. Grants are given to students based on their financial need, and they do not need to be repaid. Some grants are specific to a particular academic major. Students meet academic qualifications for grants by being admitted to a college and

maintaining grades that are acceptable to the grant provider.

A *scholarship* is money from the college or another source that supports a student's education and does not have to be repaid. Some scholarships are need based—that is, they are awarded on the basis of both talent and financial need. *Talent* can refer to past accomplishments in the arts or athletics, potential for future accomplishments, or even where students are from. Some colleges and universities place importance on admitting students from other states or countries. *Need* in this context means the cost of college minus a federal determination of what you and your family can afford to contribute toward that cost. Your institution might provide scholarships from its own resources or from individual donors. Some donors stipulate characteristics of scholarship recipients, such as age or academic major.

Other scholarships are known as *merit scholarships*. These are based on talent but do not require students to demonstrate financial need. It can be challenging to match talents with merit scholarships. Most merit scholarships come through colleges and are part of the admissions and financial aid processes, which are usually described on the college's website. Web-based scholarship search services are another good source to explore. Be certain that the website you use is free, will keep your information confidential unless you release your name, and will send you a notice (usually through e-mail) when a new scholarship that matches your qualifications is posted. Also be sure to ask your employer; your family's employers; and social, community, or religious organizations about any available scholarships.

Work-study programs allow students who receive financial aid to have part-time jobs to earn extra money if their aid amount is not enough to cover all their education costs. Students receive work-study notices as part of the overall financial aid notice and then can sign up to be interviewed for work-study jobs. Although some work-study jobs are relatively menial, the best options provide experience related to students' academic studies while allowing them to earn money for college. The salary will be based on the skills required for a particular position and the hours involved. Keep in mind that you will be expected to accomplish specific tasks while on duty, although some supervisors might permit you to study during any downtime. In addition to the money, work-study positions give you the opportunity to develop and test out some or all components of your personal work ethic, such as honesty, personal initiative, sense of responsibility, discipline, and willingness to work in a team toward a common goal.

Cooperative (co-op) education allows you to alternate a term of study (a semester or quarter) with a term of paid work. Engineering co-op opportunities are among the most common, and the number of co-op programs in health-care fields is growing. Colleges make information about co-ops available through admissions and academic departments.

Navigating and Qualifying for Financial Aid

The majority of students need help in paying for college, and various types of financial aid are available: scholarships, grants, loans, and paid employment. Financial aid professionals refer to this combination as a *package*.

Financial aid seems complex because it can come from a variety of sources. Each source may have a different set of rules about how to receive the money and how not to lose it. The financial aid office at your college or university can help you find the largest amount of money that doesn't need to be repaid, the lowest interest rate on loans, and work possibilities that fit your academic program. Do not overlook this valuable campus resource. It is the best place to begin looking for all types of financial assistance.

Most financial assistance requires some form of application. The application used most often is the Free Application for Federal Student Aid (FAFSA). All students should complete the FAFSA by the earliest submission deadline among the colleges they are considering. The FAFSA website (search "FAFSA") is very informative. If additional forms are required—such as the College Board's CSS Profile form (search "College Board Financial Aid Profile") or individual scholarship applications—they will be listed in colleges' financial aid or admissions materials or by organizations that offer scholarships.

Read "Steps to Qualify for Financial Aid," which outlines the steps you must take to qualify for most scholarships and grants, especially those sponsored by the federal government or state governments. The amount of financial aid you receive will depend on the cost of your academic program and what you or your family can pay as determined by the FAFSA. The cost of your program includes average expenses for tuition and fees, textbooks and supplies, room and board, transportation, and personal expenses. The financial aid office will subtract from that total the amount you and your family are expected to pay. In some cases, that amount can be as little as zero. Financial aid is designed to make up as much of the balance, or need, as possible.

How to Keep Your Funding

If you earn average or better grades, complete your courses each term, and finish your program or degree on time, you should have no trouble maintaining your financial aid. It's a good idea to check with the financial aid office before you drop classes to make sure you won't lose any aid.

Some types of aid, especially scholarships, require that you maintain full-time enrollment and make satisfactory academic progress. Dropping or failing a class might jeopardize all or part of your financial aid unless you are enrolled in more credits than the minimum required for financial aid. For full-time financial aid, that minimum is often defined as twelve credit hours per term. If you initially enrolled in fifteen credit hours and dropped one three-hour course, your aid should not

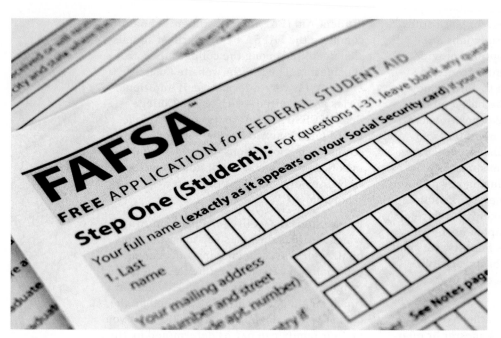

change. Even so, talk with a financial aid counselor before making the decision to drop a course, just to be sure. Remember that, although the financial aid office is there to serve you, you must take the following steps to be your own advocate:

- **File for financial aid every year.** Even if you don't think you will receive aid for a certain year, you must file annually in case you become eligible in the future.

- **Meet all filing deadlines.** Students who do not meet filing deadlines risk losing aid from one year to the next.

- **Talk with a financial aid officer immediately if you or your family experiences a significant loss** (such as the loss of a job or the death of a parent or spouse). Don't wait for the next filing period; you might be eligible for funds for the current year.

- **Inquire every year about criteria-based aid.** Many colleges and universities have grants and scholarships for students who meet specific criteria. These might include grants for minority students, grants for students in specific academic majors, and grants for students from single-parent families.

- **Inquire about campus jobs throughout the year**, as these jobs might be available at any time, not just at the beginning of the term. If you do not have a job but you want or need to work, keep asking.

- **Consider asking for a reassessment of your eligibility for aid.** If you have reviewed your financial aid package and think that your circumstances deserve additional consideration, you can ask the financial aid office to reassess your eligibility. The office is not always required to do so, but the request might be worth your effort. ■

TRY IT!

SETTING GOALS ▷ Exhaust All Avenues

Set a goal to learn about possible sources of financial support on your campus in addition to those you may already be receiving. The best single source for this information is your institution's financial aid office. You may also want to check with your employer (if you work off campus), your parents' employers, houses of worship, and civic organizations, such as the Rotary or Kiwanis clubs in your hometown. Be prepared to share your findings in class.

Steps to Qualify for Financial Aid

1. **Enroll half-time or more in a certificate or degree program** at one of the more than 4,500 colleges and universities certified to distribute federal financial aid. A few aid programs are available for less than half-time study; check with your department or college.

2. **Complete the FAFSA.** The first FAFSA you file is intimidating, especially if you rush to complete it right before the deadline. Completing the FAFSA in subsequent years is easier because you only need to update items that have changed. To make the process easier, get your personal identification number (PIN) a few weeks before the deadline. This PIN will be the same one you'll use throughout your college career. Try to do the form in sections rather than tackling all of it at once. Most of the information is basic: name, address, driver's license number, and other information you will know or have in your personal records and files. The financial section will most likely require your own and your parents' information from tax materials. However, if you are at least twenty-four, are a veteran, or have dependents, you do not need to submit your parents' tax information. If you are married, your spouse's tax information will be needed.

3. **Complete the College Board's CSS Profile form if your school or award-granting organization requires it.** Review your college's admission information, or ask a financial aid adviser to determine whether this form is required.

4. **Identify any additional applications that are required.** These are usually scholarship applications with personal statements or short essays. The organizations that are giving the money will provide instructions about what is required. Most have websites with complete information.

5. **Follow instructions carefully, and submit each application on time.** Financial aid is awarded from a fixed pool of funds. Once money is awarded, there is usually none left for those who file late.

6. **Maintain your GPA.** Complete the classes for which you were given financial aid with at least a minimum grade point average as defined by your academic department or college or the organization that provided you the scholarship.

Achieving a Balance Between Working and Borrowing

After you have determined your budget, decided what (if anything) you can pay from savings, and taken your scholarships and grants into consideration, you may find that you still need additional income. Each term or year, you should decide how much you can work while maintaining good grades and how much you should borrow from student loans.

Advantages and Disadvantages of Working

The majority of students today find that a combination of working and borrowing is the best way to gain experience, finance college, and complete their educational goals on time. Paid employment while you are in college has benefits beyond the money you earn. Having a job in a field related to your major can help you develop a credential for graduate school and make you more employable later because it shows that you have the capability to manage several priorities at the same time. Working while you are in college can help you determine whether a particular career is what you really want to pursue after you graduate. And students who work a moderate amount (fifteen or twenty hours per week) typically get better grades than students who do not work at all.

However, it's almost impossible for students to get outstanding grades if they work full time while taking a full-time course load. Some first-year students prefer not to take a job until they've adjusted to their new academic environment. You might find that you're able to work some terms but not others, depending on your course schedule. And family obligations or challenging classes can sometimes make the added burden of work impractical or even impossible.

Part-time off-campus jobs that relate to your major or career plan are hard to come by. You'll likely find that most part-time employment has little or no connection to your career objectives. A better option may be to seek a job on campus. In addition to the feeling of connectedness that on-campus jobs often offer, students who work on campus develop relationships with instructors and staff members who can help them negotiate the academic and social sides of campus life and make plans for the future. While off-campus employers are often unwilling to allow their student employees time off for study and exam preparation, college employers will want you to put your studies and exam preparation first. The downside to on-campus employment is that you'll likely earn less than you would in an off-campus job, but if

TRY IT!

MANAGING TIME ▷ Be Realistic

You might already have a job or be looking for one. However, many college students try to do the impossible by taking on too many time commitments—working one or even two jobs while maintaining a full load of courses. Be realistic about what you can do in twenty-four hours a day, seven days a week. The better alternative might be reducing your expenses instead of adding more time commitments. Reflect on your current situation. Are you able to get everything done? If you are feeling stressed from trying to juggle it all, brainstorm some solutions to make cutting back on your work hours feasible.

success in college is your top priority, the upside of working on campus outweighs the downside.

Student Loans

Although you should be careful not to borrow yourself into a lifetime of debt, avoiding loans altogether could delay your graduation and your progress up the career ladder. For most students, some level of borrowing is both necessary and prudent.

The following list provides information about the most common types of student loans. The list reflects the order in which you should apply for and accept loans to get the lowest interest rates and best repayment terms.

- **Subsidized federal student loans** are backed by the government, which pays the loan interest on your behalf while you are enrolled in undergraduate, graduate, or professional school. These loans require at least half-time enrollment and a submitted FAFSA application.

- **Unsubsidized federal student loans** may require that you make interest payments while you are enrolled. If not, the interest is added to the amount you owe; this is called *capitalization*.

- **Parent Loan for Undergraduate Students (PLUS) loans** are applied for and owed by parents but disbursed directly to students. The interest on PLUS loans is usually higher than the interest on federal student loans but lower than that on private student loans. Parents who apply must provide information on the FAFSA.

- **Private student loans** are offered through banks and credit unions. Private loans often have stricter credit requirements and higher interest rates than federal loans do, and interest payments on private loans begin immediately.

Student loans are a very important source of money for college, but like paid employment, loans should be considered carefully. Loans for costs such as textbook purchases and tuition fees are good investments. Loans for a more lavish lifestyle are likely to weigh you down in the future. As one wise person put it: If by borrowing you live like a wealthy graduate while you're a student, you'll live like a student after you graduate. Student loans can be a good way to begin using credit wisely, a skill you are likely to need throughout your life. ∎

> ❝ Student loans are a very important source of money for college, but like paid employment, loans should be considered carefully. ❞

TRY IT!

FEELING CONNECTED ▷ Search Party

When job searching, you probably want to find the best-paying job possible. Earning money while you're in college provides income to help with your expenses, and hopefully you are already getting in the habit of budgeting. Remember, too, that the ideal job will not only pay well but also move you toward your long-term career objectives. Connect with other students in your class who need or want to find jobs. Investigate what on-campus and part-time off-campus jobs are available for students, and share ideas for searching for jobs that make sense considering the competing responsibilities of work, college, and other personal and family commitments. Compare the wages, hours, and working conditions of available jobs. Share leads, and share your perspectives with one another and with your whole class.

Plan for the Future

It's never too early to begin thinking about how you will finance your life after graduation and whether you will begin working immediately or pursue a graduate or professional degree. Your work, whether on or off campus, will help you make that decision. Here are some tips that will help you plan now for your future.

- **Figure out your next step—more education or work?** If you are working on campus, get to know faculty or staff members, and seek their advice about your future plans. If you are working off campus, think carefully about whether your current job is one that you would want to continue after you graduate. If not, keep your options open and look for part-time work in a field that more closely aligns with your career plans or long-term educational objectives.

- **Keep your address current with the registrar.** Even when you have finished your degree or program, and especially if you stop classes for a term, alert the registrar of any changes in your address. This is doubly important if you have a student loan; you don't want to get a negative report on your credit rating because you didn't receive some information about your loan.

- **Establish a savings account.** Add to it regularly, even if you can manage to deposit only a few dollars a month. The sooner you start, the greater your returns will be.

Your education is the most productive investment you can make for your future and that of your family. Research shows that the completion of programs or degrees after high school increases future earnings; opens up career options; leads to greater satisfaction in work; results in more engaged citizenship, such as voting and community service; and greatly increases the probability that your children will go to college. Although college is a big investment of time and money, it's an investment you'll be glad you made.

Managing Credit Wisely

When you graduate, you will take two significant numbers with you. The first is your grade point average (GPA), which represents the level of academic success you attained while in college. The second, your credit score, is a numerical representation of your fiscal responsibility. Although this second number might be less familiar to you than the first, it could be a factor that determines whether you get your dream job, regardless of your GPA. In addition, twenty years from now you'll likely have forgotten your GPA, whereas your credit score will be more important than ever.

Your credit score is derived from a credit report that contains information about accounts in your name. These accounts include credit cards, student loans, utility bills, cell phones, and car loans, to name a few. This credit score can determine whether or not you will qualify for a loan (car, home, student), what interest rates you will pay, how much your car insurance will cost, and your chances of being hired by certain organizations. Even if none of these things is in your immediate future, now is the time to start thinking about your credit score.

Although using credit cards responsibly is a good way to build credit, federal law prohibits college students under the age of twenty-one from obtaining a credit card unless they can prove that they are able to make the payments or unless the credit card application is cosigned by a parent or guardian.

Understanding Credit

Even if you can prove that you have the means to repay credit card debt, it is important for you to thoroughly understand how credit cards work and how they can both help and hurt you. Simply put, a credit card allows you to buy something now and pay for it later. Each month you will receive a statement listing all the purchases you made with your credit card during the previous thirty days. The statement will request a payment toward your balance and will set a payment due date. Your payment options will vary: You can pay your entire balance, pay a specified portion of the balance, or make only a minimum payment, which may be as low as $10.

Beware: If you pay only the minimum required, the remaining balance on your card will be charged a finance fee, or interest charge, causing your balance to increase before your next bill arrives even if you don't make any more purchases. Paying the minimum payment is almost never a good strategy and can add years to your repayment time. In fact, assuming an 18 percent interest rate, if you continually pay only $10 per month toward a $500 credit card balance, it will take you more than seven years to pay it off. Plus, you'll pay an extra $431 in interest, almost doubling the amount you originally charged.

Avoid making late payments. Paying your bill even one day late can result in a finance charge of up to $30, and it can raise the interest rate not only on that card but also on any other credit accounts you have. If you decide to use a credit card to build credit, you might want to explore the automated online payment options that are available to you. Remember that the payment due date is the date that the payment should be received by the credit card lender, not the date that you send it.

> " It is important for you to thoroughly understand how credit cards work and how they can both help and hurt you. "

△ **In Case of Emergency**
Having a credit card for emergencies is a good practice. Circumstances that might warrant the use of credit include paying critical expenses to care for yourself or your family, dealing with an auto accident or an unforeseen medical expense, or traveling on short notice to handle a crisis. Remember: Spring break is not an emergency. © Britt Erlanson/Getty Images

If you decide to apply for a credit card while you're in college, remember that it should be used to build credit and for emergencies. Credit cards should not be used to fund a lifestyle that you cannot otherwise afford or to buy wants (see the "Living on a Budget" section in this chapter). If you use your credit card just once a month and pay the balance as soon as the bill arrives, you will be on your way to a strong credit score in just a few years.

Debit Cards

Although you might wish to use a credit card for emergencies and to establish a good credit rating, you might also look into the possibility of applying for a debit card (also called a check card). The big advantage of a debit card is that you don't always have to carry cash and thus don't run the risk of losing it. Because the amount of your purchases will be limited to the funds in your bank account, a debit card is also a good form of constraint on your spending.

The only real disadvantage is that a debit card provides direct access to your checking account, so it's very important to keep your card in a safe place and away from your PIN. The safest way to protect your account is to commit your PIN to memory. If you lose your debit card or credit card, notify your bank immediately. ∎

Frequently Asked Questions about Credit Cards and Identity Theft

- **I have a credit card with my name on it, but it is actually my parents' account number. Is this card building credit for me?** No. You are considered an authorized user on the account, but your parents are the primary account holders. To build credit, you must be the primary account holder or at least a joint account holder.

- **I have a credit card and am the primary account holder. How can I resist abusing it?** Use your credit card to help you build credit by making small charges and paying them off each month. Stick to two expense categories only, such as gas and groceries, and don't make any exceptions unless you have an emergency.

- **I choose the "credit" option every time I use my debit card. Is this building credit for me?** No. Using the credit function of your debit card is more like writing an electronic check because you are still taking money directly out of your checking account. Even if your debit card features the logo of a major credit card (Visa, MasterCard, Discover), it is not building credit for you.

- **I have a few store credit cards (Target, Best Buy, and Old Navy). Are these accounts included on my credit report?** Yes. While they will affect your credit score, store credit cards do not carry as much weight as major credit cards. It is OK to have a few store credit cards, but a major credit card will do more to help you build credit.

- **Where can I apply for a major credit card?** A good place to begin is your bank or credit union. Remember that you might have to prove your ability to make payments in order to obtain a card. Use your credit card to build credit by making small charges and paying them off each month.

- **If one credit card will help me build credit, will several build my credit even more?** Research shows that there is no benefit to having more than two major credit cards. And even if you're able to pay the required monthly amounts, having too many accounts open can make you appear risky to the credit bureaus determining your credit score.

- **What if I forget and make a late payment? Is my credit score ruined?** Your credit report reflects at least the past seven years of activity but puts the most emphasis on the most recent two years. In other words, the farther you get from your mistakes, the less impact they will have on your credit score. There is no quick fix for improving a credit score, so beware of advertisements that say otherwise.

- **If building credit is a wise decision, what's so bad about using credit cards to buy some things that I really want but can't afford right now?** It is not wise to use credit cards to purchase things that you cannot afford. Living within your means is always the way to go.

- **What is identity theft?** In this insidious and increasingly common crime, someone assumes your identity, secretly opens up accounts in your name, and has the bills sent to another address.

- **How can I protect myself from identity theft?** *Be password savvy.* The more sensitive the information, the stronger your password should be. Aim for passwords with eight to fourteen characters, including numbers; both upper- and lowercase letters; and, if allowed, a few special characters, such as @ and #. Never use an obvious number like your birthday or wedding anniversary. Don't use the same username and password for every site. Change the password to your online credit card or bank account at least once a year. If you must keep a written record of your usernames and passwords, keep the list in a secure place at home, not in your wallet.

- ***Beware of scams.*** Lots of them are out there. Don't make yourself vulnerable. A few tips: Research a company or organization before submitting your résumé. Do not transmit personal information (social security number, bank details, credit or debit card numbers, passwords etc.) through e-mail. Doing so could put you at risk of identity theft. Don't answer questions about vital personal information over the phone if you didn't originate the call. Don't reply to e-mails, pop-ups, or text messages that ask you to reveal sensitive information. Don't send sensitive data by e-mail. Call instead, and deal only with businesses you trust. Never click on links in unsolicited e-mails or paste URLs or lines of code into your browser bar. If an offer sounds too good to be true—like a huge line of credit at 0 percent interest—it probably is.

- **Where can I get my credit report?** You can keep an eye on your credit report by visiting the free (and safe) website www.annualcreditreport.com at least once a year. Regularly reviewing your credit history pays off in major ways. It alerts you to any new accounts that might have been opened in your name. It also lets you catch unauthorized activity on accounts that you've closed or haven't used lately. Everyone is entitled to one free credit report a year from each of the three major credit bureaus.

Chapter Review

Reflect on Choices

Successful college students learn to manage their money. They are careful to manage their income and their expenditures. Write about the choices you have already made about how to spend your money. This chapter offers lots of good strategies for handling your finances. Which of them will you practice this term?

Apply What You've Learned

Now that you have read and discussed this chapter, consider how you can apply what you have learned to your academic and personal lives. The following prompts will help you reflect on the chapter material and its relevance to you, both now and in the future.

1. Sometimes it's hard to plan for the future. Describe two ways that you can save money each week, such as using public transportation to reduce the expense of owning a car.

2. Money is a difficult subject to talk about, and sometimes it just seems easier not to worry about it. Ask yourself some hard questions. Do you spend money without much thought? Do you have a lot of debt? Describe your ideal financial picture.

Use Your Resources

GO TO ▷ The financial aid office: If you need help understanding financial aid opportunities and how to apply for scholarships. Also, if you are a veteran, an underrepresented student, or an adult student, your institution may have special scholarship opportunities for you.

GO TO ▷ Your local United Way office: If you need credit counseling. Many communities have credit counseling agencies within their local United Way.

GO TO ▷ The student affairs office: If you need help finding programs on money management. These programs are often offered in residence halls or through the division of student affairs.

GO TO ▷ The business school or the division of continuing education: If you need help finding a course in personal finance. Check your college catalog or website, or call the school or division office.

GO TO ▷ The counseling center: If you need help managing money problems that are related to compulsive shopping or gambling.

GO TO ▷ Your campus library or bookstore: If you want additional print resources about money management. A good book to look for is Susan Knox's *Financial Basics: A Money-Management Guide for Students* (Columbus: Ohio State University Press, 2004).

GO ONLINE TO ▷ The Budget Wizard: If you want to use a free, secure budgeting tool from the National Endowment for Financial Education.

GO ONLINE TO ▷ The Free Application for Federal Student Aid: If you want to access the online application for federal student aid. You can set up an account, complete the application electronically, save your work, and monitor the progress of your application.

GO ONLINE TO ▷ Fastweb: If you are interested in using a free scholarship search service and discovering sources of educational funding you never knew existed.

GO ONLINE TO ▷ Bankrate: If you are interested in unbiased information about the interest rates, fees, and penalties associated with major credit cards and private loans. This site also provides calculators that let you determine the long-term costs of different kinds of borrowing.

 **LaunchPad Solo** macmillan learning — LaunchPad Solo for *Step by Step* is a great resource. Go online to master concepts using the LearningCurve study tool and much more. **launchpadworks.com**

12

Staying Healthy

Fenton one/Shutterstock

The first year of college can be one of life's most interesting and challenging transitions. Much of what you experience will be new—new friends, new freedoms, and new responsibilities. You will notice that many students use sensible and healthy coping strategies to handle the transition to college successfully. They watch what they eat and drink, exercise regularly, and get enough sleep. However, some students go in the opposite direction; they stay up late, drink too much, smoke, overeat, or engage in risky sexual behaviors. Many students gain weight during the college years, and much of that weight gain happens in the first year.

This chapter explores the topic of staying healthy, which includes taking care of your mind, body, and spirit; making healthy choices; and achieving balance. The college experience shouldn't only be about studying; it's also important to spend time with friends and enjoy the freedom and all the activities your college has to offer. But the freedoms you experience in college bring challenges and risks, and your success in college will depend on your ability to make sensible decisions about your personal habits and behaviors.

Review Your ACES Score

Take a moment to reflect on your **Personal and Financial Health** ACES score, and insert it in the box to the right. Now let's take action!

Did you score in the high, moderate, or low range? Are you surprised by your score? This score will help you learn more about your strengths and weaknesses in understanding how to manage your personal and financial health. In this chapter, we will focus on your personal health and wellness. Even if you already feel strong in this area, be open to learning new strategies to help you improve your score as you move through the chapter. This chapter will further your understanding of why this topic is essential to your success in college.

Score:

☐

○ High
○ Moderate
○ Low

To find your ACES score, log on to LaunchPad Solo for *Step by Step* at **launchpadworks.com**.

Preview the topic headings in this chapter. Then, in a journal or a readily accessible file, reflect on your current skills by answering the following questions:

▶ **What are your current strengths and challenges?**
▶ **What do you hope to learn from this chapter?**

Making Time to Be Healthy

Gino Santa Maria/Shutterstock

When I started attending the University of West Florida, I was expecting to have a lot of fun. However, when I received the syllabi for each of my classes, I could tell I was going to have to work really hard. To make study time, I cut back on going to the gym each week. I also started skipping lunch and eating snacks from vending machines between classes instead. Those days, I was sleeping less and eating more junk food.

I was particularly stressed out about an upcoming presentation in my psychology class. The day of the presentation finally came, and I was really nervous. I stumbled through the presentation, my voice shaking and my face flushed. I was so disappointed in myself. I hardly slept at all that night, knowing that I had two more presentations to complete that term.

The next day I went to see my instructor, Dr. Wilson, to tell her I was dropping the class. Dr. Wilson tried to persuade me otherwise. "Lots of people are afraid of public speaking, and their stress causes them to perform poorly. But please keep in mind that the goal of my class is to help you get better. I can help you, Rahm," she assured me.

I was really embarrassed, but Dr. Wilson convinced me that I couldn't escape public speaking for the rest of my life and that I needed to learn how to control my anxiety. She helped me make an appointment at the counseling center. I was surprised to learn that dealing with anxiety starts with eating, exercising, and sleeping well—healthy behaviors that I had been neglecting for a while. The professionals at the counseling center helped me deal with my public speaking fears and also taught me a lot about resilience—the ability to bounce back—so that I won't automatically want to quit when things get hard. Now I feel ready to take on that next presentation!

Rahm experienced a common pitfall of first-year students when he stopped taking care of his health because he was busy and stressed. Why is it important for students to eat properly, get regular exercise, and maintain a regular sleep schedule? What strategies do you use to stay healthy? When do you slip up?

Understanding Wellness

Wellness is a concept that encompasses the care of your mind, body, and spirit. Wellness involves making healthy choices and achieving balance throughout your life. It includes reducing stress in positive ways, keeping fit, fostering your spirituality, deepening your self-knowledge, maintaining good sexual health, and taking a safe approach to alcohol and other drugs—assuming that you are of legal age to consume them.

Take this short quiz. As you consider each question, rate yourself on a scale of 1 to 5, with 1 being "never" and 5 being "always."

1. Are you able to manage your stress successfully? _____

2. Do you eat a wide range of healthy foods?

   _____

3. Do you exercise at least once a day? _____

   _____

4. Do you get seven or more hours of sleep each night? _____

5. Do you say no to others in order to manage your obligations? _____

6. Do you seek help from friends, family, or professionals when you need it? _____

7. Are you in control of your sexual health?

   _____

8. Do you avoid abusing alcohol, tobacco, or other substances? _____

9. Do you live a balanced life? _____

In what areas did you mark 4 or 5? _____

_____

_____

In what areas did you mark 1 or 2? _____

_____

_____

As you read the following preview of the nine components of wellness, pay special attention to the areas that you scored as 1 or 2.

1. **Managing Stress.** Occasional stress is a normal reaction to being a new college student. Recognize when your stress level is getting out of control, and seek help before stress gets in the way of your academic performance.

2. **Paying attention to diet and nutrition.** Eating fast food will often increase your cholesterol and your weight. Substitute water for diet sodas, and opt for fresh, unprocessed foods.

3. **Exercising regularly.** Exercising helps relieve stress and control weight. If you don't have time to work out every day, start with a smaller goal of three or four times a week.

4. **Getting enough sleep.** Going without sleep will negatively affect your overall health and ability to perform academically. Seven or eight hours of sleep per night can significantly improve your ability to handle stress.

5. **Saying no when you need to.** In order to manage your obligations, sometimes you have to say no to friends or even family members. Know what your priorities are and stick to them.

6. **Seeking help for emotional problems.** If your emotions are out of control, you're feeling depressed, or you're becoming anxious about what's happening in your life, consider talking to a friend or family member or seeing a professional counselor.

7. **Maintaining your sexual health.** Be sure that you practice safe sex. Understand the resources available to you when you have questions or problems.

8. **Avoiding substance abuse.** During your college years, you will encounter alcohol, tobacco, and drugs. Be sure you know the laws that govern the use of these substances in your state. If you are of legal age, remember that moderation is key. Are you a smoker? If so, quit now. There is no such thing as a safe level of smoking.

9. **Achieving balance.** Wellness is about mind, body, and spirit. When you take care of all aspects of your personal wellness, it will be easier for you to handle problems when they develop.

Managing Stress to Maintain Wellness

Everyone experiences stress at one time or another—it's a normal part of being a human being—but the level of stress that affects college students can undermine their ability to succeed academically. Consider the level of stress you feel today. Rate your current stress level on a scale of 1 to 5, with 1 being "little or no stress" and 5 being "extremely stressed."

My current stress level: _____

If your stress level is 3 or higher, describe the symptoms of stress that you are experiencing.

_____

_____

Can you identify *why* you are feeling this level of stress?

_____

_____

If your stress level is 1 or 2, can you identify why?

_____

_____

Is the stress rating you gave yourself consistent most of the time, or does it fluctuate from day to day? If you have a high level of stress almost every day, you should seek some assistance from a counselor or health professional.

When you are stressed, your body undergoes physiological changes. Your breathing becomes rapid and shallow; your heart rate increases; the muscles in your shoulders, forehead, neck, and chest tighten; your hands become cold or

TRY IT!

MAKING GOOD CHOICES ▷ Have You Reached Your Limit?

Are you so stressed out that you can't concentrate or study, or you're irritable with your roommate or best friend for no good reason? Have you always been this way, or is stress something new? Whatever your history with stress, now is the time to make a decision to learn more about it and get it under control. A first step is to read the material on this page and apply these strategies. A second step might be to develop an exercise regimen that includes yoga. Meditation is another tried-and-true stress-reduction technique. Give yourself a couple of weeks, and if your stress level is still high, seek external help from your college counseling center. By reducing or eliminating your stress and worry, you can improve your academic performance and even your relationships with others.

sweaty; your hands and knees may shake; your stomach becomes upset; your mouth goes dry; and your voice may sound strained. Over time, stress can develop into chronic health issues, such as irritable bowel syndrome, common colds, migraines, and fatigue.

A number of psychological changes also occur when you are under stress. You might experience confusion, trouble concentrating, memory lapses, or have difficulty solving problems. As a result of stress, you might make decisions that you later regret. High stress levels can lead to anger, anxiety, depression, fear, frustration, and irritability, which might cause you to lose sleep. These stress-related changes can turn into more serious psychological ailments, such as anxiety, depression, or panic attacks.

Stress has many sources, but two are prominent: life events and daily hassles. Life events are occurrences that represent major adversity, such as the death of a parent, spouse, partner, or friend. Researchers believe that an accumulation of stress from life events, especially if many occur over a short period, can cause physical and mental health problems. Daily hassles are the minor irritants that you experience every day, such as losing your keys, having three tests on the same day, quarreling with your roommate, or worrying about money.

The best starting point for handling stress is to be in good physical and mental shape. If you pay attention to your body and mind, you will be able to recognize the signs of stress before they escalate and become uncontrollable.

Take Control

Sometimes stressful situations are beyond your control; but other times your stress is directly related to your own behavior. Modifying your lifestyle is the best overall approach to stress management. You have the power to change your life so that it is less stressful. To begin, identify the parts of your life that do not work well, make plans for change, and then carry out those plans. For example, if you are stressed because you are always late for classes, get up ten minutes earlier. If you get nervous when you talk to a certain negative classmate before a test, avoid that person when you have an exam coming up. Learn test-taking skills so

that you can manage test anxiety. If doing poorly on a test causes you to give up or become depressed, develop your resilience and belief in yourself. Learn from your mistakes, and trust yourself to do better in the future.

Another way to take control of your lifestyle is by knowing your limits and making priority lists. This might mean saying no to friends or family members who distract you from your tasks and obligations. It is OK to say no, and you don't have to feel guilty about doing so. You will have many obligations—including classes, clubs, and friends—and you will have to work hard to manage all these obligations and still maintain good grades.

> ❝ If you pay attention to your body and mind, you will be able to recognize the signs of stress before they escalate and become uncontrollable. ❞

TRY IT!

SETTING GOALS ▷ Use Stress to Your Advantage

Do you get stressed before an exam or graded presentation? Some level of stress might motivate you to do well, but a high stress level can have the opposite effect. The next time you are stressed before a test or presentation, note how you feel, both physically and mentally. Are you more energized and more alert? Or does your stress negatively affect your concentration or self-confidence? Set a goal to manage your stress so that it helps, not hurts, your preparation and performance.

The Importance of Good Nutrition

What you eat and drink connects to your overall health, well-being, and stress level. Eating a lot of junk food will reduce your energy. When you can't keep up with your work because you're slow or tired, you will experience more stress.

Caffeine is probably the best example of a common substance that is linked to high stress levels. College students, like many adults, use caffeine to enhance their productivity. Caffeine helps increase alertness and reduce fatigue if used moderately. Up to 400 milligrams (mg) of caffeine a day appears to be safe for most adults. That's roughly the amount of caffeine in four cups of coffee, ten cans of cola, or two "energy shot" drinks.[1] However, too much caffeine can cause nervousness, headaches, irritability, upset stomach, and sleeplessness—all symptoms of stress. Monitor and limit your daily use of caffeine, especially if you consume energy drinks. Using coffee or energy drinks when you're cramming for exams—or even to get through the day—can become a crutch. Find other sources of energy, such as jogging or power napping.

Many of us find that gaining weight is really easy; a few days of donuts, pizza, and soft drinks can pack on unexpected pounds. Losing weight, even a small amount, is far more difficult. Let's face it—food is one of life's greatest pleasures, and having the self-discipline to say no to a giant piece of birthday cake is difficult.

But weight gain will almost always reduce your energy and interest in exercise. If you are gaining weight and losing energy, what can you do about your eating habits? It might not be easy at first, but if you start making small changes, you can build toward a new way of eating. You will not only feel better but also be healthier and probably happier. Here are some common sense suggestions:

- Limit snacks to healthy options, such as fruit, vegetables, yogurt, hummus, and small portions of nuts, like pistachios, almonds, cashews, or walnuts.

- Be careful about fad diets. Before using diet pills or beginning a diet regimen such as the Paleo, Atkins, or South Beach diet, check with your physician. These diets might cause you to miss essential nutrients, especially if you are an athlete. Changing your portion sizes can be a first step toward weight loss.

- Drink plenty of water. Drinking 64 ounces of water a day helps flush your system, keep your skin healthy, and manage your weight. A rule of thumb: To keep hydrated, drink water before and after a workout and between meals.

- Add variety to your meals. Cafeterias offer options, and the most important strategy is to eat a meal that includes protein, vegetables, grains, salad, and fruit. Stay away from fried and sugary foods. A good reference is ChooseMyPlate.gov, shown in Figure 12.1. Watch your portion sizes. Avoid large, jumbo, or king-sized fast-food items and all-you-can-eat buffets.

- Eat a healthy breakfast! Your brain will function better if you eat a power-packed meal first thing in the morning. Try oatmeal, eggs, and foods high in protein.

- Always read the nutrition label on packaged foods; look for the number of grams of fat, sugars, protein, carbohydrates, and sodium. Sodium (table salt) will make you retain water, which increases your weight and can possibly increase your blood pressure. Do not let items marketed as "nonfat/low-fat" options fool you. Often, these products contain chemicals and by-products that are worse for you than their full-fat counterparts.

- If possible, take time to cook your own food, bring your lunch, and pack your own snacks. Preparing your own meals and snacks is almost always healthier and more cost-effective than eating out or buying snack food.

[1] "Caffeine: How Much Is Too Much?," Mayo Clinic, accessed January 13, 2016, www.mayoclinic.org/healthy-lifestyle/nutrition-and-healthy-eating/in-depth/caffeine/art-20045678?reDate=01022018.

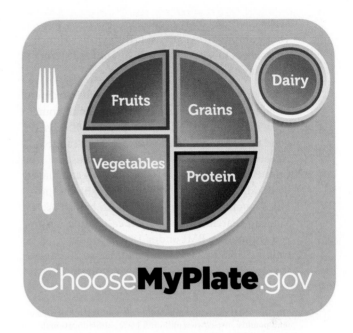

Figure 12.1 ▷ MyPlate Eating Guidelines
In 2011, the federal government introduced the MyPlate icon to replace the Food Guide Pyramid. ChooseMyPlate.gov provides tips and recommendations for healthy eating and for understanding the plate's design. Source: Courtesy of USDA

Exercising to Maintain Wellness

Exercise is an excellent stress-management and weight-management technique and the best way to stay fit. Whether it's walking to class, going to the campus recreation center, or taking a bike ride, it is important to be active every day. Choose activities you enjoy so that you look forward to your exercise time and make it a regular part of your routine.

Besides doing wonders for your body, aerobic exercise keeps your mind healthy. When you do aerobic exercise, your body produces hormones called beta-endorphins. These natural narcotics cause feelings of contentment and happiness and help manage anxiety and depression. Your mood, energy level, sleep, and sense of competence will improve with regular aerobic exercise. Think about ways to combine activities efficiently. Leave your car at home and walk or ride a bike to class. If you drive, park at the far end of the parking lot to get in extra steps. Go to the gym with a friend, and ask each other study questions while you're on the treadmill. Take the stairs whenever possible. Wear a pedometer, and aim for a certain number of

Risky Eating Habits

Although we advise you to think about what you eat each day, we also advise you not to overthink your diet. Remember that the key to good health is achieving balance, and an obsession with how much you eat may be a sign that things are out of balance. Over the last few decades, an increasing number of both male and female college students have developed eating disorders, such as anorexia nervosa (an extreme fear of gaining weight), bulimia (overeating followed by self-induced vomiting or laxative use), and binge eating (compulsive overeating long past the feeling of being full).

Anyone who is struggling with an eating disorder should seek immediate medical attention. Eating disorders can be life-threatening if they are not treated by a health care professional. Contact your student health center or the National Eating Disorders Association (www.nationaleatingdisorders.org or 1-800-931-2237) to find a professional in your area who specializes in treating eating disorders.

steps each day. Play organized sports, or use your campus fitness center. Remember that exercise is most effective if you make it part of your day-to-day life.

Another way to monitor your weight-management progress during exercise is to be aware of your body mass index (BMI). Knowing your BMI is a good way to understand your optimum range. According to the U.S. Centers for Disease Control and Prevention (CDC), BMI is calculated by dividing your weight by your height and provides an effective way to screen for health issues. You can search online for BMI calculators[2]. As you will note, a BMI under 18.5 is "underweight," 18.5 to 24.9 is "normal," 25 to 29.9 is "overweight," and 30 or higher is "obese."

[2] The NIH BMI calculator allows for calculations in feet, inches, and pounds: https://www.nhlbi.nih.gov/health/educational/lose_wt/BMI/bmicalc.htm

MANAGING TIME ▷ Making Time to Stay Fit

For many of us, the statement "I just don't have enough time" is our excuse to avoid an exercise routine. Making exercise a daily habit helps you control your weight and increases your energy level, but unless you schedule exercise on a regular basis, you will soon see unwelcome pounds and inches. One of the most common challenges in college is staying fit. Find a way to schedule a few hours each week dedicated to fitness. There are many devices available today that will help—Fitbit, Moves, and Argus, for example, are free apps that will make it easy for you to keep track of your activity level.

△ Get Moving!
Whether it is running, walking, or playing a sport, every student needs to get moving. What are your exercise habits? Remember that daily exercise can be a great no-cost way to reduce stress while keeping you in good physical and mental shape. Michael Doolittle/Alamy

Use Technology to Stay Fit

We all want to be healthy and look fit, but we live in a world that makes us inactive and presents us with convenient but unhealthy food options. Many of us spend lots of time in front of television and computer screens. Even when we aren't watching a particular show or presentation, we view videos on our phones, at the gas pump, in restaurants, or while we wait for the elevator. When we are bored, we have game systems and games on our phones that often keep us sitting in one spot. It seems as though we are in front of digital screens almost twenty-four hours a day. So instead of letting technology make you a couch potato, how can you use it to help you become—and stay—fit?

▶ the GOAL

Enlist technology to get moving and make healthier choices.

▶ how TO DO it

- **Learn how to filter out the fiction.** When it comes to fitness and nutrition, there's a lot of conflicting advice and bad information out there, and more than a few scams. Zero in on a few reputable, well-vetted sources of information. You can find everything from healthy menu plans to yoga training to fitness tips on the following websites and smartphone apps:

Fitness Websites

Site Name	Function
FitDay	Tracks diet and exercise activity
Fitness.com	Provides fitness tips and recipes, suggests exercises, and more
Livestrong	Contains articles offering diet, nutrition, and exercise tips
Nutrition Data	Offers nutrition facts, recipes, and more
Weight Watchers	Provides weight-loss and diet plans

Health-Related Phone Apps

App Name	Function
Argus	Tracks physical activity
Human	Tracks activity and calories
Fooducate	Features shopping guide that helps users find healthier food
Diet Point	Helps track food/calorie intake
HealthyOut	Finds healthy dishes when eating out or getting takeout

- **Use your electronic calendar to send periodic alerts to your cell phone to take breaks or work out.** You don't necessarily have to go to the gym. Sometimes all it takes is a brisk walk or fifteen minutes of stretching and relaxed breathing to reset your body and your mind.
- **Make some of the time you spend in front of a screen active time.** Clear some floor space, and use YouTube or online services like Netflix to stream workout programs. Video gaming systems like Xbox let you enjoy real-life workouts in the virtual world.

▶ your TURN

Although all of these resources above will direct you to good information, you may like some better than others. Pick one favorite from each of the two categories, "Fitness Websites" and "Health-Related Phone Apps." Share this information, along with any other favorite app or website, with other students in a small group.

△ **Catch Some Zs**

When you aren't getting enough sleep, you cannot do your best. A brief nap of twenty minutes or so can revive you when you're feeling tired during the day. Establish good sleeping habits, and grab opportunities for power naps when you can. © Fuse/Getty Images

Getting Enough Sleep to Maintain Wellness

Getting adequate sleep is another way to protect yourself from stress. According to a 2013 Gallup poll, almost 50 percent of individuals aged eighteen to twenty-nine get less than the recommended seven hours of sleep per night.[3] Lack of sleep can lead to anxiety, depression, and academic problems. Research has shown that students who stay up late partying or pull all-nighters studying earn lower grades.[4] Try the following suggestions to establish better sleep habits:

- Avoid daytime naps that last more than thirty minutes.

- Try reading or listening to a relaxation tape before going to bed. Avoid looking at your electronic devices for at least a half hour before going to bed.

- Exercise during the day.

- Get your clothes, class materials, and food together for the next day before you go to bed.

- Sleep in the same room and bed every night.

- Stick to a regular weekday schedule for going to bed and getting up.

Spirituality

Many students find that maintaining a connection to their spiritual life helps them maintain strong emotional health. Spirituality is a broad term that includes not only religion but also an exploration of questions about life's meaning and ultimate value. For some college students, spirituality is linked to attendance at a church, temple, mosque, or synagogue. Others feel that they have a personal and private relationship with God, or they may explore spirituality through meditation, yoga, or a strong connection to nature or art. Maintaining your sense of spirituality will help you achieve a healthy perspective on whatever difficulties come your way.

Emotional Health

Your emotional or mental health is an important component of your overall wellness. Particularly in the first year of college, some students have difficulty establishing positive relationships with others, dealing with pressure, or making wise decisions. Other students are optimistic and happy and seem to believe in their own abilities to address problems successfully. Your ability to deal with life's challenges is based on your emotional intelligence (EI), a topic addressed in chapter 2, "Cultivating Motivation, Resilience, and Emotional Intelligence."

[3] Jeffrey M. Jones, "In U.S., 40% Get Less Than Recommended Amount of Sleep," December 19, 2013, http://www.gallup.com/poll/166553/less-recommended-amount-sleep.aspx.

[4] "College Students Sleep Longer but Drink More and Get Lower Grades When Classes Start Later," press release, June 8, 2011, http://www.aasmnet.org/articles.aspx?id=2327.

Depression. Depression is one of the most common psychiatric disorders in the United States. According to the National Institute of Mental Health, an estimated 17 million adult Americans suffer from depression during any one-year period.[5] College students are at especially high risk for both depression and suicide because of the major life changes and high stress levels some of them experience.

Depression is not a weakness; it is an illness that needs medical attention. Feelings of depression are often temporary and may be situational. A romantic breakup, a disappointing grade, or an ongoing problem with another person can create feelings of despair. Although most depression goes away on its own, if any of the following symptoms last for more than two weeks, it is important to talk to a health care provider:

- Feelings of helplessness and hopelessness
- Feeling useless, inadequate, bad, or guilty
- Self-hatred, constant questioning of one's thoughts and actions
- Loss of energy and motivation
- Loss of appetite
- Weight loss or gain
- Difficulty sleeping or excessive need for sleep
- Loss of interest in sex
- Difficulty concentrating for a significant length of time

Suicide. The CDC reports that students aged fifteen to twenty-four are more likely than any other age group to attempt suicide.[6] Most people who commit suicide give a warning of their intentions. The following are

common indicators of someone's intent to commit suicide:

- Recent loss and inability to let go of grief
- Change in personality—sadness, withdrawal, indifference
- Expressions of self-hatred
- Change in sleep patterns
- Change in eating habits
- A direct statement about committing suicide (e.g., "I might as well end it all")
- A preoccupation with death

If you or someone you know threatens suicide or displays any of these signs, it's time to consult a mental health professional. Most campuses have counseling centers that offer both one-on-one sessions and support groups for students, usually for free.

Finally, remember that there is no shame attached to having high levels of stress, depression, anxiety, or suicidal tendencies. Unavoidable life events or physiological imbalances can cause such feelings and behaviors. Proper counseling, medical attention, and in some cases prescribed medication can help students cope with depression and suicidal thoughts.

Cyberbullying. Instances of cyberbullying have increased in recent years, not just in grade school and high school, but also on college campuses. Experts define *cyberbullying* as "any behavior performed through electronic or digital media by individuals or groups who repeatedly communicate hostile or aggressive messages intended to inflict harm or discomfort on others."[7] According to a recent study, the prevalence of cyberbullying among college populations ranges from 10.0 to 28.7 percent.[8]

---

[5] *Depression: How Psychotherapy and Other Treatments Can Help People Recover*, American Psychological Association, July 2010, http://www.apa.org/topics/depress/recover.aspx.

[6] National Center for Injury Prevention and Control, *Suicide: Facts at a Glance*, 2015, http://www.cdc.gov/ViolencePrevention/pdf/Suicide-DataSheet-a.pdf.

[7] Peter K. Smith et al., "Cyberbullying: Its Nature and Impact in Secondary School Pupils," *Journal of Child Psychology and Psychiatry* 49, no. 4 (2008): 375–76.

[8] Carlos P. Zalaquett and SeriaShia J. Chatters, "Cyberbullying in College: Frequency, Characteristics, and Practical Implications," *SAGE Open* (January–March 2014): 1–8, http://sgo.sagepub.com/content/4/1/2158244014526721.

△ **Difficulty Coping**
Many events in life can trigger feelings of despair. Know the signs of depression. If you or someone you care about seems to be having trouble, reach out. College campuses have resources to help.
© Wavebreakmedia Ltd/Getty Images

These may seem like low numbers, but cyberbullying can go unreported because of embarrassment or privacy concerns. Recently, tragic cyberbullying stories that have resulted in the victim's clinical depression or suicide have been reported.

Cyberbullying is a serious issue and a crime that harms individuals in many ways; thus, it should be dealt with immediately. If you or someone you know has experienced cyberbullying, report it as soon as possible. Do an Internet search for the following foundations and resources, which are available to help students report cyberbullying:

- Stopbullying.gov
- Megan Meier Foundation
- National Crime Prevention Council ■

Maintaining Sexual Health

Survey data reported in 2015 by the American College Health Association found that about 66 percent of traditional-age college students reported having intercourse in the previous twelve months.[9] Whether or not you are sexually active, it can be helpful to consider your sexual values and whether sex is right for you at this time in your life. If you decide to become sexually active, you should adopt strategies for avoiding the unwanted consequences of unprotected sex.

Communicating about Safe Sex

Communication is the most important aspect of sexual relationships. You and your partner must share your backgrounds, needs, and how to be safe. Without communication, intentions can get confused, and emotions can become muddled. Here are some communication strategies:

- **Discuss testing for sexually transmitted infections (STIs).** Make sure both partners have been tested recently. The rule of thumb for a sexually active person is to get tested at least once a year and after any unprotected encounter.

- **Share expectations.** Partners should talk about what they expect from the sexual encounter. Partners should be clear about their comfort level and what they want from the experience.

- **Use protection.** Protecting yourself and your partner from unwanted consequences—pregnancy or the transmission of STIs—is important, and so is communicating about protection ahead of time. Do you and your

partner have what you need, or does one of you need to buy it? One unprotected encounter can change your entire life, so make sure you are prepared.

- **Communicate in "I" statements.** "I" statements help facilitate open communication. When you use "I" statements, you accept responsibility for your feelings, and you do not accuse or threaten each other. The statement "I feel like we need to explore our options" is more useful than "You don't know what you're talking about."

> " Communication is the most important aspect of sexual relationships. "

Avoiding Sexually Transmitted Infections

You can avoid STIs and unwanted pregnancies by abstaining from sex entirely. Many college students choose this option, finding that masturbation is a reasonable alternative to sex with a partner.

If you are having sex with a partner, you're more likely to avoid STIs if you have only one partner. Whether you're monogamous or not, you should always protect yourself by using a condom or making sure your partner uses one.

In addition to being a contraceptive, a condom can help prevent the spread of STIs—including human immunodeficiency virus (HIV) and human papillomavirus (HPV)—during anal, vaginal, and oral intercourse. The most up-to-date research indicates that condoms are very effective at both preventing the transmission of STIs and preventing pregnancy when used correctly and

[9] American College Health Association, *ACHA-NCHA II: Undergraduate Students: Reference Group Executive Study, Spring 2015*, 2015, http://www.acha-ncha.org/docs/NCHA-II_WEB_SPRING_2015_UNDERGRADUATE_REFERENCE_GROUP_EXECUTIVE_SUMMARY.pdf.

consistently when you have sex. Note that only latex condoms and polyurethane condoms—not lambskin or other types of natural membrane condoms—provide this protection. Use a water-based lubricant such as K-Y Jelly rather than an oil-based lubricant, which can cause a latex condom to break.

In recent years, the number of STIs on college campuses has increased dramatically, faster than other illnesses on campuses today. Approximately 5 to 10 percent of visits by U.S. college students to college health services are for the diagnosis and treatment of STIs. HPV, a sexually transmitted infection that is closely linked to cervical cancer, is the most common STI.[10] In fact, the CDC estimates that 79 million Americans are currently infected with HPV. Gardasil, a vaccine that became available in 2006, provides protection for both men and women against the strains of HPV that cause genital warts, anal cancer, and cervical cancer. For more information about this vaccine or to receive the three-injection series, contact your college or university health services or your local health care provider.

[10] *General HPV Infection—CDC Fact Sheet*, July 11, 2017, http://www.cdc.gov/std/hpv/stdfact-hpv.htm.

Using Birth Control

Sexually active heterosexual students have to take steps to prevent unwanted pregnancies. The best method of contraception is any method that you use correctly and consistently each time you have intercourse. Always discuss birth control with your partner so that you both feel comfortable with the option you have selected.

Remember, birth control only protects against pregnancy. Use condoms for protection against STIs, in addition to your chosen method of pregnancy prevention. What if the condom breaks or you forget to take your birth control pill? Emergency contraceptive pills can reduce the risk of pregnancy. According to the Planned Parenthood Federation of America,[11] if emergency contraceptive pills are taken within five days (120 hours) of unprotected intercourse, they can significantly reduce the risk of pregnancy. ■

[11] Planned Parenthood, "Emergency Contraception," https://www.plannedparenthood.org/learn/morning-after-pill-emergency-contraception.

Protecting Yourself and Others Against Sexual Assault and Violence

Sexual assault on college campuses is a problem that has existed for many years. Everyone is at risk for becoming a victim of sexual assault, but the majority of victims are women. The results of a recent study conclude that during their first year in college, one in seven women will have experienced incapacitated assault or rape (under the influence of alcohol or drugs), and nearly one in ten will have experienced forcible assault or rape.[12] According to statistics, more than 80 percent of survivors will have been assaulted or raped by someone they know[13]—and most will not report the crime. Alcohol is a factor in nearly 75 percent of these incidents.[14]

Interventions to reduce sexual violence on campus are urgently needed. In 2013, the federal government instituted an initiative called the Campus Sexual Violence Elimination (SaVE) Act. The act mandates that all colleges and universities must provide sexual assault, violence, and harassment education to students. The Campus SaVE Act provides an amendment to the Clery Act of 1990, which the federal government implemented after a college student, Jeanne Clery, was raped and killed. The Clery Act required postsecondary institutions to report existing sexual crimes and related statistics, and the Campus SaVE Act expanded those requirements by extending them to dating violence, domestic violence, and stalking, in addition to sexual assault. As always, the victim's identity must remain confidential in such reports. You can find out more about the Campus SaVE Act by visiting campussaveact.org, contacting your campus security or public safety office, or contacting your student judicial office. It is always up to the survivor to decide how he or she would like to proceed after a sexual assault has occurred.

Whether sexually assaulted by an acquaintance or by a stranger, a survivor can suffer long-term traumatic effects as well as depression, anxiety, and even suicidal thoughts. Many survivors blame themselves, but the only person at fault for a sexual assault is the perpetrator. If you are a survivor of sexual assault, seek help by contacting a counselor, a local rape crisis center, the campus public safety department, student health services, women's student services, or a local hospital emergency room. If you know a survivor of sexual assault, here are some steps you can take to help:

- Remain empathetic and nonjudgmental.
- Keep information private and ensure the survivor's confidentiality.
- Listen.
- Ask the survivor how he or she would like to proceed; discuss options like contacting the campus police or the campus counseling center.
- Seek out advice from a professional on how to help the survivor.
- Stay in touch, and follow up to see if the survivor is getting the help he or she needs.

Many sexual assaults on college campuses happen early in the first term. Moving to college can bring you into contact with new people and new places that are unfamiliar and may be unsafe. You should maintain a heightened sense of awareness when going to social events during your first few months on campus. Always take a friend with you, bring your cell phone, carefully monitor what you are drinking, trust your intuition, and be sure to become familiarize yourself with your surroundings so that you know how to leave or get help if needed. If you observe a sexual assault or a potential sexual assault, make your presence known. Don't be a bystander; intervene in any way you can. For instance, create a distraction by accidentally spilling your drink, or offer those at risk a ride home or a way out. If you need help, ask for it.

---

[12] Kate B. Carey et al., "Incapacitated and Forcible Rape of College Women: Prevalence across the First Year," *Journal of Adolescent Health* 56 (2015): 678–80, http://i2.cdn.turner.com/cnn/2015/images/05/20/carey_jah_proof.pdf.

[13] Christopher P. Krebs et al., *The Campus Sexual Assault (CSA) Study* (report prepared for National Institute of Justice), October 2007, https://www.ncjrs.gov/pdffiles1/nij/grants/221153.pdf.

[14] Meichun Mohler-Kuo et al., "Correlates of Race While Intoxicated in a National Sample of College Women," *Journal of Studies on Alcohol* 65, no. 1 (2004): 37–45, http://www.jsad.com/doi/10.15288/jsa.2004.65.37.

Alcohol and Other Substances

In this section, our purpose is not to make judgments but to warn you about the ways in which the irresponsible use of substances can have a negative impact on your college experience—and your life. In today's world, it is easy to obtain substances—both legal and illegal—that can cause serious harm to your health and well-being. For college students, tobacco, alcohol, and marijuana are the substances most commonly used and abused.

The Use and Abuse of Alcohol

In college, many students will encounter alcohol. Of course, there are legal age restrictions on consuming alcohol, and you should not drink alcohol if you are under age twenty-one. If you decide to

△ **Consider the Consequences**
This party looks like fun. But if you drink too much, you may find yourself hooking up with someone you hardly know. What started off as a good time could end up being your worst nightmare. © Digital Vision/Getty Images

consume alcohol, you can still make responsible decisions by using the harm-reduction approach. Following are some simple harm-reduction approaches to consuming alcohol:

- **Slow down drinking.** One way to maintain a "buzz"—the euphoric sensation you experience from drinking—is by drinking one beer or glass of wine per hour or less. Pacing yourself and limiting your drinks help prevent you from attaining a high blood alcohol content (BAC).

- **Eat while you drink.** Sometimes eating while you consume alcohol helps slow down your drinking and slows down the processing of alcohol. Body weight and gender play a large role in this as well.

- **Drink water.** Alcohol dehydrates your body, so it is important to drink plenty of water while consuming alcohol.

- **Designate a driver before you go out.** Walking is always a better option than driving a vehicle, but if you are going to take a vehicle to a destination where you will drink, designate a sober driver before you leave.

Many college students report having to help a friend who is drunk; therefore, it's important that all students learn about the effects of alcohol consumption. Alcohol can turn drinkers and nondrinkers into victims. You might have heard news reports about college students who died or were seriously or permanently injured as a result of one incident of excessive drinking.

People experience the pleasurable effects of alcoholic beverages as the alcohol begins to affect the brain. How fast you drink makes a difference, too. Drinking more than one drink an hour may cause a rise in BAC because the body is absorbing alcohol faster than it can eliminate it. And popular home remedies for sobering up—like drinking coffee or water or taking a cold shower—don't work.

Driving is measurably impaired even at BACs lower than the legal limit of .08. In fact, a safe level for most people may be half the legal limit, or .04. As BAC climbs past .08, people become less coordinated and less able to exercise good judgment. Most people become severely uncoordinated at a BAC higher than .08 and may fall down, slur their speech, and, if driving, be unable to maintain lane position and brake appropriately.[15]

Most people pass out or fall asleep when their BAC is above .25. At a BAC higher than .30, most people will show signs of severe alcohol poisoning, such as an inability to wake up, slowed breathing, a fast but weak pulse, cool or damp skin, and pale or bluish skin; these people need immediate medical assistance. ■

[15] CDC, "Impaired Driving: Get the Facts," http://www.cdc.gov/motorvehiclesafety/impaired_driving/bac.html.

TRY IT!

FEELING CONNECTED ▷ Sharing and Comparing Experiences

List three ways that your quality of life has been influenced by another person's drinking or smoking. In small groups, share your lists. What did you find out when you compared your experiences with those of others? What did you learn about handling situations that involve drinking and smoking?

Tobacco and Marijuana

Tobacco is a legal drug that contains nicotine, a highly addictive substance, and is the cause of many serious medical conditions, including heart disease, lung disease, and some forms of cancer. One concern that particularly relates to college students is social smoking. This term describes smoking by students who do so only when hanging out with friends, drinking, or partying. Most college students believe that they will be able to give up their social smoking habit once they graduate, but some find that they have become addicted to cigarettes.

You may have noticed advertisements for electronic cigarettes (e-cigarettes or e-cigs) or seen them in stores. E-cigarettes are battery-operated products designed to deliver nicotine, flavors, and other chemicals in the form of vapor. Vaping, the term for using e-cigarettes, has not been fully studied, so consumers currently don't know the potential risks.

A final reason for smokers to quit, and for others never to start, is the out-of-pocket cost, which varies by state. A pack-a-day smoker spends more than $1,500 annually on cigarettes (ranging from $1,662 in Missouri, where cigarettes are cheapest, to $3,674 in New York, where cigarettes are most expensive). A pack-a-day smoker over the course of a lifetime will have spent more than $84,000 on cigarettes (from $84,754 in Missouri to $187,379 in New York).[16] Contact your campus health center for more information about quitting.

Recently, California, Maine, Massachusetts, Nevada, Colorado, Washington, Oregon, Alaska, and Washington, DC, legalized recreational marijuana use for individuals twenty-one years of age or older. However, it is still illegal in other states and federally. College students sometimes get caught with marijuana, and as with tobacco, there are health risks associated with smoking it. Some affects of marijuana use include an increase in anxiety, paranoia, short-term memory loss, and depression. In addition, much like tobacco, marijuana smoke increases your risk for lung cancer.

[16] Richie Bernardo, "The Real Cost of Smoking by State," January 17, 2018, https://wallethub.com/edu/the-financial-cost-of-smoking-by-state/9520/#main-annual.

Chapter Review

Reflect on Choices

Successful college students focus on their wellness and reflect deeply on their experiences. From the strategies you learned in this chapter, what do you remember as being most important? How will you change your behaviors and check in with yourself in the future? Reflect on the information found in this chapter.

Apply What You've Learned

Now that you have read and discussed this chapter, consider how you can apply what you have learned to your academic and personal lives. The following prompts will help you reflect on the chapter material and its relevance to you, both now and in the future.

1. Identify one area in your life where you need to make changes to become healthier. How do you think becoming healthier will improve your performance in college? What are the challenges you face in becoming healthier?

2. If you could make only three recommendations to an incoming first-year college student about managing stress in college, what would they be? Use your personal experience and what you have learned in this chapter to make your recommendations.

Use Your Resources

GO TO ▷ The counseling center: If you need help with anxiety and stress. Professionals here will offer individual and group assistance and lots of information. Remember that their support is confidential, and you will not be judged.

GO TO ▷ The campus health center: If you need to discuss a health-related issue. On most campuses, the professionals who staff the health center are especially interested in educational outreach and practicing prevention. You should be able to receive treatment as well.

GO TO ▷ Campus support groups: If you need help dealing with problems related to excessive alcohol and drug use, abusive sexual relationships, and other issues. If you are a member of a minority group on campus in terms of your age, sexual orientation, race or ethnic group, or veteran or active-duty status, seek out services that are designed specifically for you.

GO ONLINE TO ▷ Go Ask Alice!: If you need advice about health issues related to being in college. This website, sponsored by Columbia University, has answers to many health questions.

GO ONLINE TO ▷ The American Cancer Society: If you want to learn more about the health effects of tobacco.

GO ONLINE TO ▷ The American Dietetic Association or Nutrition.gov: If you need help finding information on healthy eating and nutrition.

GO ONLINE TO ▷ The American Institute of Stress: If you need help combating stress.

GO ONLINE TO ▷ The Center for Young Women's Health: If you want to find helpful advice on sexual health and other issues.

GO ONLINE TO ▷ The National Eating Disorders Association: If you want to learn more about online screening, treatment, and support for an eating disorder that you or someone you care about is struggling with.

GO ONLINE TO ▷ The National Clearinghouse for Alcohol and Drug Information: If you want to access up-to-date information about the effects of alcohol and drug use.

LaunchPad Solo
macmillan learning

LaunchPad Solo for *Step by Step* is a great resource. Go online to master concepts using the LearningCurve study tool and much more. launchpadworks.com

Appendix
Using the ACES Progress Report

Taking ACES again

Now that you've reached the end of the term, it's time to take ACES again to receive your Progress Report. The Progress Report gives you an updated report on the strengths and growth areas you've previously evaluated with ACES. By comparing your ACES Initial Report from the beginning of the term with your Progress Report scores, you can reflect on the progress you've made.

To take the ACES again and obtain your Progress Report, log on to LaunchPad Solo for *Step by Step* at **launchpadworks.com**.

Understanding Your Progress Report

Your Progress Report score follows the same format as your initial ACES score. Your report (sample below) will show where you fall in relation to the average incoming college student.

▶ Low scores appearing in red fall between the 1st and 25th percentile. For any scores in this range, you should set goals for development in these areas.

▶ Moderate scores appearing in yellow fall between the 26th and 75th percentile. For any scores in this range, you should continue your development in these areas.

▶ High scores appearing in green fall between the 76th and 99th percentile. For scores in this range, you should capitalize on these strengths.

Your Results

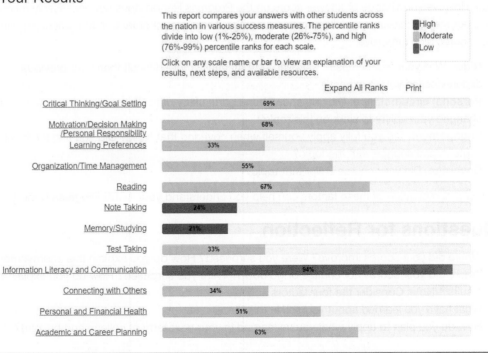

This report compares your answers with other students across the nation in various success measures. The percentile ranks divide into low (1%-25%), moderate (26%-75%), and high (76%-99%) percentile ranks for each scale.

Click on any scale name or bar to view an explanation of your results, next steps, and available resources.

High
Moderate
Low

Expand All Ranks   Print

Critical Thinking/Goal Setting	69%
Motivation/Decision Making /Personal Responsibility	68%
Learning Preferences	33%
Organization/Time Management	55%
Reading	67%
Note Taking	24%
Memory/Studying	21%
Test Taking	33%
Information Literacy and Communication	94%
Connecting with Others	34%
Personal and Financial Health	51%
Academic and Career Planning	63%

Comparing Your Progress and Initial Report Scores

Chart your percentile scores for each skill area from your Initial and Progress Reports. (See sample chart below, or use the online chart in LaunchPad Solo for *Step by Step* at launchpadworks.com.)

Scale	My ACES Initial Score	My ACES Progress Score
Critical Thinking/Goal Setting		
Motivation/Decision Making /Personal Responsibility		
Learning Preferences		
Organization/Time Management		
Reading		
Note Taking		
Memory/Studying		
Test Taking		
Information Literacy/Communication		
Connecting with Others		
Personal and Financial Health		
Academic and Career Planning		

How to Read These Results

A higher score on the Progress Report can represent the real improvement you've made in that skill area. However, no change or a lower score on the Progress Report does not necessarily mean you have not strengthened your skills or made progress. There are other factors that could explain why your scores didn't improve:

1. **Rigor.** Was your first semester of college substantially more difficult than your previous experience led you to expect?
2. **Personal circumstance.** Did you encounter a particularly difficult personal circumstance that changed your ability to work on this topic?
3. **Engagement.** Did you fully apply yourself when covering that topic? Did you find it difficult to relate to and engage with the topic?
4. **Coverage.** Did your course cover that topic?

Any or a combination of these factors can help you understand your ACES Progress Report scores.

Questions for Reflection

1. Where did your scores improve? Were you surprised? How do you explain this improvement?
2. Where did your scores not change or go down? Were you surprised? How do you explain these results? (Note: Consider the four factors above)
3. What have you learned about yourself in this term?
4. How do you plan to apply what you've learned in your next term of college and beyond?

Index

A

Abbreviations, in note taking, 80
Abstract concepts, 60
Abstracts of articles, reading, 97
Academic advisers, 142–43
Academic databases, 128, 168
Academic honesty, 115–17
Academic plans, 142
  changes in, 7
  readiness and procrastination, 41
Accommodations, for learning disabilities, 59
Accountability
  of study partners, 49
  in workplace, 145
Active learning, 71
  group discussions, 79
  online classes, 74
Active reading
  of essay questions, 111
  flash cards, examples of, 92
  four-step plan for, 87–91
  improving, 93–94
Activism on campus, 170
Adaptability
  competencies associated with, 29
  emotional intelligence, 25
  and higher grades, 30
  in multimodal learning, 56
  valued, in workplace, 145
ADD, 59
ADHD, 59
Adjunct instructors, 13
Administrators and staff, connecting with, 14
Age, diversity of, on campus, 164
Alcohol use and abuse, 206–7
Alertness and active reading, 91
American College Health Association, 203
American Psychological Association, "10 Ways to Build Resilience," 23
Analysis
  of research topic, 127
  as fourth level of learning, 66
  guidance, in choosing courses, 5
Anger management, 26
Annotating while reading, 89–90
Anorexia nervosa, 197
AP credits, applying toward major, 143
Appealing to false authority, as faulty reasoning, 63
Applying, as third level of learning, 66
Apps
  budgeting, tools for, 179
  flash cards, 108
  mind maps, 108
  note taking, 73–74, 81
  review sheets, 108
  staying fit, 199
  style guides, 132
  time management, 48
Aptitude
  self-knowledge of, 147
  tests, 142
Argument, developing, 62
Artistic career fields, 149
Artistic personality and career types, 148–49
Assigned reading
  and listening critically, 72
  preparing for class, 71
  strategies to keep up with, 93–94

Associate's degree and effects on earnings, 3
Assuming truth, as faulty reasoning, 63–64
Assumption, challenging, 61
Assumptions, questioning, in an argument, 62
Asterisks, used in online searches, 128
Asynchronous sessions, in online learning, 12
Athletes, optimism and, 30
Attacking the person, as faulty reasoning, 63
Attendance
  full-time *versus* part-time, 43
  policy, 13
Attention disorders, learning with, 59
Attitude, 19–22
Audience, identifying, for public speaking, 133
Aural learners, 55, 72
Authority of information, 126–27

B

Bachelor's degree and effect on earnings, 3
Backing up answers for online tests, 114
Balance, finding, and time management, 36–37
Bandura, Albert, 53
Bandwagon, as faulty reasoning, 63
Bar-On, Reuven, 28
Begging, as faulty reasoning, 63
Beliefs
  examining, 61
  systems, diverse, 167
Biases
  identifying, to avoid fake news, 67
  of information, evaluating, 127
Binders, for note taking in quantitative courses, 80
Binge eating, 197
Bio, professional, for job searching, 155
Birth control, 204
Blair, Jayson, 116
Block scheduling, 47
Blocks of time for active reading, 91
Blood alcohol levels (BACs), 206–7
Bloom, Benjamin, 66
Bloom's taxonomy, 66
Body mass index (BMI), 198
Books and library resources, 125
Boolean operators, 128
Brain, human
  memory, strategies for improving, 107–8
  neuroplasticity, 53
  rehearsal, as part of memory, 81
Brainstorming, 65
Branching map, 88
Brand building, for yourself, 153–54
Breakups of romantic relationships, 160
Breathing deeply and taking tests/exams, 111
Budgeting
  apps and online services for, 179
  benefits of, 178
  cutting costs, 176–77
  living expenses, 175–76
Bulimia, 197

C

Caffeine, 196
Calendar, term-length, 44
Cameron, Jae, 167
Campus counselor, and discussing sexual harassment, 167
Campus jobs and financial aid, 180–182
Campus learning assistance center, 94
Campus organizations and groups, 169–71
Campus Sexual Violence Elimination (SaVE) Act, 205
Career center
  skills assessments, 146
  internship opportunities, 152
  off-campus employment, 151
  website, 144
Careers
  and economy, 139–41
  Holland method for personality and career types, 147–49
  meeting deadlines, 36
  opportunities for graduates, 139
  values-based recruitment, 145
Catching up with reading, 93–94
Categorizing, and listening critically, 73
Certificate programs, 183
Challenges
  attitude toward, 20–21
  motivation to overcome, 19–22
Change, acceptance of, 23
Chat function, for online learning, 14
Cheating, consequences of, 116–17
ChooseMyPlate.gov, 196–97
Chronological résumé, 154
Citing sources, three rules for, 132
Classes. *See also* Online learning
  block scheduling, 47
  discussions, participating in, 74
  homework, completing, 82
  preparation for, 71
  selecting, 143
  taking notes during, strategies for, 79
  websites, for lecture materials, 79
Class notes and homework, reviewing, 83
Class participation, in online learning, 74
Clery, Jeanne, 205
Clubs on campus, 168
Cognitive disorders, learning with, 59
Cognitive and noncognitive skills, 1, 17
Collaboration
  and critical thinking, 63
  and learning, 58–59
  on online tests, 114
College
  costs for, budgeting, 175–78
  databases, and broader experiences, 168
  diagnosing learning disabilities, 59
  opportunities in
  part-time work in, 151
  research projects, 126–27
  success courses, 30
College Board's CSS Financial Aid Profile, 181
College chaplain, 162

College counselors and relationship breakups, 160
College graduates, career opportunities for, 139
Communication
  clear and respectful, 171
  in collaborative learning, 58–59
  e-mails to instructors, 15
  "I" statements, 203
  offline, or face-to-face, 134–35
  online methods, 134–35
  with parents, 162
  about safe sex, 203–4
  as transferable skill, 146
Community service, 36, 170
Competition among companies, 139
Comprehension
  monitoring, while active reading, 91
  of online reading, 92
  strategies to enhance metacognition, 57
Computer centers, 46
Computer literacy, 121
Concentration, and active reading, 90–91
Conclusions, in problem-solving, 65
Condoms, types of, 203–4
Confidence and resilience, 23
Connecting with others, 10–14, 23, 157–71. *See also* Relationships
Constructivism, 54
Contraception, 203–4
Conventional career fields, 149
Conventional personality and career types, 148–49
Cooperation, in workplace, 145
Cooperative (co-op) education, 181
Cooperative education experiences, 150–51
Corequisites for courses, 143
Cornell format for note taking, 75, 78
Costs, cutting, 176–77
Costs of education and online learning, 12
Counseling center, 108
  assistance with learning disabilities, 59
  stress management, 108
Course catalogs, reviewing, 142
Course materials for online learning, 12
Courses
  cost of, 82
  credit hours and financial aid requirements, 181–82
  expectations, as stated in syllabi, 13
  schedule, managing, 46–47
  withdrawing from, 117
  workload, 143
Cover letters, 154–55
Creating, as sixth level of learning, 66
Creativity, 65, 140
Credit cards, 187–89. *See also* Identity theft
Credit hours, and financial aid requirements, 181–82
Crediting sources, 116, 127
Credit report, 189
Credits, applying toward major, 143
Credit score, managing wisely, 187–89
Critical listening
  suggestions for, 72–73
  taking notes during lectures, 79